KEITH HARDING

Going International

English for Tourism

OXFORD UNIVERSITY PRESS

2

4

Tour operation
page 43

5

Air travel
page 60

6

Travel by sea and river – cruises and ferries
page 74

Contents

10

Guiding
page 137

11

Promotion and marketing in tourism
page 150

12

Developments in tourism
page 164

1

The history and development of tourism

SECTION 1 — An introduction to tourism

Listening 1 — Personal experiences

❶ Listen to these four people talking about themselves and their experiences of travel and tourism.

▲
Juan Menacho González

is a 21-year-old trainee travel agent from Seville.

▲
Ulla Lindström

is 36, comes from Stockholm, and is the Marketing Manager of a Swedish tour company.

▲
Anita Clayton

is 18 years old, comes from Manchester, and is unemployed.

▲
Paola Gallizia

is a 21-year-old flight attendant with Alitalia. She lives in Milan.

Find the answers to the following questions as quickly as possible.

1 Who likes paintings?
2 Who has been to the carnival?
3 Who is working in their first job in tourism?
4 Who has a sister who has worked in Turkey?
5 Who has been to Japan?
6 Who works on aeroplanes?
7 Who is interested in ancient civilizations?
8 Who wants to work in another country?

2 Listen again and complete this profile chart for each person. Then add information about yourself.

Name	Juan	Ulla	Anita	Paola	you
Nationality					
Age					
Home town					
Occupation					
Interests/hobbies					
Countries visited					
Favourite place					
Plans for the future					

Speaking

Tourist attractions

1 Look at these pictures of well-known tourist attractions. Can you identify them? In which of the ten countries listed below are they located?

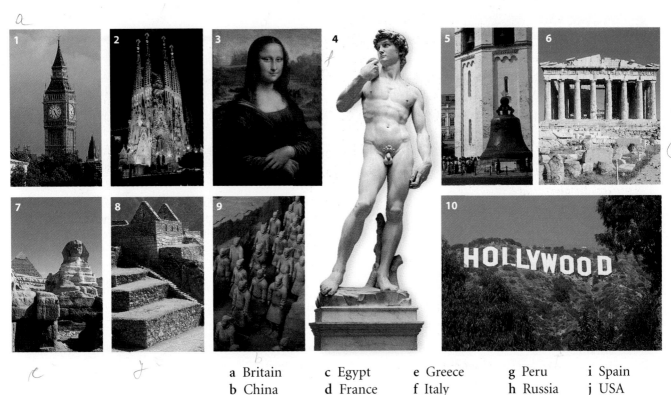

a Britain	**c** Egypt	**e** Greece	**g** Peru	**i** Spain
b China	**d** France	**f** Italy	**h** Russia	**j** USA

2 In pairs, put the tourist attractions in chronological order, with the oldest one first. Look at the chapter titles of a book on the history of civilization on the next page, and decide which chapter you would find them in. Compare your answers with another pair.

3 In your new groups, discuss which of the places and works of art you would like to visit. Put them in an order (1 = like most, 10 = like least). Imagine you are travelling together and agree an order for the whole group. Compare your views with another group.

Language focus 1

Talking about likes and dislikes

Look at these sentences. Which ones (a) express a strong like or dislike, and (b) express a mild like or dislike?

I love helping people to decide which places to visit.
I'm very interested in ancient civilizations.
I like travelling.
I'm not very fond of flying.
I can't stand airline food.
I don't mind it most of the time.
I love art galleries.

Can you think of any other phrases for expressing likes and dislikes?

Talking about past experiences

1 Look at these examples of the simple past and the present perfect tenses which Juan uses to talk about his life and experiences.

I finished my studies at the School of Tourism in Spain last year.
I've just started my first job in a travel agency.
I've been to most parts of Europe.
I went there last year and had a wonderful time.
I saw the Pyramids, the Sphinx, and the Valley of the Kings.

Remember that we use the present perfect tense

a to talk about the past and the present together, often where there is a present result of a past action
I've just applied for a job as a tour rep.

b for a state which has continued up to the present
I haven't travelled a lot.

c for actions in a period of time up to the present
I've been to most parts of Europe.

We use the simple past tense

a to talk about completed actions in the past
I went there last year and had a wonderful time.

b for actions in the past in a period which is finished
I went to Paris when I was a little girl.

2 Look at the tapescript on page 183 and find similar examples in the other profiles. Match each sentence with one of the uses outlined in exercise 1.

3 Which of these time expressions are used with the present perfect, and which are used with the simple past? Which can be used with both tenses?

last year	ever
just	several hours ago
for eight years	already
when I was younger	since 1997
recently	yesterday

Practice

1 Expand these notes into sentences using the correct tense.

a I/never/travel/abroad/before.
b you/ever/eat/snails?/you/like/them?
c she/visit/Barcelona/last year.
d he/be/in India/since January.
e I/go/to the USA first/then/I/travel/to Mexico.
f Oh no! We/arrive/too late. The art gallery/just/close.

2 Using the notes you made about yourself in the profile chart on page 7, and the information in **Language focus 1**, write a profile of yourself.

Contractions and linking

1 Look at these two pairs of sentences. What is the difference in pronunciation?

a I've visited a lot of different places.
I visited a lot of different places.

b She's spent the last three summers in Turkey.
She spent the last three summers in Turkey.

2 In the sentence *I've always loved travelling*, the /v/ sound on the contraction *I've* moves to the front of *always* – there is no pause or boundary between the sounds (I – valways …). Say these sentences. What happens to the underlined sounds?

a I'm very interested in ancient civilizations.
b Have you ever eaten snails?
c I've only been to Venice in the winter.

Output task

Class survey and profiles

You are going to produce a profile form for another member of the class. The form will contain the following information.

Personal information
Name
Nationality
Age
Home town
Occupation
Interests/hobbies
Home town
Name
Location
Sights/places of interest
Hotels/accommodation
Restaurants
Night-life/entertainment
Other information
Travel/holiday experiences (include favourite countries/places)
Ambitions/career plans
Level of English/hopes for the course

❶ In groups, prepare the questions you will need to ask in order to get this information.

❷ Work with someone from another group and ask your questions. Take notes, and then write a profile for that person. For further practice, interview other people outside your class.

Vocabulary

The language of tourism

❶ Complete this word puzzle using the clues below. All the words are related to travel and tourism.

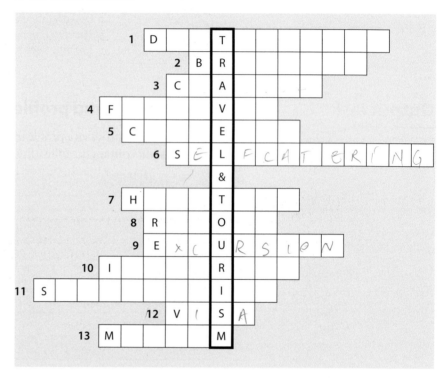

1 When you get to your _____ you'll be met by our representative.

2 If you want to choose a holiday the best way to start is to read a _____.

3 Hiring transport (for example, a plane) for a special purpose.

4 Every year the villagers celebrate their _____ with fireworks, a procession, and a huge meal.

5 You'll need to change your money into local _____.

6 If you don't want to eat the hotel food you could always go _____ and prepare your own meals.

7 The environment, including the countryside, historic buildings, etc., seen as something good to be passed on to future generations.

8 Place where people regularly go for holidays.

9 Short visit, often no longer than a day, returning to the place you started from.

10 A list of places to be visited on one journey.

11 I want to see everything in the city, so I've booked a _____ tour on an open-top bus.

12 For some countries you need to have a _____ before you're allowed in.

13 Building in which collections of rare objects are exhibited.

② Match one word from column **A** and one word from column **B** to make a typical combination (for example, *travel* + *agent*). Give each combination of words a definition, or use it in a sentence as in exercise 1.

A		B	
boarding	package	view	policy
check-in	panoramic	lounge	season
departure	passport	tour	card
guided	room	desk	holiday
high	terminal	cheques	building
in-flight	travel	entertainment	control
insurance	traveller's	agent	service

Note When learning new words it is important to (a) organize them in categories, and (b) try to give them an English definition, or use them in a sentence in English.

③ Put all the items of vocabulary from exercises 1 and 2 into different 'tourism categories'. Look at the titles of the units in this book. Which units would you expect the vocabulary to appear in?

Pronunciation focus 2

It is also important when learning new words to remember how they are pronounced. In English, all words of two syllables or more have one syllable which is stressed more than the others.

For example: O o o   O o
               tourism   travel

Listen to these words from exercise 1 on page 10, and mark the stress pattern in a similar way. Say each word out loud.

destination	brochure	charter	festival
currency	self-catering	heritage	resort
excursion	itinerary	sightseeing	visa
museum			

Speaking

Key events in the development of tourism

① Look at this list of important developments affecting travel and tourism. Put them in chronological order. What effect did they have on the development of tourism?

a the invention of television
b the invention of steam engines and railways
c the invention of the motor car
d the introduction of computer technology
e the introduction of holidays with pay
f the invention of the jet engine
g the building of roads (Romans)
h the building of great pyramids, temples, and cathedrals
i the introduction of traveller's cheques
j the development of the stagecoach and horses transport system
k the Second World War
l an increased standard of living and a rise in disposable incomes

② Here are some of the possible effects of these key events. Match them with the correct event. Try to think of some more of your own.

– air travel became quicker and cheaper
– faster booking and reservations systems
– tourists didn't need to carry cash (therefore safer to travel)

❸ In groups, discuss what you think were the five most important events in the development of tourism.

'Footprints in the sands of time'

❶ You are going to read a magazine article about the history of tourism. When did tourism begin? Who were the first tourists?

❷ Now read the article and list the key events mentioned for each of these periods.

– ancient Greece   – early Christianity   – 19th century
– the Romans   – 17th and 18th centuries – post-World War Two

FOOTPRINTS IN THE SANDS OF TIME

I DO IT, you do it, even the ancient Greeks did it. Travelling for pleasure, travelling to experience new places and events, travelling to relax and get away from it all – in other words, tourism.

Ever since man first emerged from his cave-dwelling, it seems he felt the urge to travel. But tourism had to wait for the civilization of ancient Greece before it really got moving. The Olympic Games of 776 BC were the first international tourist event, with people travelling from many countries to watch and take part.

Of course, if you want to travel from A to B, a good road is always an advantage, and we have a lot to thank the Romans for here. During the heyday of the Roman Empire they built thousands of roads. Some of the first people to take advantage of these roads were religious travellers visiting cathedrals, shrines, or holy sites – the word 'holiday', after all, originally comes from 'holy day'. Pilgrims like Geoffrey Chaucer would tell each other stories to entertain themselves on the road. Nowadays we have the in-flight movie – in medieval times they had the *Canterbury Tales*!

Gradually, more and more people caught the travel bug. At first it was the nobility who set out in the 17th and 18th centuries on their Grand Tours – an essential part of every young gentleman's education. At the same time the upper classes were flocking to spa towns like Bath and Cheltenham. They also enjoyed the healthy pleasures of sea-bathing at Brighton and other resorts.

> A BIT OF TIME OFF WORK, A LITTLE TOO MUCH TO EAT, SOME RELAXING ENTERTAINMENT, LOOSE COTTON CLOTHES, AND A PAIR OF SANDALS – THE TOURIST OF TODAY ISN'T VERY DIFFERENT FROM THOSE OF NEARLY 3,000 YEARS AGO.
>
> CHARLIE HOWARD TAKES A GENTLE LOOK AT THE HISTORY OF THE WORLD'S LARGEST INDUSTRY.

But it was developments in transport that really opened up the tourist industry. First there were stagecoaches and coaching inns. Then came steam, and suddenly the world was a smaller place. Steamboats crossed the English Channel, and railways stretched their iron webs across the civilized world. No sooner had the first railways been built in the 1830s than enterprising men like Thomas Cook in England began to exploit their potential by selling organized tours.

With excursions across continental Europe, the building of hotels and resorts to cater for the tastes of the pleasure-seekers, and the introduction of hotel vouchers and traveller's cheques, the tourist industry in its modern form was born. By the end of the 19th century the middle classes had joined the tourist classes, and mass tourism was a reality.

If the 19th century saw the birth of mass tourism, then the post-war years have witnessed its coming of age. Soon after the end of the Second World War, paid holidays became normal in Britain and many other countries. People now had more disposable income to spend on leisure time, and travel and tourism were available to the many rather than the élite few. Holiday camps sprang up, offering the masses an affordable accommodation-and-entertainment package. Television sets were appearing in more and more homes, bringing the attractions of distant lands into people's living rooms. Package holidays abroad began to appear in the 1950s. But it wasn't until the introduction of the first commercial jet airliners that the idea of foreign holidays really took off.

In recent decades things have only got better for the tourist: faster and cheaper travel options, a wider range of suitable accommodation, more time and money to spend on their holidays. Tourism has come a long way from its distant, humble beginnings. So when you're next wandering along a sun-kissed foreign beach, sipping your cocktail, gazing at the sunset, and trying to forget your worldly cares, remember – you may be treading in the footprints of a 19th-century adventurer, a gentleman on his Grand Tour, a pilgrim or a crusader, or even a Roman soldier or an ancient Greek!

3 Read the article again and answer these questions.

1 What reasons are given for people wanting to travel?

2 Find four examples of improvements in transport.

3 What were the *Canterbury Tales*?

4 What did Thomas Cook do?

5 Why was the introduction of hotel vouchers and traveller's cheques so important?

6 Why were holiday camps so popular?

7 What technical development helped the expansion of package holidays abroad?

8 Explain these expressions:

a *travelling to relax and get away from it all* (paragraph 1)

b *more and more people caught the travel bug* (paragraph 4)

c *the idea of foreign holidays really took off* (paragraph 7)

d *trying to forget your worldly cares* (paragraph 8)

Output task

Pioneers of tourism

The text on page 12 mentions one person, Thomas Cook, who was an important influence on the development of tourism. Do you know any other 'pioneers of tourism' from any of the periods described? Have you heard of Freddie Laker or César Manrique?

1 Divide into three groups. Each group is going to read about one of these three pioneers of tourism – Thomas Cook, Freddie Laker, and César Manrique.

In your groups, fill in the information for your person in this chart.

Name	
Dates	
Job or role in tourism	
Achievements/events (with dates)	
General contribution to development of tourism	
Any other important information	

2 When you have made notes, get together with members of the other groups and find out about the other pioneers of tourism. Discuss the different contributions made by each of the pioneers. Who do you think made the most valuable and important contribution? Why?

Thomas Cook

For millions of people around the world, the name Thomas Cook means traveller's cheques and travel agencies – but who was Thomas Cook? He was the first person to develop mass tourism. He organized excursions and tours which opened up the world of travelling for pleasure to the middle classes. Many of the things which we now take for granted in modern tourism date back to Thomas Cook – things like traveller's cheques, hotel vouchers, and chartered transport.

Thomas Cook lived in Leicester in the centre of England in the mid-19th century. He organized his first tour, a railway excursion from Leicester to Loughborough, in 1841. A total of 570 passengers joined it. The excursion was so successful that Cook organized other similar events. All of the early tours used the newly-invented railways.

Cook organized his first major continental tour in 1855 but it lost money. However, by 1862 he had managed to negotiate cheaper rates for crossing the English Channel. The cheaper rates were in return for a guarantee that he would bring large numbers – the essence of mass tourism. Tours to France and to Switzerland became regular events. The Swiss in particular quickly recognized the need to build the things that the tourists wanted – hotels and other facilities – so a whole tourist industry began to develop. After the opening of the Suez Canal in 1869, Egypt also became a popular destination for Cook's tours. In the early 1870s he organized the first round-the-world tour, lasting 222 days.

So in a little over thirty years the foundations of modern mass tourism were established.

Freddie Laker

Freddie laker was one of the pioneers of modern passenger air travel. He was born in England in 1922, and from an early age he was involved with aircraft. He was an aircraft engineer in the Second World War and also learnt to fly.

Laker's business ability appeared soon after the war ended. In the Berlin airlift of 1948 he was one of a number of businessmen who bought and chartered planes to take food and supplies to the people of Berlin when the city was blockaded by the Russians.

This early entrepreneurial experience led Freddie Laker to increased business activity in the 1950s. He was one of a number of businessmen who helped the rapid expansion of air travel, using recent developments in aircraft technology. In 1955, for example, he set up an air service carrying passengers and cars across the Channel between England and France.

It was in the 1960s and 1970s that the real growth in charter air travel happened, as more and more people wanted to go on package holidays. Laker was at the forefront of this. He ran British United Airways from 1960 to 1965, and Laker Airways from 1966 to 1982. His main achievement was to set up companies which were independent of the big state corporations, and to offer cheap flights for thousands of people. Perhaps the best example of this was the Skytrain passenger service to the USA which started a price war on the transatlantic routes from 1977 to 1982. Freddie Laker helped to make air travel a realistic and fairly cheap possibility for many travellers and tourists.

César Manrique

The tribute most often paid to César Manrique is that without his efforts tourist development on Lanzarote would have followed the high-rise, high-density route and the island would have lost its identity. In the environmentally conscious 1990s Lanzarote is studied by other countries who are developing tourism, and is used as a role model.

Manrique was born in Arrecife in 1919 and studied art in Madrid and New York, at a time when surrealism was a major influence. He returned to his beloved island in 1968, determined to preserve its natural beauty in the face of tourism. His major set-piece visitor attractions, Jameos del Agua, Mirador del Río, and Jardín de Cactus are masterpieces of design which are totally in harmony with the landscape.

The hallmarks of any Manrique project are the use of local materials, integration with nature, and a completely peaceful atmosphere (often helped by ethereal 'mood music'), all finished with a flourish of his own brand of surreal art.

Manrique was far more than just an artist and designer, however. He was the driving force behind the island's whole tourism development philosophy. He was a fiery orator and a tireless promoter of the island, and it is thanks to him that almost all the architecture on Lanzarote is in traditional style, and that there is still a total ban on advertising hoardings.

César Manrique died in a car accident just outside his Taro de Tahiche home in September 1992. His influence has been so pervasive throughout Lanzarote that his philosophy is sure to live on.

Festivals

Imnarja festival

❶ You are going to listen to a tour guide describing a festival to a group of tourists on a coach. Before you listen, discuss these questions.

1 What do you know about Malta? Think about: geography, location, people, language, culture, religion, food and drink.

2 Look at the photograph. What do you think happens during the Imnarja festival?

3 The following words are all used in the guide's talk. How do you think they are connected to the festival?

harvest   crops   torches   bonfires   procession   banners   rabbit

❷ Now listen to the guide's talk. Were your predictions correct?

❸ Listen again, and complete the gaps in these notes used by the guide to remind her of the details of the festival.

Name of festival is [1] *Imnarja.*

Official name is Feast of [2] _____.

'Imnarja' means [3] _____.

Opening ceremony ('Bandu') is procession of brightly-coloured
[4] _____.

Main part of festival is [5] _____ on last day.

Display of vegetables, fruit, poultry, [6] _____.

Stalls sell local cakes, pastries, and [7] _____.

Special Maltese dish of [8] _____.

During races the horses are ridden [9] _____.

Winners receive [10] _____ which they display in their
[11] _____.

To reserve a place on the excursion go to [12] _____.

Describing procedures – present simple passive

Look at these examples from the talk about Imnarja.

the crops are laid out on display
the festival is opened by a simple ceremony
there are stalls which are set up
a lot of Maltese wine is drunk
horse and donkey races are held
the banners are handed out

The present simple passive is often used to describe events and procedures – the person or people doing the action is not as important as the event itself.

Practice

1 Match the nouns in column **A** with the verbs in column **B** and produce a sentence which describes something that could happen in a festival. You will need to put the verb in the correct form. For example:

Flowers are displayed.

A		B	
flowers	music	bake	light
speech	lanterns	carry	make
costumes	money	collect	play
candles	children	display	put up
special cakes	decorations	dress up	wear

2 Try to continue each sentence. For example:

Flowers are displayed at the windows of all the houses.

Structuring a talk

Look at these examples from the talk about Imnarja.

***I want to tell you about** one of the local island festivals.*
***Let me start by saying** that this is probably one of the most exciting festivals on the island.*
***What happens is** this.*
***You're probably wondering about** food and drink.*
***Now, moving on to** the climax of the festival.*
***Another interesting thing is** that the winners take their banners ... .*
***So, as you can see,** it's well worth visiting.*
OK. Let's move on.

The highlighted expressions are used by the guide to give her talk a structure.

Practice

Now use the expressions above, and your notes from exercise 2 on the previous page, to retell the information about the Imnarja festival.

Output task

Other festivals

1 Are there any festivals or traditional events in your own country which are celebrated every year? If you are studying with students from other countries, you should be able to find out about a large number of different festivals. For each festival, make notes under the following headings.

Name
Where does it take place?
When does it take place?
What are its origins? (to do with religion, agricultural seasons, historical event, other)
What exactly happens during the festival?

2 If you don't know about any festivals, your teacher will provide some notes on three festivals from different parts of the world. Prepare a short talk about one of them. Structure it like the talk on the Imnarja festival.

The geography of tourism

Tourism is a world industry, but different parts of the world offer different attractions for the tourist. Divide into groups. Each group will be given a different part of the world to work with.

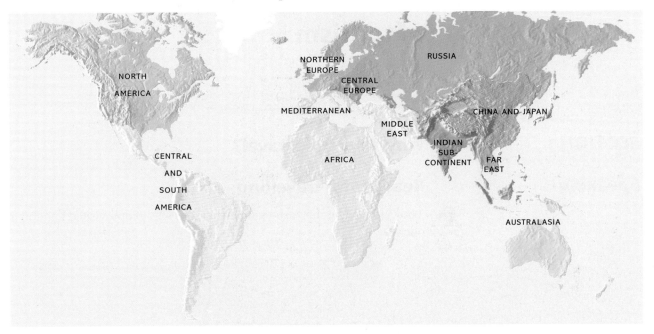

① Think about the countries and cities in the area you have been given. What tourist attractions do they offer? Can you name any particular places?

② Why do tourists visit this area? Analyse your area in terms of what it offers in the following categories:

– history	– sport/leisure activities	– climate
– culture and religion	– typical entertainments	– landscape

③ When you have made a detailed list, divide up into new groups with one person from each of the first groups. Compare what you have found out about the different regions of the world.

Vocabulary			
ambitious	currency	insurance policy	self-catering
ancient	departure lounge	itinerary	sightseeing
art gallery	deposit	long-haul flight	spa
banners	destination	museum	steam
boarding card	disposable	night-life	terminal building
bonfire	income	package holiday	torch
brochure	excursion	panoramic view	tour rep
carnival	festival	passport control	tourist attraction
century	flight attendant	pilgrim/pilgrimage	travel agent/
charter	guided tour	pioneer	agency
check-in desk	heritage	procession	traveller's cheque
chronological	high-rise	pyramids	unemployed
civilization	high season	railway	visa
climate	in-flight	resort	voucher
crops	entertainment	room service	

2

The organization and structure of tourism

SECTION 1	Why do people travel?

Speaking · **Reasons for travelling**

❶ Look at these pie charts showing the reasons why people visited London in one year.

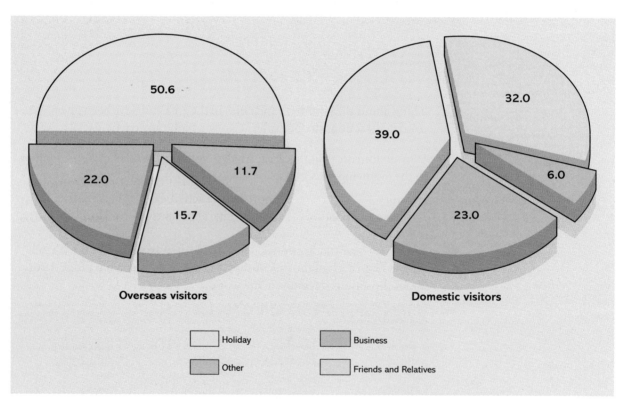

Overseas visitors

Domestic visitors

Holiday   Business

Other   Friends and Relatives

1 What are the main points shown by the charts?
2 The 'other' section is quite large. What do you think it could include?
3 Do you think the charts would be very different for your city or country?

❷ Think of four people – family or friends – that you know well. Make a list of all the places they have travelled to in the past two years, and have stayed in for at least one night. In groups of three or four, put your lists together and make a pie chart similar to the ones above. Then compare with other groups.

Listening 1

A passenger survey at an airport

1 Listen to this woman conducting a passenger survey at a busy airport. She is asking people why they are travelling and other details about their journey. As you listen, complete the chart below.

	Passenger 1	Passenger 2	Passenger 3	Passenger 4
Destination				
Purpose of visit				
Length of stay				
Size of party				
Mode of transport to airport				
Occupation				
Age				

2 Listen again and note down the different question forms the woman uses. Organize the questions into groups according to the way each is formed.

Language focus 1

Question forms

This is one possible way of grouping the questions the interviewer asks. What do you notice about the word order in the three different types of question?

Questions using question words – *what, where, how*
Where are you going?
What is the purpose of your visit?
How long are you staying in Corfu?
How did you get to the airport?

Yes/No questions
Do you have a few minutes to answer some questions?
Are you travelling on business?
Is there anyone else in the party?

Indirect questions
I wonder if you'd mind answering some questions?
Could you tell me how you got to the airport?
Could you tell me where you are going?
Can I ask which of these age groups you're in?
Would you mind telling me how old you are?

Pronunciation focus 1

Intonation

1 When we ask people for information that might be personal, we are more likely to choose an indirect question form. Compare:

How old are you?
I wonder if you'd mind telling me how old you are?
Which sounds more polite?

2 Intonation is very important. Listen to the different versions of these questions and decide which is more polite.

a *Could you tell me where you're going?*
b *Would you mind filling in this form?*
c *Could you tell me how old you are?*
d *Could you possibly turn the radio down?*

Note the intonation pattern in the polite form.

Could you tell me where you're going?

When you respond to a polite question or request your intonation should start high and the tone should fall:

Could you tell me where you're going?

Of course. I'm flying to Brussels.

Practice

1 Convert these direct questions into indirect questions.

a What's the time?
b When is the next flight to Amsterdam?
c Is this your suitcase?
d When does the flight from Istanbul arrive?
e How many times a year do you fly?
f Have you got any seats on the ten o'clock flight?
g Is there a phone near here?
h Why are there no trains on Sundays?

2 Now take turns to ask your partner each indirect question. Try to ensure that your intonation is polite. Your partner should only reply if the question is asked politely.

Class passenger survey

① Choose one of the pictures and imagine you are that person. Don't tell anyone which picture you have chosen. You are at the airport, about to travel somewhere.

Complete the chart below.

Destination	
Purpose of visit	
Length of stay	
Size of party	
Mode of transport to the airport	
Occupation	
Age	

② Now go round the class and conduct a survey to find out the same information about other 'travellers'. Try to guess which of the pictures each person chose.

Statistical information about travel and tourism

Displaying statistical information

1 These three graphs and charts give different statistical information related to tourism and travel. Which one is (a) a pie chart, (b) a block graph, and (c) a line graph?

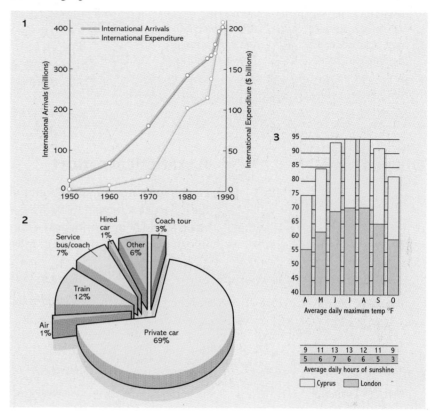

Decide what is the most important fact shown in each graph or chart. Why is the information presented in these different ways? What other ways of displaying statistical information can you think of?

2 Now answer these questions.

1 What was the total international expenditure on tourism in 1985?

2 Which decade saw the biggest increase in international arrivals?

3 What is the most popular form of transport used by tourists in Britain?

4 Which is the hottest month in Cyprus?

5 In which month is there the greatest difference between the temperature in Cyprus and the temperature in the London?

3 What do you think?

1 Why did the 1970s see so many international arrivals?

2 Why does air transport only account for 1% of tourist transport in Britain?

3 Do you think the chart showing tourist transport would be very different for your country?

Language focus 2

Describing graphs and statistics

1 Describe the graphs and charts in the previous section. Use the words and expressions from the list to complete the sentences.

went up gradually	a small percentage of
levels off	from ... to ...
more than double	a fairly sharp fall
rose dramatically	the most popular
a gradual increase	the vast majority of

a There was ____ in international arrivals between 1950 and 1960 ____ 25.3m ____ 69.3m.

b International expenditure on tourism ____ from 1950 to 1970 and then ____ from 1970 to 1980.

c ____ tourists in Britain travel by car.

d ____ tourists in Britain travel by coach.

e ____ mode of transport in Britain is by private car.

f There is ____ in the temperature in Cyprus in October.

g The temperature in Cyprus ____ in July and August at 95 degrees.

h The number of hours of sunshine in Cyprus in July is ____ that in London.

2 Make some more sentences of your own.

Output task

A statistical report

1 Here is some information about tourism in Britiain. At the moment it is in the form of a series of tables. With a partner, decide which type of graph or chart would be appropriate as a more visual way of presenting the information. Then draw the graphs and charts.

A Top ten attractions in London

British Museum	5.8m visitors
National Gallery	3.8m
Madame Tussaud's	2.4m
Tower of London	2.3m
St Paul's Cathedral	1.9m
Tate Gallery	1.8m
Natural History Museum	1.7m
Chessington World of Adventure	1.5m
Science Museum	1.3m
Victoria and Albert Museum	1.1m

B Tourist spending breakdown

Accommodation	£6,520m
Eating out	£4,388m
Shopping	£3,576m
Travel within the UK	£2,564m
Entertainment	£1,008m
Services, etc.	£497m
Total	**£18,553m**

C Recent trends in tourism

Visitors to London

	1992	1994	1996 (millions)
Visits			
domestic	7.0	7.5	8.0
overseas	10.0	7.5	8.0
all	17.0	18.2	19.5
Nights			
domestic	19.4	19.0	18.5
overseas	68.7	74.0	80.0
all	88.1	93.0	98.0
Expenditure (£)			
domestic	640	900	1,325
overseas	4,150	4,825	5,700
all	4,790	5,725	7,025

2 Write a brief report to accompany each of your graphs or charts. The report should include all the important information. Use phrases from **Language focus 2**. Present one of your graphs or charts to the class.

SECTION 3

Reading

Working in tourism

The structure of the tourism industry

1 Discuss these questions with a partner.

1 What are the different sectors of the tourism industry? Make a list.
2 Is tourism an 'industry'?
3 In what ways is tourism a 'product'?
4 How is this 'product' distributed to the consumer?

2 This diagram from J. Christopher Holloway's *The Business of Tourism* shows the structure of the tourism industry. Fill in the gaps with words and phrases from the list.

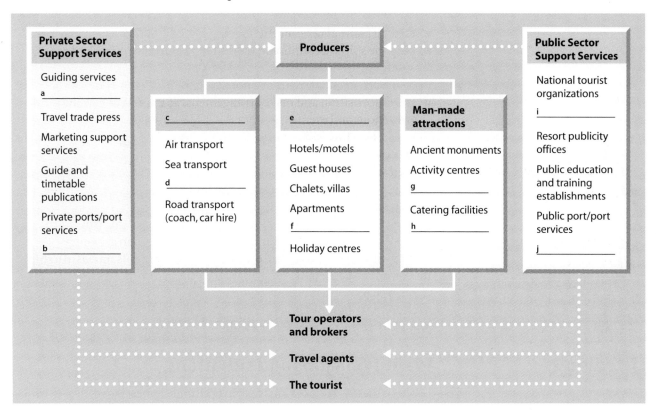

The list of words and phrases:

accommodation
camping and caravan sites
carriers
rail transport
regional tourist organizations
stately homes

theme parks
travel insurance and finance services
visa and passport offices
private education and training establishments

How many of the sectors did you have on your list from exercise 1?

3 Think of a real example of each of the sectors in the place you are studying, or for your own country. For example, for air transport, write down the name of an airport and an airline. When you have finished, choose a different country.

Jobs in tourism

1 Look at this list of jobs related to tourism, and decide which sector of the tourism industry they belong to. Use the diagram from the previous section to help you.

a baggage handler   f purser
b curator   g air traffic controller
c warden   h entertainments officer
d guard   i concierge
e marketing consultant   j tour manager

2 Now make a list for each of the other sectors. Compare your lists with those made by other students.

3 Who would carry out the activities below?

a direct a plane at take-off and landing
b keep the ship's accounts and look after passengers' rooms and general comfort
c deal with people arriving at a hotel
d give information and make arrangements at a hotel concerning local attractions and events
e look after a museum
f fly a plane
g look after the passengers on a plane
h take suitcases and bags on and off planes
i help hotel guests with their suitcases and bags
j give advice on how to promote a region or sector of tourism
k check suitcases and bags for illegal items on arrival in a country
l help arrange concerts, dances, and other social events on board a ship
m look after a game park
n be in charge of arrangements for a group of tourists travelling together
o clean the rooms in a hotel
p look after the passengers on a train

Identifying jobs and situations

1 Listen to these extracts from five conversations. For each one, decide who is talking to whom, and where the conversation takes place.

Conversation 1 _____

Conversation 2 _____

Conversation 3 _____

Conversation 4 _____

Conversation 5 _____

2 What qualities and qualifications are needed for each of the five jobs? Which of the five would you expect to need these qualifications, personal qualities, and experience?

– keyboard/computer skills   – the ability to speak three languages
– a university degree   – an attractive and pleasant personality
– the ability to swim   – experience of dealing with the public

Output task

Producing a CV

❶ When you apply for a job it is usual to include a curriculum vitae, or CV (US résumé). This is a list of your personal details, educational history, qualifications, experience, and interests – in other words, the story of your life from a professional point of view.

Here are some headings that might appear on a typical CV.

Name

Personal statement
(a brief summary of your status)

Personal details
(address, date of birth, nationality, etc.)

Education
(including dates, places, and examinations)

Professional qualifications
(including dates and places)

Work experience

Languages

Interests and hobbies

Referees

Match each of the headings with the jumbled up sections of this CV. What job do you think this person might be applying for?

a

Argentinian

b

Spanish (*mother tongue*)
English (*advanced level*)
Portuguese (*intermediate level*)

c

1993–94
Higher Institute of Tourism, 'Perito Moreno'.
Graduated in Hotel Management.

1995–96
Diploma in Protocol and Ceremonial,
Association of Hotels in Buenos Aires, including
training at the Plaza Marriott, Buenos Aires.

d

July 1997–December 1997
Conte Hotel (five-star), Buenos Aires.
Started as bell-boy, trained as telephone
operator and worked on switchboard; final
position, reception assistant on front desk.

e

An enthusiastic and hard-working hotel
management graduate looking for a
challenging junior management position in a
top-class hotel.

f

Film and music (playing the guitar)

g

10 April 1974

h

12 Selbourne House,
Canterbury Street,
London SE1

i

Leonel Jorge García

j

Manager, Plaza Marriott, Buenos Aires
Personnel Manager, Conte Hotel, Buenos Aires

2 Look at these two job advertisements. Work in groups and discuss what experience and qualifications potential candidates would need to have.

| APPOINTMENTS | A | B |

SENIOR ENTERTAINMENTS OFFICER

TO WORK ON CARIBBEAN CRUISE SHIP

RESPONSIBLE FOR
– *planning and running an entertainment programme for over 1,000 passengers*
– *managing a staff of 20*
– *experience essential*
– *nine-month contract (renewable)*

APPLY TO
Charlotte Goldsmith, Leisure Recruitment Services, 329–31 Farringdon Road, London EC1 2AW

EMPIRE STATE BUILDING

New York's most famous skyscraper is seeking a Director of Tourism Services

The successful candidate will have responsibilty for:
▸ managing the observatory, shops, and exhibition
▸ recruiting and managing a team of 15 employees
▸ publicity and marketing

Apply in writing with current résumé to:
Executive Appointments, 268 Madison Avenue, New York, NY 10016

3 Now write a CV of your own in response to one of the job advertisements. Try to base it as much as possible on your own details and experience. You can add things such as qualifications and work experience which you hope to get in the future. Don't be too modest!

4 In groups, look at the CVs of another group and decide who has the best qualifications and experience for each job.

ACTIVITY   Tourism in The Gambia, Sierra Leone, and Belize

1 What do you know about The Gambia, Sierra Leone, and Belize? What facilities for tourists would you expect to find in these countries – or any other developing country? What facilities might they need to develop?

2 Read this introduction to the three articles below. What impression does it give of the current state of tourism in the developing world?

Introduction

Although it may help to boost a country's economy, the international tourism industry is fragile. For most people, foreign holidays are a luxury, and when a country is in recession some people will save money by cutting out holidays.

This can be economically disastrous for countries which rely heavily on income from tourism. In other parts of the world, from Central America to Western Europe, the development of tourism has also caused widespread environmental damage.

3 Divide into three groups. Each group is going to read about the tourism industry in one of the three countries. As you read, make notes about your country in the table below. After you have read your article, find out from members of the other groups about the other two countries.

	The Gambia	Sierra Leone	Belize
Geography			
Location			
Size			
Climate			
Tourism			
When tourism started			
Number of visitors			
Where from			
Facilities offered			
Facilities needed			
Advantages of tourism			
Problems brought by tourism			

Belize

MEXICO

Atlantic Ocean

BELIZE

Pacific Ocean

SOUTH AMERICA

Belize, which lies on the east coast of Central America, is a former British colony and has a population of approximately 2 million.

The climate of Belize is sub-tropical and the country has an average temperature of 20˚C. Running the length of the coastline of Belize is a barrier reef, which is second only in size to the Australian Great Barrier Reef.

In a similar way to tropical rain forests, coral reefs are among the most complex and delicate of all ecosystems. As well as protecting the coastline from hurricane damage, Belize's barrier reef has always been an essential source of food and income for local fishermen.

Like the governments of other developing countries, the Belizean government has actively encouraged the development of tourism as a way of earning foreign exchange. Last year, over 200,000 tourists visited the country. But the growth of tourism is now threatening the delicate marine life of the coral reef.

In order to make room for hotels to be built and to provide beaches, the swamps of tropical mangrove trees have had to be cleared. As a result, shore erosion has occurred and vital areas which are home to rare reef plants have been destroyed. The coral reef itself is also under threat – from pollution, from the physical damage caused by the anchors of cruise ships and boats chartered by tourist divers, and from the activities of some of the divers themselves.

Additionally, over-fishing has seriously reduced the populations of fish and shellfish such as conch, grouper, and lobster. The anticipated rise in sea level as a result of global warming is also expected to damage the coral and fish reserves.

The government of Belize has responded to these problems by setting up a Coastal Zone Management Plan, with the aim of carrying out regular surveys to monitor the effects of tourism and fishing on reef life. But because Belize has a foreign debt of about $100 million, it has had to rely on support from environmental groups to continue with this important work.

One particular environmental group is Coral Cay Conservation, a voluntary team of divers and marine biologists, which is currently working on a project to establish a marine reserve at the southern end of the barrier reef.

The government has also agreed to provide funds to establish a new Conservation Division which will establish and manage a number of new conservation areas in Belize.

The Gambia

AFRICA

—THE GAMBIA

Surrounded by the former French colony of Senegal, The Gambia forms a narrow strip of land on either side of the River Gambia. The country is low-lying and extends inland for 320km; it is never more than 50km wide. The Gambia has a population of just 800,000 and is the smallest country in West Africa.

The tourist season runs from November to April and visitors come mainly from Britain, Sweden, France, and Germany. Since it began developing its tourism industry in the late 1960s, the number of visitors to the country has increased from just 20 in 1965 to well over 100,000 in the early 1990s. This growth may partly be due to the American best-seller *Roots*, in which the writer Alex Haley claimed to have traced his ancestors back to the Gambian village of Juffure. The village is now a major tourist attraction.

Most of the country's 17 resort hotels are concentrated on the coastline around the town of Bakau; several of them are wholly or partly owned by the Gambian government. An estimated 7,500 Gambians are directly employed in the tourism industry as cooks, receptionists, bookkeepers, drivers, and guides. In 1990, tourism brought The Gambia $15 million in foreign exchange, or 10 per cent of Gross National Product.

The government also earns income from the sale of land, taxes paid by the companies which own the hotels, and customs duties on foreign equipment such as construction machinery. Alongside the benefits tourism has brought to The Gambia's economy, many of the problems associated with it are also beginning to be felt.

Sierra Leone

AFRICA

— SIERRA LEONE

With a long stretch of coastline on the Atlantic Ocean, Sierra Leone is bordered by Guinea to the north and Liberia to the south. Its natural features are varied: the coastal region is low-lying and sandy, whereas inland the terrain is more mountainous. The country has a population of about four million, and 7,000 people are currently employed in the tourism industry.

Sierra Leone is a late arrival on the tourist scene. In 1989, the foreign exchange earned from tourism was $17.4 million, or just 2 per cent of Gross National Product. In that year, most of the 25,000 holidaymakers who arrived in the country by air came from France, followed by North America and the United Kingdom.

At the moment, the country has just eight hotels, concentrated on the 38km of coastline around the capital, Freetown. With funding from the European Union, the government is expanding the limited telephone system and hopes to build a network of hotels, roads, and service stations across the country. Plans are also under way to develop safari-type holidays, together with forest explorations, game-hunting, and bird-watching.

But the tourism industry in Sierra Leone has a number of problems to overcome.

Like other developing countries, it does not yet have the resources to provide the kind of facilities Western tourists expect, such as good roads, modern hotels, and airports.

Roads linking the airport to the capital and the surrounding beaches are poor, pitted with holes, and dangerous to drive along at night. There is also an acute shortage of petrol and the country's postal service remains basic.

To develop better facilities, a country like Sierra Leone needs to attract foreign investors, and provide incentives in the form of tax relief or exemption from customs duties. Recently, the government passed a Tourism Development Bill to encourage the expansion of tourism. The Bill identifies particular areas which might be developed for tourism, provides much-needed incentives for foreign investment, and introduces controls on the number and quality of new buildings.

Vocabulary

accommodation	climate	guard	receptionist
advertisement	concierge	keyboard	referee
air-traffic controller	conference	land/landing	return ticket
apartment	consultant	level off	stately home
average	continental breakfast	marketing	suitcase
baggage handler	contract	manager	supplement
bell boy	curator	motel	survey
blanket	curriculum vitae	overseas	take-off
cabin	(CV)	passport	temperature
camp-site	domestic	percentage	theme park
captain	expenditure	pie chart	tour operator
caravan site	facilities	port	travel agent
carrier	flight attendant	porter	villa
chalet	graph (block graph,	purser	warden
chef	line graph)	qualifications	

3
Travel agents

SECTION 1	**What kind of holiday?**
Speaking and vocabulary	**Holiday types**

1 In pairs, discuss the following questions.

1 How many holidays have you had in your life? Make a list.
2 Which ones did you enjoy most/least? Why?
3 Put them into categories. Think of as many different types of holiday as possible.

2 Look at this list of types of holiday. Match each one with the correct drawing/icon, and with the appropriate phrase from a publicity brochure.

a adventure	e farmstay	i safari/wildlife
b camping	f fly-drive	j self-catering
c cruise	g independent/backpacking	k skiing
d driving /touring	h package/beach	l trekking

i 'Sun, sea, and sand – and all you pack is your suitcase'
ii 'A floating five-star hotel'
iii 'Route maps provided'
iv 'Escape the crowds – go where the mood takes you'
v 'A unique game-viewing experience'
vi 'Tents available for hire'
vii 'Discover a world of excitement'
viii 'Your car will be waiting at the airport'
ix 'Each suite has basic cooking facilities and a fridge'
x 'Breathtaking views from the snow-capped Himalayas'
xi 'Sun glistening on the white Alpine slopes'
xii 'Experience the working life of the countryside'

❸ What do people do on these types of holiday (e.g. beach holiday – sunbathing)? Who goes on them? Is there a 'typical tourist' for each one?

Reading

Four holidays

❶ Here are the names of four different holidays. What do you think will happen on each?

Earthwatch   Adventure Nepal   Eurobus   Rural tourism in Spain

❷ These words and phrases appear in the four texts. Which words would you expect to appear in each text?

bazaar	elephant	pass
beaches	extinction	pony-trekking
camp-sites	farmers	predetermined circuit
cheetah	farmhouse	project
co-existence	itinerary	researchers
cottage	jeep	snow-capped
drop-off point	jungle lodge	white-water rafting

Now read the texts to see if you were right.

DO YOU CARE ENOUGH TO JOIN AN EARTHWATCH PROJECT?

Your help is urgently needed now. The world is changing faster than ever before. Researchers are providing the data on which crucial decisions about our future will be based, but they cannot do it all on their own. That's where you come in. The funds that you contribute directly help the projects you join – but far more important is your own insight, enthusiasm, and willingness to help get the job done. We will get you there and back safely, mostly comfortably, sometimes not, in some of the most fascinating company you're ever likely to meet, people of all ages and abilities. We guarantee it's an experience you will never forget.

CHEETAH

HALTING THE CHEETAH'S RACE TOWARDS EXTINCTION

NORTHERN NAMIBIA – The fate of the cheetah lies in the hands of the farmers here whose land it shares. You can help Laurie Marker-Kraus (Cheetah Conservation Fund) examine, tag, release, and radio-track cheetahs caught in farmers' traps, and aid her educational campaign to show farmers the advantages of peaceful co-existence with the cat they love to hate.

Eurobus

★ ★ ★ ★ ★ ★ ★ ★ ★ ★ ★ ★ ★ ★ ★ ★ ★ ★

Budget travel designed for 16 to 38s– hop on, hop off

This innovative concept in Europe utilizes modern coaches operating around predetermined circuits, taking in the most popular destinations. Coaches depart daily from all Eurostops.

Consider the advantages:

★ You can tailor your own itinerary by choosing a pass or passes which best suit your travel plans. Choose to travel just one zone, link up two, or if you have plenty of time take the All Zones! Take it fast, take it slow, it's up to you. From your first day of travel you have up to four months to complete your pass.

★ You will be travelling with people from all parts of the world, a great opportunity to **make new friends** but also the opportunity to go it alone if and when you choose.

★ Eurobus stops outside accommodation points in each city, including **hostels**, **hotels**, and during the summer months also drops at selected **camp-sites**.

★ Eurobus has well-trained and experienced drivers and guides available to answer any questions you may have and to offer advice on the best sights to see, where to change money, all the small but important details which take so much time.

★ With your ticket you will be provided with information on how to make your Eurobus reservations, how to join Eurobus, and the pick-up and drop-off points in Europe.

Adventure
NEPAL
20 DAYS

8-DAY WALK IN THE ANNAPURNA FOOTHILLS

WHITE-WATER RAFTING

CHITWAN JUNGLE WILDLIFE

This action-packed trip will take you walking in the foothills of the snow-capped Annapurnas, rafting on the turbulent Trisuli river, and elephant-riding in the jungles of Chitwan reserve.

Kathmandu & Pokhara

After our arrival in Kathmandu, we'll be introduced to some of the city's ancient Buddhist and Hindu temples and shrines. There's also time to wander in its fascinating bazaars at your own pace before we fly to Pokhara.

Annapurna Foothills Trek

We cross Phewa Tal by boat, and are met by our Sherpa porters to begin our walk in the magnificent Annapurnas. Our route takes us off the tourist path, through lush forests and small villages. We'll visit the charming settlement of Gandrung and ascend Panchase Peak at 2,509m (7,400ft) for superb views of Annapurna II and the sacred 'fishtail peak', Machapuchhare.

Rafting & Chitwan Jungle

Returning to Pokhara, we drive south to our raft-point. Our qualified raft crew will brief you on the safety aspects and paddling techniques required to take part in the thrilling sport of white-water rafting. Then, from our jungle lodge in Chitwan Reserve, we set out by jeep or elephant in search of one-horned rhino and perhaps even Bengal tiger. Finally, we drive to the Everest Panorama resort for a relaxing day in wonderful hill country. On a clear day we may have views of eight of the world's ten highest mountains – from Everest in the east to Dhaulagiri in the west.

✳ SPANISH NATIONAL TOURIST OFFICE

Information sheet–Rural Tourism in Spain

In response to the ever-increasing demand for holidays close to nature, the regional autonomous governments and the private sector in Spain are now offering a comprehensive programme of rural facilities. These range from low-cost holidays at farmhouses and country cottages to sophisticated holidays in splendidly renovated country mansions and palaces. The common attraction is their location in some of the most beautiful parts of the Spanish countryside. A complementary range of activities such as pony-trekking, walking, and canoeing are normally on offer, and information is available from the establishments.

Here's an example from Asturias in Northern Spain.

La Quintana de la Foncalada

Management: Severino García and Danièle Schmid

This honeysuckle-clad farmhouse lies in the heart of the coastal 'marina' area of Asturias. Severino and Danièle love the land, its people, and traditions. Nearly everything is home produced: organic vegetables, honey, cheese, juices, and jams. The inside of the house is light and spacious, with cheerful and uncluttered bedrooms (smallish bathrooms), furnished with table lamps, and other things made by Danièle herself. You are welcome to make yourself hot drinks in the large kitchen. Upstairs there is a guest lounge with wicker furniture and masses of information on walks and visits. Severino will happily advise you on the best beaches, where to eat, and the best excursions from La Foncalada by bike or pony. A perfect place for a family holiday.

Rooms: 5 with shower & WC, 1 en suite with bath & WC

Price: D/TW 4,700 pesetas; ST 8,500 pesetas for 2; extra bed 400 pesetas Breakfast: 400 pesetas Dinner: 1,500 pesetas (M) – low season only Closed: never

3 In groups, decide which of the four holidays on pages 30 and 31 you would recommend for the following people.

a A family of four – a couple in their thirties with two children aged eight and four. They are not particularly rich, but not poor either. They have two weeks available.

b A group of young people (students). They don't have much money, but they have plenty of time (one or two months), and they want to 'go somewhere different'.

c A retired couple in their sixties, healthy and active, interested in culture and nature.

d A single woman. She has a very well-paid but stressful job as a lawyer. She likes outdoor sports and restaurants.

Which holiday would you choose for yourself? Why?

4 In pairs, write down some more client profiles. They could be real or imaginary people or groups. Discuss the type of holiday that you think would be suitable – include any of the holiday types listed in the vocabulary section.

Listening 1

Booking a holiday

1 Listen to this conversation which takes place in a travel agency. The customers want to travel to somewhere hot for a beach holiday in November. Which of these places do they choose – The Gambia, Spain, Tenerife, Lanzarote, La Gomera, or France? What is wrong with the places they don't choose?

2 Listen again and complete this customer enquiry form.

Real Holidays Ltd. Customer enquiry form

Resort	Playa Blanca
Hotel	
Room	☐ single ☐ twin ☐ balcony ☐ sea view
Meal-plan	☐ self-catering ☐ bed & breakfast ☐ half-board ☐ full-board
Airport	from _____ to _____ Departure on _____ November Dep: 09.35 Arr:_____ Return on _____ Dep: _____ Arr: _____
Client name	1 _____ 2 _____
Contact phone number	_____
Booking reference	_____

Language focus 1

Taking a booking

1 Here are some of the expressions the travel agent uses when taking the booking.

Can I help you?
I'll check availability for you.
There's availability on the 14th of November.
Do you want to confirm it?
Can I take some details?
I'll just give you the booking reference number.

2 Listen to the conversation again and note down exactly what is said immediately after each of the examples above (it may be said by either the travel agent or the customer).

Making suggestions and giving information (spoken)

Look at these examples from the conversation.

Suggestion	Add information	Add further comment
OK, what about going to the Canaries?	They're warm throughout the year	and they're very interesting.
… have you thought of going to The Gambia?	It's very reasonably priced	and you're guaranteed sun.
How about La Gomera?	It's a small island, very quiet but with things going on	and it's very pretty.
You could try Lanzarote.	There are some very peaceful parts.	I think you'd love it.
If I were you I'd choose B&B.	Then you can eat out in the restaurants at night.	That way you'll see a bit of the local life.
Why don't you reserve it for 24 hours?	I can put a 24-hour hold on it.	You can let me know tomorrow.

3 Use the expressions above to make suggestions, give information, and make comments in response to these statements. You can use your own ideas, or the ideas in brackets if you want.

a I don't like flying.
(take the train – fairly quick – interesting views)

b We want to go skiing.
(Switzerland – many different resorts – beautiful scenery)

c Where can I find the cheapest flights?
(look in the Sunday papers – all the companies advertise there – I've got a copy)

d I'd like to send my parents on a cruise.
(Mediterranean – ....)

e How can we get to see more of the island?
(hire motorbikes – ....)

f We want a holiday with a difference.
(...)

Pronunciation focus 1

Listen again to these sentences from **Listening 1**. What do you notice about the pronunciation of the underlined words or syllables?

Can I help you?
OK, well, what about going to the Canaries?
Have you thought of going to The Gambia?
Can I just take some details?

Where is the main stress in each sentence?

Output task

Travel agent role-play

Divide into two groups – half of you are travel agents, half of you are customers. After you have finished change roles and repeat the role-play, using the second set of holiday types you are given.

Travel agents **A**

You will be given a list of the holiday types you specialize in. Think about the details of the holidays you are offering. Customers will come to you with particular holiday requests. Try to sell them a holiday that suits their needs, but is also one of the holidays you specialize in.

Feedback
How many holidays did you sell with a definite reservation? How many did you put on a 24-hour hold?

Customers **B**

You will be given one or two holiday types in which you are interested. Try to find a travel agent who can provide you with the same holiday or a similar one. Visit as many travel agents as possible so that you can be sure you have got the best holiday for you.

Feedback
Customers – Did you find the holiday you wanted? How helpful did you find the travel agent?

Vocabulary and listening 2

The business traveller

The needs of the business traveller

1 In groups, discuss the following questions.

1 From the travel agent's point of view, what differences are there between dealing with a business traveller and an ordinary tourist?

2 What does a business traveller look for when arranging a trip?

3 When arranging (a) a flight and (b) a hotel, which of these things are most important for the business traveller?

flight	hotel
a choice of flight times	express reservation
a choice of airlines	corporate discount rate
express check-in	express check-in/check-out
automatic upgrade	access to fax
good food with free champagne	modem point in room
lots of leg-room	mini-bar
reclining seats	close to airport
air miles incentive scheme	free newspaper
immediate car hire pick-up on arrival	room for business meetings
limousine service from airport to hotel	sports centre

2 Now listen to a travel agent who specializes in corporate travel describing the particular needs of the business traveller. Before you listen, think about the meaning of these phrases:

at short notice   *client history*   *extended credit*
a complete package   *to settle up*   *en suite facilities*

1 What does he think are the main differences between a business traveller and an ordinary tourist?

2 What does he think are the most important things for the business traveller?

Reading and speaking

Holiday Inn Priority Club

1 In the listening on page 34, Mark mentioned that business travellers often like to join hotel chain 'priority clubs'. What do you think would be the benefits of joining such a club?

2 Read this leaflet giving information on the Holiday Inn Priority Club.

MAKE THE MOST OF YOUR TRAVEL

Join Holiday Inn Priority Club now and benefit from the awards and privileges that membership can bring. As a member you will receive special benefits every time you stay at a Holiday Inn hotel worldwide. At hotels in Europe, the Middle East, and Africa the benefits include:

- Corporate rate*
- Express reservations
- Your family can stay FREE, up to four people in the same room, when you pay corporate rate
- Express check-in (advance reservation required) and check-out
- Extended check-out time until 2.30 p.m. upon request
- 20% discount on specific hotel business services
- Special Priority Club rate for business and leisure car rentals from Hertz – just quote CDP 500166 and rate code 'FTR' at time of reservation
- Free weekday newspaper
- Regular special offers

EARN POINTS NOW

You will earn Priority Club points every time you stay on most business and leisure room rates, which you can exchange for personal awards ranging from free in-house movies, store vouchers, and Holiday Inn Executive Bedroom upgrades to free weekend stays and exciting special activity awards.

There are over 140 hotels to select from for your free weekend and a wide range of special activities – the choice is yours. Just imagine, you could soon be in Paris enjoying a romantic weekend, touring Michelangelo's masterpieces in Florence, or experiencing a Broadway show and dinner in New York.

Excludes Holiday Inn Garden Court® hotels in South Africa, Zambia, and Zimbabwe and specific fair periods.

HOW TO JOIN

Priority Club membership normally costs US$10 per year (or local currency equivalent). For FREE Priority Club membership until 31 December just complete the enclosed application form and hand it to reception before 30 September, so you can start earning your points and enjoying your special benefits right now.

Your temporary membership card is enclosed. Please quote your membership number when you make your next reservation at a Holiday Inn hotel, and show the card at check-in to receive your points.

We will send you your full membership pack after your second night at a Holiday Inn hotel. A quarterly statement will be sent to you, detailing your personal points balance and special offers when you stay at a Holiday Inn hotel during the preceding three months.

AIRLINE OPTIONS

If you belong to any of the following airlines' frequent flyer programmes, you can choose to receive airline credits instead of Priority Club points.

American Airlines®	Lufthansa
Delta Airlines	Sabena
Northwest Airlines	Swissair
United Airlines	Ansett Australia
Air Canada	Asiana Airlines
El Al	Qantas
Finnair	Thai Airways International
KLM	

Simply indicate your preferred airline and enter your frequent flyer number on the application form. Please remember to quote your airline alliance number when making a reservation. Your stays at Holiday Inn will appear on your airline programme statement. YOU WILL ONLY RECEIVE CORRESPONDENCE FROM PRIORITY CLUB IF YOU CHOOSE TO EARN PRIORITY CLUB POINTS. You may switch to earning Priority Club points by contacting the Priority Club Service Centre.

3 Which of the things listed in exercise 1 on page 34 (hotel) are available through the Holiday Inn Priority Club?

4 A business traveller has contacted his travel agent to ask about the Holiday Inn Priority Club. How should the travel agent answer these questions?

a How do I get points?
b What sort of things can I spend my points on?
c Do I get a discount at all Holiday Inn hotels?
d How much does membership cost?
e What do I have to do to qualify for membership?
f I'm also a member of the KLM frequent fliers club. Can I get air mile credits instead of priority points?
g If I do this will I still get Holiday Inn Priority Club points as well?
h OK, I'd like to join. What do I do now?

5 In pairs, role-play a conversation between a travel agent and a business traveller.

1 As a business traveller, decide what company you work for, your position, the countries you visit, how often you travel, and your preferences for flights and hotels.

2 Take turns to be the travel agent and the customer. Fill in the Holiday Inn Priority Club application form for your 'business traveller' partner.

LAST NAME _____

FIRST NAME _____ INITIALS _____

MALE   FEMALE   TITLE _____

HOME/BUSINESS   ADDRESS _____

POSTCODE   CITY _____

COUNTRY _____

COMPANY NAME _____

HOME/BUSINESS   TEL. _____ FAX _____

☐ AMERICAN	☐ EL AL	☐ SWISSAIR
☐ DELTA	☐ FINNAIR	☐ ANSETT
☐ NORTHWEST	☐ KLM	☐ ASIANA
☐ UNITED	☐ LUFTHANSA	☐ QANTAS
☐ AIR CANADA	☐ SABENA	☐ THAI

AIRLINE MEMBERSHIP NUMBER
You will only receive correspondence from Priority Club if you choose to earn Priority Club points.

ID CARD NUMBER _____ ISSUING COUNTRY _____

PASSPORT NUMBER _____ ISSUING COUNTRY _____

Date of Birth   DAY   MONTH   YEAR

American Express (AX)   Visa (V)   Eurocard (EC)
Mastercard (MC)   Diners Club (DC)

Valid to: MONTH   YEAR

Please tick here if you want this credit card number to be used to guarantee your Holiday Inn hotel reservations.

Signature . . . .   Date . . . .

Room preference

king-size bed   standard   smoking   non-smoking

Are you a member of any other hotel loyalty programmes? Please tick.

Hilton	Sofitel	Intercontinental	Novotel
Sheraton	Forte	Best Western	Marriott

Your age   18–25   26–35   36–45   46–55   56+

Nights spent in hotel accommodation on business last year

1–5   5–15   16–25   25+

Which countries/regions do you visit regularly? Please tick.

Eastern Europe	United Kingdom
France	Africa
Germany	Israel
Italy	Middle East
Scandinavia	Asia/Pacific
Spain	USA/ Canada
Netherlands/Belgium/	Caribbean/Latin America
Luxembourg	

What are your main leisure interests? Please tick.

Fishing	Soccer/Rugby
Sailing/Watersports	Motorsports
Skiing	Food and wine
Golf	Theatre/Arts
Athletics	Other

Do you take short breaks and holidays?

Alone   With other adults   With the family

Comparing facilities at three hotels

Stage 1

In groups of three or four, look again at the imaginary business travellers you each invented in exercise 5 of the previous section. Make sure you have detailed information about each of them, including their personal details and the company they work for. Invent more information if necessary.

All four of the travellers have to go to Vienna for business. Decide:

– exactly what business they will be doing (e.g. meeting clients, attending a conference, planning a sales promotion, etc.)
– what type of hotel each of them will be looking for in Vienna
– what facilities they will need
– how important the location is
– what recreational facilities they will want
– how important the price is

Stage 2

Now imagine you are travel agents specializing in business travel. You have been approached by each of the four business travellers for information on suitable hotels in Vienna. Look at the information on three Vienna hotels. Discuss which hotel would be most appropriate for each of your clients.

Description four-star hotel with 107 suites (see room facilities).
Location near to shops and underground system. About twenty minutes from the city centre.
Hotel facilities the hotel is an American-style 'all-suite' hotel, so there are few facilities – reception, café (for breakfast).
Room facilities each suite has lounge (TV), bedroom (TV), bathroom and toilet, bar area, kitchenette (microwave, refrigerator – with drinks), and office centre.
Business facilities each suite has spacious desk, telephone and PC, fax and modem connections. The suite is big enough for small meetings.
Conference rooms for up to forty people are available.

Radisson /// ISAS
PALAIS

Description luxury five-star hotel in attractive old-fashioned building (246 rooms).
Location on 'the Ring', ten minutes from the city centre.
Hotel facilities restaurants and bars, fitness centre, and sauna.
Room facilities cable and satellite TV, air-conditioning, mini-bar, telephone, fax point.
Business facilities Business Service Centre in the foyer with fax, telephone, personal computer, and secretarial services.
Fourteen conference rooms.

Description large modern five-star hotel (600 rooms).
Location near the City Air Terminal, ten minutes' walk from city centre.
Hotel facilities restaurants and bars, fitness club, and sauna.
Room facilities en suite rooms, cable TV, individually-controlled air-conditioning, telephone, mini-bar.
Business facilities Business Service Centre in the foyer providing secretarial services, fax, photocopying, personal computer, notebooks, laser printer, modem points, worldwide courier service.
Conference and banqueting facilities for up to 500 people.
Meeting rooms for 10 to 20 people available.
Limousine transfer service from airport.

Stage 3

In pairs, act out the roles of PA and travel agent.

Personal Assistant	**A**

You are the Personal Assistant of one of the business travellers you invented in Stage 1. You are speaking to your travel agent about the best hotel for your boss. Make certain all the facilities you require are there.

Travel agent	**B**

You are the travel agent. You are speaking to the Personal Assistant of a business person who does a lot of travelling. Find out about the needs of your client and recommend the most suitable hotel.

Visas

US visa requirements

1 Have you ever travelled to a country where you needed a visa? How did you apply for it? Why do some countries require visas? Have you ever been to the United States? Did you need a visa?

2 Listen to a recorded telephone message giving information on visa requirements for travellers to the United States. Decide whether the following statements are true or false.

1 A British citizen only requires a visa if he or she is staying for more than nineteen days.

2 Citizens from Japan can participate in the visa-waiver programme.

3 You are allowed to work while in the US.

4 You can enter on any airline or sea carrier.

5 You are allowed to make return trips to Mexico while you are in the US.

6 If you need a visa for a holiday the correct visa is a B1/B2 visa.

7 You should get your visa before you buy your travel ticket.

8 If you have already been refused a visa you will not get one when you apply again.

9 Postal applications take about three weeks.

10 You will need to send your passport when you apply for a visa.

3 The following people have all contacted your travel agency for advice on visas for travelling to the US. What information would you give them? Listen to the recorded message again.

a Masato Suzuki from Japan, flying to San Francisco for four weeks' holiday in California, followed by a trip to Canada, and then home to Japan.

b Greg Sheldon from New Zealand, planning a six-month world trip. He'll probably arrive in the US from Mexico and stay a month or so. He hasn't got much money.

c Mr and Mrs Henderson, a retired British couple travelling for a two-week holiday in the US and then staying with their son and his family in Canada for an unknown period (probably 3 to 6 months).

d Mehmet Ozgun, a Turkish national resident in the UK, who needs to visit the US on business in two weeks' time.

e Annika Johansson and Carina Lundgren, two students from Sweden who want to spend three to four months over the summer travelling round the US. They hope to find some casual work to help finance their trip.

Obligation and permission

1 Look at these sentences from the visa information recorded message.

Obligation

You must hold a return ticket.
You need to complete a visa-waiver application form.
A visa is required if you're staying more than 90 days.
You have to send a completed visa application form.

Lack of obligation

A visa is not required for British citizens for most holidays.

If you're entering the US from Canada you don't need to have a visa.

Permission

You may make side trips to Canada, Mexico, and the Caribbean Islands.

Citizens of twenty-three countries are able to travel to the US without a visa.

Lack of permission

You cannot perform productive work.
You are not allowed to accept paid or unpaid employment.

2 Although a recorded information message is spoken, the style is often like that of written language. Match these spoken statements with the four language functions. They all refer to laws and customs in the UK.

a You can get married at 16 provided your parents agree.
b You've got to drive on the left.
c Children under 16 aren't allowed to buy cigarettes.
d You don't have to have an ID card.
e You can't drink alcohol in pubs if you're under 18.
f When you're 18 you can vote in elections if you want – but you don't have to if you don't want to.

Which words or phrases are different in the spoken version?

Practice

1 Think about your own country. Discuss the following areas using spoken register.

– driving a car/motorcycle   – drinking alcohol
– wearing seat-belts/crash helmets   – smoking
– getting married   – military service

2 Now write a brief paragraph on laws and customs in your country – to be used in a guidebook.

Telephone language

1 Look at these expressions which are often used or heard when telephoning. Which three are from recorded messages?

a Going Greek reservations. Jane speaking. Can I help you?
b Can you put me through to your Accounts Department?
c This is the American Embassy visa information line.

d I'll just transfer you. Hold on a moment.
e I'll just see if he's in. Can I ask who's calling?
f All our operators are busy at the moment. Please hold.
g I'm afraid the office is closed at the moment. Please leave your name and number after the tone and we'll get back to you as soon as possible.
h Can I speak to Judith Vine, please?
i I'm afraid it's a bad line. Could you speak up?
j I'll get her to call you back.

2 Of the remaining seven expressions, which involves
 – asking the caller to wait?
 – asking to speak to someone?
 – speaking to the switchboard operator?
 – identifying themselves?
 – offering to take a message?
 – asking for repetition or clarification?
 – promising action?

3 Here are some similar expressions. Match them with the functions in question 2.

a Is Mario Ferrara there, please?
b I'll just put you on hold.
c Can I have extension 4784?
d I'll make sure she gets the message.
e Would you like to leave a message?
f Sorry, I didn't catch that. Could you repeat what you said?
g This is Ruth Levine. How can I help?

4 Now match one of the sentences in question 3 with one of the following sentences to make a dialogue. In pairs, try to continue the dialogue as long as possible.

a Sorry. I said we'd like to order some more brochures.
b Speaking.
c Can you tell him it's Anna from CityTours about the group from New York?
d Hello, I'm phoning to check the availability on your winter mini-breaks.
e OK, but don't be too long – I've got a queue of people here.
f Certainly … I'm just trying to connect you.
g Thanks. It's really very important.

Pronunciation focus 2

Listen to these sentences spoken by people on the telephone. Note the pronunciation of the highlighted words, especially the way they are linked.

Could you hold on a moment?
I'll just put you through.
Could you call back a little later?
I'll get back to you this afternoon.
He's really busy, so don't be surprised if he's late.

Output task

Telephone conversations

Act out the following telephone conversations in pairs. Work with a different partner each time. Do your best to get what you want. Make sure your dialogues include some of the functions you practised in the **Language focus** section.

– introducing yourself
– asking for someone
– speaking to the switchboard operator
– asking the caller to wait
– offering to take a message
– promising action
– asking for repetition and clarification

At the end, compare with the rest of the class to see who got the best deal.

Work in pairs. **Student A** should read the information below. **Student B** should turn to the information on page 175.

1 Arranging an interview for a visa

Traveller	A

You want an appointment as soon as possible because you plan to go to America next week.

Official	B

Look at the information on page 175.

2 Phoning a travel agent

Tourist	A

You want to find out if there are any good late deals for beach holidays. You are only interested if the price is very cheap and sunshine is guaranteed.

Travel agent	B

Look at the information on page 175.

3 Asking for an upgrade

Business traveller	A

You want to be sure of an automatic upgrade when you fly to the US on your forthcoming business trip. You represent a big company which could give the travel agent a lot of business.

Travel agent	B

Look at the information on page 175.

Activity

My hols

Judith Chalmers is a television presenter. She presents the holiday programme, 'Wish you were here…?' on British TV. In the programme she travels to many different places and experiences many different types of holiday. In this article she describes her own holidays.

❶ Before you read, think about what she might look for in a holiday for herself.

2 Read through the article quickly. Note down the places she has been to and the types of holidays she has had. Which places are associated with the following things?

- car hire
- concrete mixer
- crab sandwiches
- dancing
- golf course
- good view
- high hedges
- pool
- restaurants
- lovely lawns
- market

14 TRAVEL

MY HOLS

The people of a country make the difference for JUDITH CHALMERS.

'I HAVE marvellous memories of childhood holidays – Cornwall, Devon, and Scotland. I have a younger sister, and the four of us would drive everywhere in the family Morris Minor.

My sister and I would be so excited, getting up at two or three in the morning to drive to Cornwall. I remember the hedges being high and a little rabbit scurrying along the side of the road and Daddy picking it up and letting it run off into the fields. We used to go to Looe, which had very good crab sandwiches. I went back there recently for 'Wish you were here … ?' and it's got so much more crowded.

Working on 'Wish you were here… ?' gives me ideas for where I want to go on holiday. We certainly don't get our holidays free, but we get an upgrade sometimes, which is where my job can help.

Last winter we went to Cape Town, where I think we had our best-ever holiday. We spent three weeks over Christmas and New Year and I was so thrilled with it.

We rented a house through a friend, which is always a risk because we did that in Corsica once and arrived to find a concrete mixer in the drive. But it was magnificent – comfortable, not grand – in a suburb of Cape Town called Bishopscourt. We had lovely lawns, a pool, and a view out to Table Mountain. The restaurants were good – our favourite was called Uitsig in Constantia. The waterfront has been developed cleverly and is full of life – a little bit like Covent Garden.

We hired a car and Neil and I went off for four days along the Garden Route to Plettenberg Bay. We stayed at a wonderful little Edwardian-style B&B at Mossel Bay and had a good breakfast there with the owner.

We've always gone for self-catering or rented houses. I like the freedom and I stay in so many big hotels for work. I like to know we can get up when we want and I can potter in the garden or go down to the shops. I don't like the regimentation of a hotel and I don't want someone on the landing with a Hoover waking me up.

Inevitably, I do get recognized when I'm away. People want to tell me about their holidays or ask where they should go next. I enjoy meeting them – as long as I'm not working and trying to concentrate on doing my next piece to camera.

I know I've got a good job and I love it. Packing and unpacking is a bit of a chore, but I've got that fairly well sorted now. I have sections of the bedroom – if I'm going on safari I have my khaki gear and my Timberland boots here; and then I have my shorts and summer trousers there. I still agonize over it at times, and the times I've made mistakes are when I've had to pack too quickly.

I enjoy flying and I still get a buzz arriving at an airport. I use the time on the plane to catch up with films and reading. I don't sleep well on planes and I sometimes suffer from jet lag. I suppose I should just drink water but I like a glass of champagne. I don't bother with spirits, but I do

like good wine with a meal. We go away for about three weeks in the winter, to somewhere warm, and again in the summer to the Algarve, where we own a house. We bought it about nine years ago because we found ourselves going back every summer and renting somewhere. It's not big – three bedrooms and two bathrooms – but it has a pool and it is on the golf course with a lovely view over the fairway to the lights of Quarteira.

I get up early in the morning, at about 7.30, sling on a cotton bathrobe and creep out to deadhead the geraniums. I love the beaches there, but I can't sit on a beach for long. I like walking along the sand with a breeze in my face. We always rent a car and sometimes we'll take off into the mountains. I like the market at Loulé which, despite all the tourists, maintains its Portuguese identity. There is a square near the house and a wine bar where we have a dance in the evenings. At night we sit on the little terrace and have supper. I sometimes buy fish at the market in Quarteira and cook it that night.

I think I'll always travel. I don't know Italy well at all and I'd love to wander around Tuscany. I'd also love to go to the Galapagos Islands. The people in a country make so much difference – which is why I love Ireland. We were in Egypt recently, too, and the people there were wonderful.

I do have concerns about the environment. You have a lovely place, everybody wants to see it, but by the very fact that they go, they spoil it. My idea of an absolute hell holiday is to be surrounded by people who don't care where they are and shout and drink themselves silly and throw their cans of lager about. I can't abide bad manners. If I see people dropping litter I will pick it up, and if I'm in the car and I see somebody throw something onto the road I will toot them to hell.

I hope there is a growing awareness within the industry of the need to protect the environment. People are trying not to build high-rise hotels and even Benidorm has been cleaned up. But how do you control it? You can only do your bit.'

3 Now read the article again and answer these questions.

1 What type of holidays did she go on when she was a child?
2 How does her job help when she goes on her own holidays?
3 Why was she worried before she went to Cape Town?
4 Why doesn't she like spending her holidays in hotels?
5 What does she like, and dislike, about her job?
6 What does she usually do in the mornings in the Algarve?
7 What does she usually do in the evenings?
8 What does she like about Ireland and Egypt?
9 What type of holiday would she not like?
10 Is she optimistic about the future development of tourism?

4 Look again at the section on Judith Chalmers' South African holiday (renting a house in Bishopscourt and going on a four-day driving holiday). It is going to be featured in the programme, 'Wish you were here …?'. Here is the plan for that section of the programme. Each part will probably last between thirty seconds and one minute.

1 Introduce the holiday – 'Now a holiday in South Africa, staying in a rented house near Cape Town and then taking a four-day drive along the Garden Route to Plettenberg Bay.'

2 Describe the general location (with film) – Cape Town, Table Mountain, local restaurants, facilities, places to visit, etc.

3 Describe the house – lawns, pool, and views.

4 Interview the family who are staying there (film next to pool) – their opinions.

5 Describe the Garden Route – use map.

6 Feature on the Edwardian-style B&B at Mossel Bay, including interview with the owner.

7 Give details on cost, how to book, etc.

5 Now think of a type of holiday or a resort that you know well, and plan a similar section for a travel programme. Be sure to include a description of the holiday, an interview, and some factual details.

Vocabulary

adventure (holiday)	corporate travel	full-board	special offer
air-conditioning	credit	half-board	suite
air miles	cruise	leg room	sunbathing
application form	direct flight	limousine	switchboard
appointment	discount	mini-bar	transfer
availability	embassy	modem	trekking
B&B (bed and breakfast)	en suite facilities	packing/ unpacking	twin room
	environment		unexpired
backpacking	extension	pony-trekking	upgrade
balcony	farmstay	reclining seat	valid
bazaar	ferry	reservation	venue
booking reference	fitness centre	safari	VIP
cable TV	fly-drive	satellite TV	voucher
citizen	foyer	self-catering	white-water rafting
confirm	frequent flyer	skiing	

4

Tour operation

SECTION 1

The role of the tour operator

Vocabulary

Travel agents and tour operators

What is the difference between a travel agent and a tour operator?

1 Look at the different functions listed below (a–t). Match the words in italics with the definitions (1–16).

2 Decide which function is performed by a travel agent and which is performed by a tour operator.

functions	definitions
a sell air tickets and other transport tickets	1 hire for a special purpose
b design a *brochure*	2 agreement to pay money as compensation for loss or accident
c give advice on resorts, *carriers*, and travel facilities	
d order stocks of brochures for *rack display*	3 person or company, such as a hotel or an airline, which is represented by an agent
e negotiate with *principals* for *bulk purchase* of airline seats, hotel rooms, etc.	
f record and confirm reservations, send invoices to customers	4 take someone on as an employee
g issue tickets and *vouchers*	5 publicity booklet giving details of holidays, etc.
h *charter* aircraft	6 equipment (in a shop) to hold things such as brochures
i send *flight manifest* to airline	7 legal agreements between two companies
j send *rooming list* to hotels	8 paper or ticket which is given instead of money
k provide *travel insurance*	9 buying large amounts of goods or services in order to get a lower price
l sign *contracts* with hotels, airlines, etc.	
m plan *itineraries* for customers	10 tour including travel, accommodation, and meals (like a package)
n arrange *corporate* travel	
o investigate and research new markets	11 relating to a business or company
p plan advertising and promotion *strategy*	12 planned method of work
q *recruit* and train staff, e.g. resort representatives and guides	13 company which transports passengers (such as an airline)
r arrange car hire	14 list of passengers on a ship or plane
s organize *inclusive tours*	15 list of guests in a hotel, with their room number
t sell inclusive tours	16 lists of places to be visited on a journey

Listening 1

Reading

GOING GREEK
1998 BROCHURE

Travel agents and tour operators

1. Listen to Gordon Wright of Supertravel explaining the difference between a travel agent and a tour operator. As you listen, check to see if you matched the functions to the correct jobs.

2. In pairs, use your notes to explain the roles of tour operator and travel agent to each other. **A** should explain to **B** about the role of tour operator, and **B** should ask questions and check information. Then **B** should explain to **A** about the role of the travel agent, and **A** should ask questions and check information.

3. Look again at your list of things which tour operators do. Put them in the order in which a tour operator would need to do them.

The tour operator's in-tray

1. Going Greek is a tour operator which specializes in holidays to Greece – the mainland and the islands. It organizes a variety of holidays, including ordinary Group Inclusive Tours (package tours), and specialized holidays (sports and activities, walking, holidays for senior citizens, escorted cultural tours, etc.).

    Going Greek communicates with other parts of the tourist industry, and with customers, using a number of different written media – letter, fax, phone message, e-mail, and memo. You are going to read an example of each of these, selected from a typical day at the Going Greek head office. Before you read, discuss which type of communication would be used for each of the following situations.

    a a request from a travel agent for more brochures
    b the Promotions Department arranging a meeting to discuss customer feedback
    c an enquiry from a member of the public
    d an application for the job of resort representative
    e confirmation from a Greek coach company regarding the supply of coaches for transfers

2. Read the five example texts quickly to see if you were right.

Walking tours in Greece	
	Date: Thu, 19 Nov 1998 22:10:11 GMT
From:	
To:	egoinggk@promo.co.uk
Subject:	Walking tours in Greece
Message:	I saw your page on the Worldwide Web. I am very interested in walking tours on the Greek mainland. Can you give me booking information? Is it possible to reserve via the Internet? Please reply soon. Regards, Marcus Tonino

14 Well Walk
Luton
LU6 8FT

17 November

Recruitment Manager
Going Greek
176 Green Lane
London
N22 8WX

Dear Sir/Madam

I am writing to see if you have any vacancies for resort representatives next summer.

As you can see from my CV, a copy of which I enclose, I have worked as a resort representative for Jackson Holidays for the last two years in Greece and Turkey. I am fluent in Greek.

I am available for interview immediately.

Yours faithfully

C. Brandon

Colin Brandon

(encl: CV, testimonial)

MEMO

From George Costas, Promotions Dept.

To All Managers

Date 19 November

Following our analysis of last season's customer feedback forms, it is clear that there is a growing concern over safety and security in some of our resorts.

I would like to call a meeting of all departmental managers to discuss the implications and how we can improve PR in this area. Can I suggest 11.00 a.m. next Thursday? Please confirm asap.

I will send out copies of a detailed report on the survey in advance of the meeting.

Many thanks

George Costas

George Costas

OLYMPIC COACHES
CORFU TOWN

FAX MESSAGE

TO:	Going Greek	**DATE:**	19 November
ATTN:	Rita Harris	**PAGES:**	1
FROM:	Felix Soros, Bookings Manager		

RE: Coach bookings for next season's transfers

I can confirm that Olympic Coaches will be able to supply the following coaches for transfers from Corfu Airport to the main island resorts:

1 April to 30 June	Saturdays: 4 coaches
	Wednesdays: 2 coaches
1 July to 31 Aug	Saturdays: 8 coaches
	Wednesdays: 4 coaches
1 Sept to 31 Oct	Saturdays: 4 coaches
	Wednesdays: 2 coaches

All coaches are fully air-conditioned and have 51 passenger seats.

For the above numbers we can offer the rates previously quoted. This represents a 30% discount on our published standard rates.

Can you confirm exact destinations and approximate timings as well as arrangements for return transfers?

Regards

Felix

Felix

☎ Phone message

9.10 a.m.

Peter from Broadway Travel Agency, New York phoned. They're nearly out of brochures. Can we mail 200 asap?

Jill

PS Address is on database.

3 The Director of Going Greek made these notes concerning the five items. Which item do they refer to? (There are two notes for each item.)

a Invite for interview
b Get despatch onto it
c Agreed, but prefer 10 a.m.
d Didn't we get a higher rate last year?
e Cancellation arrangements?
f Ask for referees
g Can I have a detailed report today?
h Ask for opinion of web page
i This year's or next year's? – quick call
j Jane to reply – get address to send full brochure

4 What do these abbreviations and other terms mean?

CV	testimonial
re	PS
GMT	Dept
encl	attn
asap	database
Internet	PR

Output task

Tour operator's replies

1 Write a reply for each of the five items in the previous reading section, using the same format. For example, write a letter in reply to the job application letter, a message in response to the phone message, and so on. Make sure you use the same layout. Include the points made in the Director's notes in exercise 3 of the previous section.

2 Here are some extracts which could be used in your replies. Decide which text type they belong to.

a

Thank you for your letter of 17 November.

b

Last year we received a 35% discount. I wonder why we have not been given a similar discount this year?

c

Could you also send us the names and addresses of two referees, at least one of whom should be a previous employer.

d

I have another meeting at 11.00. Could we make it 10.00?

e

I would be grateful if you could telephone this office so that we can arrange an interview.

f

As our web page is a recent means of advertising we would be grateful if you could give us your opinion on it. I am sending a brief questionnaire by post.

g

Thank you for your fax of 19 November and the confirmation of our coach bookings.

h

Make sure you check which year they want.

i

Thanks for your note. I agree we need to discuss this matter soon.

j

We will send exact destinations and timings eight weeks before the first booking.

SECTION 2 — Negotiations

Reading

Negotiation techniques

When they are putting together a tour, tour operators have to hold detailed discussions and sign contracts with a number of 'principals', such as hotels, carriers (airlines), and coach companies. During these discussions the tour operator must try to negotiate the best deal.

1 You are going to read an article giving advice on how to negotiate successfully. Before you read it, discuss how a business negotiation is different from everyday conversation.

2 The title of the article is 'Be prepared! The art of successful negotiation'. What advice do you think the writer will give? Think about these four sub-headings.

– Preparation   – Achieving your objectives
– Language and behaviour   – Follow-up

3 Now read the article on the next page to see if your predictions were correct. Work in groups of four. Each person should read one of the four sections and explain it to the other members of the group.

4 What is meant by the expressions *up your sleeve*, *a game plan*, and *hard man, soft man*?

5 You might hear the following things said during a negotiation. Which piece of advice in the text do they refer to?

a Could you just repeat that?
b Did you have a pleasant journey?
c Can I just recap on what we've agreed so far?
d If I can start with your first point …
e Yes, I see what you mean, but don't you think it would be better to … ?
f Would you like me to go over that again?

6 Do you think any of the advice is particularly important for a tour operator about to start negotiations with a hotelier or an airline company? Is any of it not relevant?

Be prepared!

The art of successful negotiation

Are you satisfied with the way you handled that last set of negotiations? Couldn't you have done just a little bit better? Are you letting down your company – and yourself? This list of helpful hints may allow you to come away from your next negotiation with a greater sense of achievement.

Preparation

Being prepared is the most important thing. If you haven't had time to prepare properly, then cancel the meeting – you'll be wasting your time.

1 Make sure you know the arrangements – the time and the place.

2 Set aside enough time for the meeting.

3 Have a clear set of objectives: what do you really want to achieve? List your main objectives and your secondary objectives. What is the minimum position you are prepared to accept?

4 Take what you need – documents, materials, people.

5 Dress appropriately. 'Power-dressing' may help, but it's more important to dress so that you feel comfortable and confident.

6 If you're hosting the negotiation, then think carefully about the arrangement of the room and the layout of the furniture.

Language and behaviour

Your behaviour should be polite and respectful – you won't gain anything by being rude. In international negotiations you may also find you're talking to someone whose first language isn't the same as yours.

1 Allow time for social conversation – and have a few topics of conversation up your sleeve.

2 Don't use threatening body language or gestures (unless you want to threaten!).

3 Be polite and civil, even when you're being tough.

4 Make sure you understand what the other person is saying. Ask for clarification if necessary.

5 Be sure the other person understands you. Offer repetition or clarification.

6 Don't patronize the other person if they don't understand your language easily. Don't treat them as if they are deaf or stupid just because their first language is not yours.

7 Show respect for different cultures and find out about them before your meeting – it may help you get what you want!

8 If the language difference is really great, then employ an interpreter.

Achieving your objectives

If you've done all of the above then you're nearly there. But you've still got to keep alert during the meeting, and respond to developments effectively.

1 Prepare a strategy – a 'game plan' – of how you want the meeting to go, but be ready to adapt. Flexibility is vital.

2 If you're negotiating in a team, then think about your different roles and strategies – you may each have a different area of expertise, or you may each decide to take a different approach (for example, 'hard man, soft man').

3 Make concessions if it helps to achieve your main objectives. The concessions can be real or apparent.

4 Avoid an atmosphere of conflict.

5 Listen to the other speaker. Don't interrupt – let them finish their points.

6 Respond to the points they make with respect.

7 Avoid saying 'No'.

Follow-up

A successful negotiation can be destroyed if you don't spend time confirming what has been agreed.

1 Keep notes of the main points as the meeting progresses – even if there's a minute-taker or it's being recorded.

2 Make sure all parties agree on what has been agreed before you leave the meeting.

3 Follow up the meeting a few days later with a letter or a contract listing the terms on which you agreed.

Preliminary negotiations

Carla Manson works for Flights of Fancy, a tour operator that specializes in holidays to far-away exotic destinations. One of her responsibilities is the negotiation of contracts with different airlines. Flights of Fancy do not charter whole planes for their long-haul flights, but buy blocks of seats on scheduled flights.

Carla is talking on the phone to Peter Nicholson, the Reservations Manager of a major airline, to arrange a meeting and set the agenda for negotiating next season's contract.

1 There are seven main stages in the conversation. What order do you think they will occur in?
   a identify areas of discussion/set the agenda
   b confirm arrangements and say goodbye
   c introduce the main reason for the call
   d arrange place for the meeting
   e arrange time of the meeting
   f introductions and polite chat
   g check who will be coming and if any special materials are needed

2 Listen to the conversation and check to see if your order was correct.

3 Listen again and complete the spaces in this meeting planner. For point 6, identify which of Carla's objectives are mentioned as agenda items. For point 7, make notes on the materials, documents, and reports which Carla will need to prepare.

Meeting planner

1 Subject: *Charter arrangements for next season*

2 Date:

3 Time:

4 Venue:

5 People present:

6 Main objectives:

– review reports on last season
– ensure exclusive deal with airline (airline not to sell to our competitors)
– get better seat rate for higher volume of business
– more favourable time slots
– better quality of plane (more modern aircraft?)
– better in-flight service (meals, drinks, etc.)
– ensure no fuel surcharge
– free ad in in-flight magazine

7 Preparation required:

Arranging a meeting

Look at these examples from the conversation.

What about next week?
No, I'm sorry, I'm busy all day.

Could you make the following Thursday?
No, that's not very convenient.

I could do the Friday, though.
Yes, that looks good.

Can you think of any other ways of arranging a meeting? Try starting with:

Are you …?   What are …?   Shall we …?

Practice

Draw or copy a diary page for next week, and write in six appointments (real or imaginary). Make appointments to see each of the other members of the class. Record each appointment as you make it. Be sure not to 'double-book' yourself!

Identifying and proposing areas of discussion

Look at these examples from the conversation.

I thought we ought to meet to discuss charter arrangements for next season.

I thought it might be useful to sort out the basic agenda now.

I think we should start with a review of last year.

I suggest we look at the question of seat rates.

Look at the tapescript on page 187. Can you find any other ways in which the speakers suggest areas for discussion?

Practice

Can you think of other ways of making proposals? Unjumble these sentences to help you.

1 on we vote propose it I
2 forward I suggestion want to following the put
3 discount offer I'd suggest we larger to like a that

Responding to points

Look at these examples from the conversation.

Accepting a point
Good point.
OK, point taken.
Yes, I agree.

Expressing reservation
I'm afraid I can't really go along with that.
I'm not so sure.

Practice

Can you think of any other ways of responding to points in a meeting? Unjumble these sentences to help you.

1 point see I your yes
2 with agree I you totally not I'm sure
3 that I yes accept
4 that sure I'm about not
5 commission yes prefer but more I'd
6 that go I'd with along

Which ones are responding positively and which ones are expressing reservation? Think about the proposal that might have preceded each one.

Contractions are used in all forms of speech, even when the language is formal. Listen to these sentences from the conversation and fill in the gaps.

1 Not too bad. _____ a pretty good year.
2 _____ know in advance _____ be coming up.
3 We _____ some better departure times.
4 _____ we can make the flight itself a selling point.

Pair work

In pairs, hold a preliminary phone call between a travel agent and a tour operator. Include these three main stages.

1 Arrange a day, time, and place for the meeting.

2 Identify and propose areas of discussion to set a basic agenda, using your list of objectives.
3 Confirm the arrangements.

Work in pairs. **Student A** should read the information below. **Student B** should read the information on page 175.

A Travel agent

Before contacting the tour operator, make a note of some appointments you have already made. You usually have to work at the travel agency every morning until 13.00, so you would prefer an appointment after that time. Make sure you leave some spaces in your diary!

Negotiations with a hotel

You are going to role-play the preliminary negotiations between a tour operator and the representative of a hotel chain. There will be three stages to the role-play:

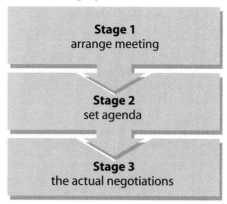

1 To prepare, divide into three groups. Tour operators (**A**) and secretaries (**C**) should read the information below. Hotel representatives (**B**) should turn to the information on page 176.

Tour operators	A

You would prefer a meeting at the hotel next week in the early morning. Friday is best for you.

Your objectives are:

– a larger allocation of rooms – 50 per night in high season
– a range of types of accommodation (e.g. self-catering, family rooms, half-board, etc.)
– shorter release dates (so you have more chance of selling your allocation at the last minute)
– a contribution to advertising costs
– hotel to provide some better photographs
– extras in the rooms (e.g. bottle of wine, basket of fruit)
– clearer idea of the hotel's recreational and leisure facilities (there was some confusion last year)

Which of these objectives do you want to set as agenda items?

Which objectives will be more difficult to achieve?

Think carefully about your tactics in the meeting. Read the article on negotiation techniques on page 48 again.

Hotel representatives	B

Look at the information on page 176.

Secretaries	C

Your role will be to monitor and record the meeting. To do this you will need to:

1 Take notes, and in particular record any decisions that are made.

2 Make sure that both sides understand each other and don't get angry or unreasonable. How will you do this?

3 Look for areas where the two sides agree – or where a compromise can be made. What do you think each side will want from the negotiations?

2 Spend some time preparing your roles in your groups. Then hold the meeting.

3 After the meeting return to your groups and discuss how well the negotiations went. Were all the objectives achieved? What compromises and concessions were made? Could the meeting have been more successful?

④ Groups A and B

Write a letter to your 'opponent' confirming the decisions you made. The letter could follow this outline:

Dear _____

It was very nice to meet you last _____ . I thought the meeting was very useful. Here is a summary of the points we covered:

1 **Allocations** It was agreed that …

2 **Accommodation types** It was decided that …

With kind regards

Group C

Write a brief report of the meeting, listing the date, time, and place of the meeting, who was present, and the main decisions made.

SECTION 3 .... # Handling complaints

Listening 3 ## Three complaints

① What things might tourists and travellers complain about? What kinds of complaints might these people have to deal with?

– a travel agent   – a flight attendant   – a hotel manager
– a tour operator   – a tour guide

② You are going to listen to three conversations. For each one, decide:

a who is complaining, and who is handling the complaint
b what they are complaining about
c what solution is proposed
d who is the most angry
e which part of the tour operator's planning is involved

③ What expressions are used to complain? Listen to the three conversations again and complete these sentences.

1 I'm afraid we're _____ .
2 In fact, to be honest, it's _____ .
3 Are you supposed to be _____ .
4 I'm sorry to _____ .
5 I'm not one _____ .

Written complaints

1 You are going to read a letter from someone complaining about a recent package holiday. You are also going to read the tour operator's reply. What things can go wrong on a package holiday? Think about: travel arrangements, transfer, the resort, the hotel, excursions. Use the list you made in **Listening 3**, exercise 1.

2 Read the first letter. What specific complaints are made?

Leah Haus
Apartment 18H
5 Washington Square
New York
NY 10012
USA

Customer Relations
Sunsearch Holidays
Highview House
14 Shepherds Street
Henford
HN3 7PP

September 14

Dear Sir,

I am writing to complain about the terrible service I received recently on a holiday arranged by your company. The holiday in question was the 'Supersun Special' departing August 20th (holiday reference: SS974/05).

My particular complaint concerns the travel arrangements, which were disastrous from start to finish. As requested we arrived at the airport two hours before departure in order to check in. However, we were told in a most impolite way that we could not check in as the flight was overbooked. We were offered no explanation by the check-in staff and we could not find any representative of your company at the airport. Surely you should employ someone to oversee the smooth running of these arrangements.

When we eventually got on a plane – four hours later! – we found that it was extremely crowded, there was very little leg-room, there was no in-flight movie as we had expected, and the meal was, quite frankly, disgusting. Again, my complaints to the flight attendant were ignored. She was most unfriendly, and even managed to spill hot coffee over my partner.

On arrival at the airport we found that there was nobody to meet us, although a representative from another company did direct us to the Sunsearch coach. After a 50-minute journey (advertised in your brochure as 20 minutes) we arrived at the hotel, exhausted and fed up.

We were reasonably happy with the resort and the hotel, although the food was not really up to the standard we are used to. However, on our return journey, we found the same disorganization and inefficiency: the coach was late, we were late checking in so that we had to be separated on the plane, and on arrival back here we found that our luggage had been mislaid.

I find such service totally unacceptable. We paid a lot of money for this holiday and I think we have a right to expect better standards of service. I would be grateful if you could give me some explanation and offer some form of compensation.

I look forward to hearing from you.

Yours truly

L. Haus

L. HAUS

3 Now read the tour operator's reply. What explanation (if any) is offered for each of the complaints? What does the tour operator offer to do?

SUNSEARCH H LIDAYS

Highview House
14 Shepherds Street
Henford
HN3 7PP

Ms Leah Haus
Apartment 18H
5 Washington Square
New York
NY 10012
USA

22 September

Dear Ms Haus

Thank you for your letter of September 14th regarding your recent holiday with Sunsearch Holidays. I was sorry to hear that you were disappointed with some of the arrangements for your flight and transfer, and I apologize unreservedly for the inconvenience you experienced.

I have investigated your complaint in detail and you may be interested in the following explanation. The problems with the flight were due to circumstances beyond our control. Unfortunately, on the day of your departure the airline experienced serious technical problems in two of its charter planes. These had to be substituted with alternatives which were not up to the same high standards. I am sure you can understand the importance ensuring that the planes are safe.

I can only apologize for the fact that the airline check-in staff were not polite to you. I have noted your point about a company representative at the airport and I will suggest that at our next planning meeting.

As far as the arrangements for the transfer at your destination are concerned, I can only assume that there was some misunderstanding, as I have been assured by our representatives at the resort that they were on duty throughout the day of your arrival. The journey took longer than expected because of the delayed flight which meant that more people had to be taken to different hotels on the same coach.

Please accept my sincere apologies for the problems you experienced on your return. These were due to local difficulties with the coach company and with the airport baggage handlers. I can assure you that we have taken steps to ensure that these problems do not occur again.

Once again I would like to apologize for the unsatisfactory service you received. As a sign of goodwill I enclose a voucher for 20% off your next holiday should you book with Sunsearch Holidays again.

Yours sincerely

Christina Macrae

CHRISTINA MACRAE
Customer Services Manager

4 Read these extracts from five other letters of complaint. Match them with the extracts from the tour operator's responses which follow.

Complaints

a
> Not only that, but the bottom of the pool was damaged, with badly chipped tiles. I heard of at least three children who suffered cuts as a result.

b
> Imagine how we felt when we found that we had been abandoned in the middle of a dangerous part of the city.

c
> The room was dirty and the sheets were not changed at all during the two weeks we were there. We didn't want to bother the rep at the time as she seemed very busy, but having returned we feel we ought to complain.

d
> The hotel we were eventually put in was of a greatly inferior quality with none of the facilities we had booked. We were offered no explanation and no discount. Indeed, we had to pay a surcharge for half-board as there were no self-catering facilities. Unless I receive a satisfactory explanation and full compensation I shall have no alternative but to take legal action.

e
> The transfer to our hotel, advertised in your brochure as taking approximately twenty minutes, in fact took over an hour.

Responses

1
> I am very sorry that you received a less than satisfactory service. However, there is very little we can do to put things right after the event. You should have mentioned the situation to our representative, who could easily have sorted out the situation for you.

2
> It is most regrettable that your accommodation had to be changed at the last minute. The representative at the resort should certainly have offered a full explanation. Please accept my sincere apologies for this unfortunate incident.

3
> Unfortunately, from time to time repairs to facilities have to be made, although we try to keep any disruption to a minimum.

4
> We will look into this matter and get back to you. Please note, however, that our brochure clearly states that all timings are approximate and cannot be guaranteed.

5
> This really should not have happened and appropriate action has been taken with the tour guide in question.

5 Do you think the customer will be happy with the tour operator's explanations and apologies? What appropriate compensation (if any) could the tour operator offer?

Language focus 2

Responding to complaints (spoken)

If you are going to work in tourism you will definitely need to deal with complaints. It is important to be able to tell how angry a person is when they complain, so that you can respond in an appropriate way. Sometimes the degree of anger will be obvious, sometimes the language they use will help you to know.

1 Look at these examples of ways of introducing a complaint.

I'm sorry to trouble you, but there seems to be a problem.
Have you got a moment?
I want to complain.
Are you supposed to be in charge here?
I was wondering if you could help me – there appears to be a little difficulty.
I demand to see the person in charge immediately.
I don't like to complain, but …

2 Put them in order from most polite to most angry. Think about an appropriate response for each one.

Responding to complaints (written)

1 When responding to written complaints, it is important to apologize, explain, give reasons, and promise action or compensation.

Introducing
Thank you for your letter …
I was sorry to hear that …

Explaining/giving reasons
I have investigated your complaint in detail.
The problems were due to …
Unfortunately, …
I am sure you can understand …

Apologizing
I can only apologize for …
Please accept my sincere apologies.

Promising action
I can assure you that we have taken steps to ensure that these problems do not occur again.
We will look into this matter.
As a sign of goodwill, I enclose …

2 Can you think of other ways of explaining, apologizing, and promising action (in writing)? What are the equivalent forms for a spoken response?

3 Choose one of the extracts from **Reading**, exercise 4, on page 55. Invent one or two more areas of complaint, and then write a full letter in response (including the extract).

Suggested responses

Initial reaction and apology	*Oh dear. I'm sorry to hear that.* *Certainly. Is there a problem?* *I'm really very sorry.*

(Decide what would be an appropriate initial reaction to each of the complaints listed above.)

Ask for clarification	*What exactly is the problem?*
Take details	*I'll just take some details.* *Could you describe …* *Let me see if I can help. I just need a few details.*
Offer explanation	*I'm terribly sorry, but there has been a bit of a problem.* *If I could just explain …*
Proposed plan	*I'll see if I can sort it out.* *I'll tell you what I'll do …* *This is what I'll do …* *Why don't you …*

Pronunciation focus 2

Using appropriate intonation can help to calm an angry or upset person. As an experiment, think of as many different ways as possible of saying *Oh dear!* or *I'm sorry*.

What is the effect of saying these with a flat intonation? (You sound rude, uninterested, and unconcerned.)

A more sympathetic sounding intonation pattern is a high falling tone:

Oh dear!   *I'm sorry.*

Practice

1 Look at the suggested responses in **Language focus 2** above. Practise saying them with a falling tone.

2 Choose one or more of the situations below and act out the conversation in pairs.

– dirty hotel room (guest to hotel reception)
– misleading advertising in brochure (holidaymaker to tour operator)
– lost suitcase at airport (passenger to baggage attendant)
– rude hotel staff (tour rep to hotel manager)
– not supplying enough brochures (travel agent to tour operator)

Feedback questionnaires

1 Most tour operators are interested in customer feedback, so that they can improve the service they offer. Read this customer satisfaction questionnaire produced by one tour operator.

THOMSON Customer Satisfaction Questionnaire

Enjoyed your holiday? We hope you have, because we work very hard to ensure that our customers have a really good time. But we need your help to make things even better. Your opinions are very important to us, and by completing this questionnaire you will help improve the standard and quality of future holidays.

Please tick ✔ appropriate box, or write in as requested.

1 YOUR HOLIDAY DETAILS

A Board arrangements:

Full-board	Flexible dining (combining B&B and H/B)
Half-board	Self-catering
Bed & Breakfast	Room only
	All inclusive (all meals, drinks, etc. included)

B The name of your resort(s) or the name of your tour/safari/cruise

C The name of your hotel(s)/villa/apartments
(name all accommodation stayed in)

D Number of nights abroad

6 or less	7–14	8–13	15–20

E How long before departure was the holiday booked?

less than 1 week	5–6 months
1–4 weeks	7–8 months
1–2 months	9–10 months
3–4 months	Longer ago

2 FLIGHTS

Please rate:	Excellent	Good	Fair	Poor
A Airport check-in arrangements				
B Resort airport check-in arrangements				
C In-flight comfort				
D In-flight food				
E Cabin crew: attitude and manners				
F In-flight audio/visual entertainment				

3 IN-RESORT SERVICE

	Excellent	Good	Fair	Poor
A On arrival: assistance at resort airport				
B Transfer journey to and from your accommodation				
C On departure: assistance at resort airport				
D Representative's availability and punctuality				
E Representative's attitude and manners				
F Representative's knowledge				
G Welcome get-together				
H Excursions choice				
I Excursions value for money				

4 YOUR ACCOMMODATION

Please give an average rating of all accommodation stayed in.

	Excellent	Good	Fair	Poor
A Location				
B Reception service				
C Bar service				
D Cleanliness and maintenance				
E Comfort of public areas				
F Bedroom comfort				
G Breakfast				
H Midday/evening meals				
I Waiter service/buffet efficiency				
J Daytime activities and leisure facilities				
K Evening entertainment				
L Villa/apartment equipment				

5 OVERALL

Taking everything into account:	Excellent	Good	Fair	Poor
A Flights				
B Holiday weather				
C Resort				
D Accommodation				
E Food				
F Representatives				
G Holiday overall				
H Holiday company overall				
I Value for money				

6 ANY PROBLEMS?

A Did you experience any problems during your holiday?

B If yes, did you contact your representative?   Yes   No

C How satisfied were you with the action taken?

   Completely   Mostly   Partly   Not at all

7 HOLIDAY EXPERIENCE

How did this holiday compare with the impression you gained from the brochure?

   Better   The same   Worse   Did not use brochure

8 ABOUT YOU

A I am: Male   Female

B I am: Married   Single

Separated/widowed/divorced   Living with partner

C Age:

Under 16	18–24	35–44	55–64
16–17	25–34	45–54	65+

D I am: In full-time/part-time employment or self-employed

A student   A full-time housewife

Retired   Otherwise not employed

② Look back at the complaints made in **Listening 3** on page 52. Which questions would the complainers have answered negatively?

③ Think of a holiday you have had (or imagine one) and fill in the questionnaire. Be sure to include at least three negative comments.

④ Show your completed questionnaire to another student. Take turns to act out the phone conversation between the holiday-maker and the tour operator. Tour operators should find out details of the complaint and say what action they will take.

⑤ In groups, look at the completed questionnaires. As tour operators, decide what areas of your planning and organization need to be looked at and improved.

⑥ Write the letter sent by the tour operator to the holiday-maker, apologizing and offering an explanation and/or compensation.

⑦ Write an internal memo, based on the comments in the questionnaire, for discussion by the tour operators at their next general meeting.

ACTIVITY

Planning a series of tours

① How many different types of transport for tourists can you think of? What kind of journey would you associate with each one?

② Look at a world map. In groups, plan a trip round the world, starting and finishing at any point you choose. Include as many different types of transport as possible. When you have finished, compare your route and types of transport with another group.

③ In groups of three or four, imagine you are a tour operator planning a series of tours to different parts of the world, using the routes and types of transport you planned in exercise 2. The tours will be marketed and sold in the country where you are studying.

You will have to make some important basic decisions. For example:

1 Which section of the population are you going to aim at (e.g. tours for young people, for families, for special interest, or any other groups)?
2 Which countries are you going to visit?
3 What type of holidays are you going to offer?
4 How many different tours are you going to arrange?

④ When you have decided these things you need to make more detailed plans.

1 Give each tour a name.
2 Summarize the basic itinerary and features of each tour.
3 Decide which principals you will need to negotiate with.

As you are making your plans, your teacher will give you extra information and news items which may mean you will have to change your ideas.

5 When you have finished your plans (and there are no more new developments!), show them to other groups. As a class, decide which group has produced the best range of tours.

Vocabulary

agenda	reservation system	inclusive tours	questionnaire
allocation	concession	Internet	rack
asap	database	interpreter	re
attn	dept	invoice	recruit
brochure	draft	memo	release date
bulk purchase	e-mail	minutes	rooming-list
campaign	encl	negotiation	scheduled flight
cancellation	feedback	objectives	specialize
coach	flexibility	overbooked	testimonial
commission	flight manifest	PR	time slot
compensation	GMT	principal	World Wide Web /
computer	hotelier	PS	web page

5

Air travel

SECTION 1	**Announcements and procedures**

Speaking

Experiences of flying

1 Have you ever travelled in an aeroplane? Divide into two groups – people who have flown before and people who haven't.

The people who have flown before should discuss these questions.

1 Who has had the longest flight?
2 Who has flown the most times?
3 Who gets bored and who gets excited on flights?
4 What part of the flight do you enjoy/dislike most?
5 Has anyone had any frightening experiences on a flight?

The people who haven't flown before should discuss these questions.

1 Would you like to fly? What would you like/not like about flying?
2 Which part of the flight do you think would be most exciting? Which part would make you most nervous?
3 What would be the best place to sit in an aeroplane – aisle seat, window seat, or the middle of a row? At the front or the back of the plane?

Discuss your answers with people from the other group.

2 Which job would you like most – pilot, flight attendant, or air-traffic controller? Why? Which is the most difficult?

Listening 1

Airport announcements

You are going to hear a series of six announcements made over the public address system of an airport.

1 As you listen, identify the type of message.

– staff announcement
– advertisement
– flight cancellation
– delayed flight arrival
– final flight call

– warning
– paging a passenger
– delayed flight departure
– security announcement

2 In five of the announcements, specific areas or parts of the airport are mentioned. Listen again and note down these places.

Announcement 1 _____

Announcement 2 _____

Announcement 3 _____

Announcement 4 _____

Announcement 5 _____

Announcement 6 _____

3 Listen to the last three announcements again. Write down the exact words which are used.

4 Write some announcements of your own. Use the notes below and the tapescript on page 188 to help you. Dictate your announcements to another member of the class.

a flight AZ207 delayed – now due 18.35
b duty-free shop open – wide range of spirits, wines, tobacco, perfumes
c final call flight AA470 to Miami
d member of security staff to check-in desk 14
e Mr González from Madrid to Information (important phone call)
f flight IB609 to Paris – two-hour delay

Reading and vocabulary

Airport procedure

1 Look at this diagram indicating basic airport procedure and layout.

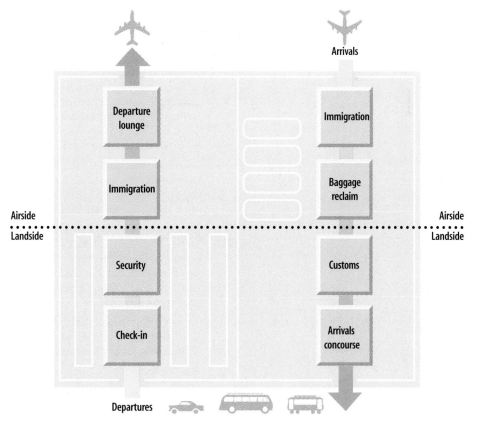

1 What happens at each point?
2 What other facilities and services do you find in an airport?

2 Read the leaflet 'Mackenzie Airport welcomes first-time fliers'. It describes the procedure for passengers at an airport. Fill in the gaps with words or phrases from the list below.

Paragraphs 1 and 2	Paragraph 3	Paragraph 4	Paragraph 5
boarding card check-in desks conveyor belt economy excess baggage hand luggage terminal building trolleys	departure lounge duty-free immigration officer passport control security check	announcement boarding departure gate departures board flight attendant ground steward	baggage conveyor belt customs escalators green channel immigration control import duty

Mackenzie Airport welcomes first-time fliers!

Welcome to Mackenzie Airport, designed to get your journey off to the right start. Whether you're flying first class, business class, or ¹_____ class, we aim to give you efficiency and comfort. For first-time fliers, we've prepared this leaflet to help you on your way.

When you arrive at the ²_____ you'll find plenty of ³_____ for your luggage. Once inside the spacious departures concourse there are over fifty ⁴_____ where your ticket will be checked and you'll be given a ⁵_____. Your luggage will be weighed and put on a ⁶_____ which takes it to the plane. Please note there is a weight limit and any ⁷_____ will have to be paid for. You can keep one small bag with you and take it onto the plane as ⁸_____.

You should then go through ⁹_____, where an ¹⁰_____ will look at your passport, and a ¹¹_____ to make sure you are not carrying any dangerous or illegal items. Now you'll find yourself in the comfort of our modern air-conditioned ¹²_____. While you're waiting for your flight to be called, why not buy some cheap ¹³_____ goods – alcoholic drinks, cigarettes, perfume, electrical goods, or souvenirs?

Soon you'll hear an ¹⁴_____ or see on the ¹⁵_____ that your flight is ¹⁶_____. It will also tell you which ¹⁷_____ to go to. Here you'll be helped by a ¹⁸_____ and on the plane a ¹⁹_____ will direct you to your seat. Bon voyage!

On your return to Mackenzie Airport we try to offer the same efficient service. After you've passed through ²⁰_____, your luggage will be waiting on the moving ²¹_____ in the ²²_____ hall. Then pass through ²³_____ where you should take either the ²⁴_____, if you have nothing to declare, or the red channel, if you have to pay ²⁵_____. Once inside the arrival concourse, lifts and ²⁶_____ will take you to all major transport services.

On behalf of everyone at Mackenzie Airport, I wish you a very pleasant journey.

Neil Thomson

Neil Thomson, Director of Mackenzie Airport

Welcome to Mackenzie!

Language focus 1

Explaining procedure – sequence linkers

Look at these phrases from the Mackenzie Airport leaflet.

When you arrive, …
Once inside, …
You should then …
Now you'll find yourself in …
While you're waiting …
Soon you'll …
On your return …
After you've passed through …
Then …

1 When explaining procedure, it is important to use sequence linkers to identify the different stages. Read this explanation by a pilot of the stages involved in flying a modern airliner. Note the highlighted expressions.

It all starts with the pre-flight briefing when we go through the detailed arrangements for the whole flight – where we're going, what route we're taking, who's doing what, and so on. Earlier, of course, we will have been given briefing notes and a flight programme to read.

The next stage is the briefing for take-off. As soon as that's over we load the computers, and then we're ready to start the engines. Once we've started the engines, and the passengers are secure and everyone's happy, we taxi to the take-off position. While all this is going on we're getting instructions from air traffic control. After this we take off and we fly the plane manually for a while before engaging the autopilot.

The next stage is the boring bit really. In effect, the plane's being controlled by the autopilot, the on-board computers, and the people down on the ground. We're just monitoring things. On long-haul flights we have two crews, so after a while we hand over to the relief crew and I'll probably meet and chat with some of the passengers before going to get some rest.

Later on, the original crew take over control again and then we go through the briefing for landing. When that's sorted out we begin our descent. Once we're down the autopilot is disengaged. The final stage is that we have to park the plane – again under instructions.

2 Look at this list of words and phrases. Which of them can be substituted for the highlighted expressions in the text?

Finally
Beforehand
To begin with
Next we have
Immediately afterwards
Next
Previously
At the same time as this
Prior to this
First of all we have
The last stage is that
Simultaneously
Before this
The first stage is

Pronunciation focus

Listen to these sentences from the pilot's description. Which one of these intonation patterns best represents the way each sentence is introduced?

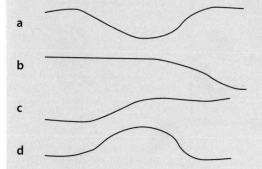

This pattern is used mainly to emphasize that a new stage of the sequence is being introduced.

Practice

1 Look back at the diagram of an airport on page 61. In pairs, ask and explain about departure and arrival procedures.

A
You've never flown before. Ask **B** what happens when you get to the airport, up to the point where you board the plane.

B
You've never flown before. Ask **A** what happens after you've landed at the airport.

2 Think of an everyday activity, such as driving a car or making a particular dish. Make a list of every stage involved in the process (your teacher will help you with necessary vocabulary). Connect the different stages on the list by using the appropriate sequence linkers. Describe the procedure to another student.

Output task

Cabin crew procedure

① Like the flight crew, the cabin crew (flight attendants) also have a procedure for the different things they need to do on a flight. Look at this list of things the cabin crew have to do on a seven-hour London to New York flight, departing at 11.30 a.m. Put them in the correct order.

a ☐ serve drinks
b ☐ check seat-belts are fastened
c ☐ give out landing cards
d ☐ welcome passengers on board
e ☐ give safety announcement
f ☐ serve tea and coffee
g ☐ get meals ready
h ☐ assist passengers leaving plane
i ☐ collect meal trays
j ☐ collect empty glasses
k ☐ assist with stowing cabin baggage
l ☐ offer duty-free goods for sale
m ☐ serve meals to passengers

② At which stage would you hear the flight attendant say the following?

a Would you like anything to drink?
b Good morning. Seat 25D is down there on the right.
c Have you finished with this, madam?
d Would you like me to put this in the overhead locker?
e Ice and lemon?
f Goodbye. Have a safe journey.
g Any wine, spirits, or perfume?
h Emergency exits are located towards the front and rear of the plane.

Can you think of any other typical things that a flight attendant might say?

③ Look at these pictures illustrating the flight safety procedure.

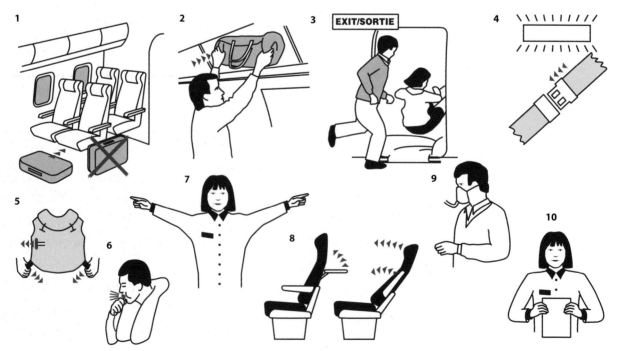

Match the following words and phrases to the appropriate pictures.

a	obstruct aisles	h	whistle
b	seat-belt	i	folded away
c	seat back upright	j	fastened
d	overhead locker	k	tapes
e	safety card	l	red toggle
f	life jackets	m	oxygen mask
g	hand baggage	n	emergency exit

4 Listen to this recorded Passenger Safety Briefing to see if you were right.

5 In groups, try to produce a full version of the safety announcement. Give your announcement to other groups.

SECTION 2

Checking in

Reading

Boarding passes and check-in screens

1 Transfer the information from this boarding pass onto the check-in desk computer screen.

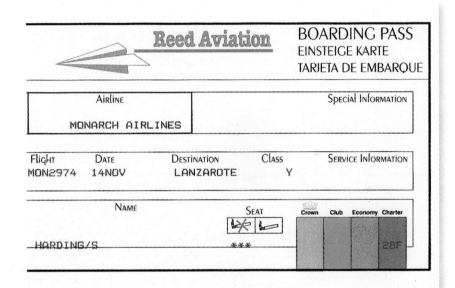

Seat plan		Economy/charter (rows 26–30)						
Flight number:		Row A	B	C	D	E	F	
Date:		26X		X	X	X	X	
Destination:		27 X X			X	X	X	
Class:		28 X X			X	X	X	X
Smoking/non-smoking:		29 S			X	X		X
Special request:		30 S X		X	X	X	X	X
			>			<		

❷ Look at the check-in desk computer screen on the previous page which indicates the seat layout. Complete the sentences spoken by the check-in steward. Use the information on the computer screen, and the words in the list.

1 OK Mr Harding, here's your boarding pass. You're in seat _____ .

2 I've got two _____ seats next to each other in row 29.

3 I'm afraid that there are no _____ seats available in the non-smoking section.

4 You've checked in two items. Your _____ are on the back of the boarding pass.

5 There are two seats together at the front which have extra _____ .

6 Row 26 is right next to the _____ . Is that OK?

7 There are two seats _____ each other in rows 27 and 28.

boarding pass	behind	leg-room	smoking
opposite	luggage tags	aisle	next to
non-smoking	window	economy	emergency exit

Listening 2

At the check-in desk

❶ You are going to listen to extracts from three dialogues which take place at an airport check-in desk. In each case there is a difficulty which has to be resolved. Before you listen, try to think of problems that might occur at check-in.

❷ Listen to the extracts and complete this chart.

extract	destination	problem	solution
1			
2			
3			

❸ Which of the passengers would you describe as

– angry and a little aggressive?
– vague and nervous?
– polite and passive?

What helped you to decide? Think about the words and expressions they used, and also their pronunciation and intonation.

Output task

Checking in

1 These are the things which the ground steward at a check-in desk usually covers in a typical conversation with a passenger. Put them in order.

a tell them the seat number
b return tickets with luggage tags and boarding card
c welcome the passenger
d ask to see ticket and passport
e say goodbye
f weigh and tag luggage
g ask passenger to put luggage on scales
h ask if they want a window seat or an aisle seat

What actual words would the ground steward use at each point?

2 In pairs, act out two check-in conversations. Take turns to be the check-in steward. Use the screen layouts and passenger requests to help you.

Conversation 1

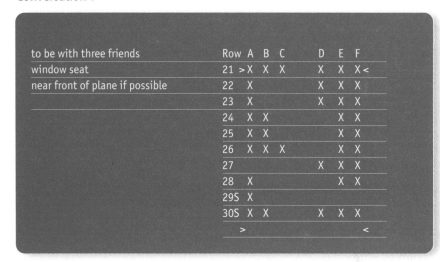

	Row	A	B	C		D	E	F	
to be with three friends	21	>X	X	X		X	X	X<	
window seat	22	X				X	X	X	
near front of plane if possible	23	X				X	X	X	
	24	X	X				X	X	
	25	X	X				X	X	
	26	X	X	X			X	X	
	27					X	X	X	
	28	X					X	X	
	29S	X							
	30S	X	X			X	X	X	
		>						<	

Conversation 2

Passenger B wants:	Seat plan:								
to be together if possible (they are a family of eight – three adults and five children, aged 3, 5, 9, and 14)	Row	A	B	C		D	E	F	
	21	>X	X	X		X	X	X<	
	22	X				X	X	X	
	23	X				X	X	X	
as many window seats as possible	24	X	X				X	X	
to be near exits	25	X	X				X	X	
	26	X	X	X			X	X	
	27					X	X	X	
	28	X					X	X	
	29S	X							
	30S	X	X			X	X	X	
		>						<	

3 Now work with a different partner. This time you should think of a particular problem, such as excess baggage, certain seats not available, special requests (e.g. for vegetarian meal, extra leg-room, a seat-belt extension). Act out the conversation.

Flight attendants

Could you be a flight attendant?

1 More myths surround the job of flight attendant than almost any other. Consequently, airlines receive thousands of enquiries every year. How do they decide who will make the grade? Kim Whittle is an experienced flight attendant trainer for British Airways. Before you hear what she has to say, make your own predictions by filling in the chart below.

flight attendant requirements	your prediction	BA requirements
Age		
Height		
Build		
Weight		
Health		
Vision		
General knowledge/education		
Languages		
Clothes at interview		
Personality		
Other		

2 Now listen to the interview with Kim Whittle to find out if your predictions were correct.

Reading

Psychology questionnaire for potential flight attendants

1 An important part of the selection procedure for an airline is to understand the psychology of an applicant. Here are ten typical questions from a pre-interview questionnaire.

1 How strong and confident are you?
2 How often can you be honest with your friends?
3 What do you look for most in a job?
4 What kind of people do you admire?
5 How do you like to spend Saturday nights?
6 What do you do when you get bad service?
7 When do you work overtime?
8 How do you feel when people criticize you?
9 What do you value most?
10 How easy is it for you to achieve your goals?

2 Match the questions to the multiple-choice options below.

a	f
It doesn't bother me at all. I don't usually mind. I don't like it very much. I hate it.	My close relationships. My personality and appearance. My intelligence. My knowledge and skills.
b	**g**
Dealing with people Security Travel Adventure and excitement	Every time my boss asks me to. Only when there is an emergency. When I want to get something finished. Never – I don't need to in my job.
c	**h**
Very – I always get what I want. I've never really had to struggle. Not very – it always takes a lot of effort. I've never really had many.	Business people Writers Police officers Film stars
d	**i**
Very – you need to be to survive. Quite – in a quiet way. I try to be but it's not easy. Not at all – I'm quite shy really.	Throwing a wild party. With family and friends. With a special person. On my own, reading.
e	**j**

Complain – more people should too.
I get embarrassed but I say something.
It depends – sometimes I do
  something.
Nothing – it doesn't really bother me.
	Very – that's what they are for.
	Quite – it depends how well I
	  know them.
	I usually try to bite my tongue.
	Rarely – people don't appreciate it.

3 Imagine you are the airline's Personnel Officer. Which of these answers would indicate a good applicant? Which would worry you? How would you deal with these worries in an interview?

4 Now complete the questionnaire for yourself. Compare your answers with your partner and see if you agree with your assessments of yourselves.

Language focus 2

Indirect questions (revision)

The questionnaire on page 68 was in written form, and the questions were therefore in a simple direct form. However, as we saw in the survey questions in **Unit 2**, it is more common to use indirect questions in speech.

Look at the ten questions again. Change them to indirect questions, starting with

Could you …, or *I wonder if …*, or *Would you mind …*.

Introducing questions and responding to answers
Here are some examples of things an interviewer might say. Which ones

a introduce a question?
b respond to an answer?

I'd like to move on to a different subject.
Can I just ask you about …
I see.
The thing I want to talk about now is …
That's very interesting.
Yes, I think that's a very good point.
Perhaps we could come back to that later.
Now, moving on …

Can you think of other phrases to add to this list?

Practice

In pairs, ask each other the ten questions from the questionnaire on page 68. **A** should ask questions 1 to 5, **B** should ask questions 6 to 10. Use indirect questions, and phrases for introducing questions and responding to answers.

Speaking

Flight attendant job interview

1 Using the information from the **Reading** section and **Language focus 2**, prepare for a role-play. Half the class are interviewers and the other half are applicants for the job of flight attendant. Before you start the interview, prepare your roles carefully in groups.

Interviewer A
Which airline do you represent? What type of person are you looking for? Which routes will they be working on? What training schedule do you propose? Now think about the detailed questions you will ask. You will be interviewing as a 'panel' of two or three, so you can each take a different approach if you want (e.g. one friendly, another tough, etc.).

Applicants B
Prepare a brief CV for yourself. What relevant experience do you have? Why do you want to be a flight attendant? Where do you want to work – which routes? What are your particular strengths and weaknesses? How will you get them across (or hide them)?

Now conduct the interview. Each panel should interview at least three candidates. Candidates who are waiting for interview can discuss why they are applying for the job and what questions they think they will be asked. Candidates who have had their interviews can discuss how well it went.

2 At the end of the interview each panel should decide who they are going to offer the job to, and announce their decision, giving their reasons.

Output task

Cabin crew role-play

❶ Divide into two groups, **A** and **B**. **Group A** (Cabin crew) should read the information below. **Group B** (Passengers) should turn to the information on page 176.

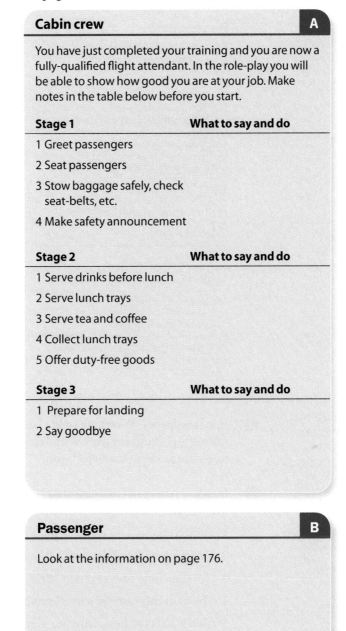

Cabin crew **A**

You have just completed your training and you are now a fully-qualified flight attendant. In the role-play you will be able to show how good you are at your job. Make notes in the table below before you start.

Stage 1	What to say and do
1 Greet passengers	
2 Seat passengers	
3 Stow baggage safely, check seat-belts, etc.	
4 Make safety announcement	

Stage 2	What to say and do
1 Serve drinks before lunch	
2 Serve lunch trays	
3 Serve tea and coffee	
4 Collect lunch trays	
5 Offer duty-free goods	

Stage 3	What to say and do
1 Prepare for landing	
2 Say goodbye	

Passenger **B**

Look at the information on page 176.

❷ When you have finished, discuss the following questions.
1 How well did the flight attendants cope with the pressure?
2 Work out some general strategies for dealing with 'difficult' passengers.
3 Has the experience changed your ideas about the job of flight attendant in any way?

Customs regulations

1 Look at the list of items in the table. Discuss which of them you think travellers are allowed to bring into the countries indicated. Fill in the first two columns.

P = permitted
X = completely banned
R = restricted

item	all countries	your country	the UK (see text)
small handgun with ammunition	☐	☐	☐
a family pet (a cat)	☐	☐	☐
antique pistol (not functioning)	☐	☐	☐
a box of 200 cigarettes	☐	☐	☐
a pornographic magazine/video	☐	☐	☐
a kitchen knife	☐	☐	☐
a flick-knife	☐	☐	☐
a salami sausage (weight = 2kg)	☐	☐	☐
two litres of vodka	☐	☐	☐
a kilo of fresh oranges	☐	☐	☐
a souvenir painting (worth £400)	☐	☐	☐
a CB radio	☐	☐	☐

2 Read the leaflet 'Travelling to the UK from outside the EU' on page 73 to fill in the column for the UK above. Assume that the passenger is travelling from inside the European Union.

3 Imagine you are a UK Customs Officer. How would you answer these questions?

1 Which channel do I have to go through?

2 I've got two litre-bottles of whisky. What should I do?

3 I'm travelling on to France. What do I do about my luggage?

4 I bought this camera when I was away. Which channel should I go to?

5 I have 400 cigarettes with me. Can my son take some through on his allowance?

4 Think about your country again and prepare the following information.

1 Tell other class members what they can and cannot bring into the country.

2 Give advice on useful items that they should bring in (for example, in Britain an umbrella is often a good idea!).

3 Suggest ideas for presents to take home from your country.

Travelling to the UK from outside the EU

You have to go through Customs if you arrive in the UK after travelling from or through a country that is not in the EU.

You must declare:

– any goods over the allowances listed on page 6 that you have bought in a country that is not in the EU

– any prohibited or restricted goods (see page 7), and

– any commercial goods (see Notice 6 - 'Merchandise in Baggage')

If you have something to declare, go to the red point or into the red channel.

Only go through the green (nothing to declare) channel if you are sure that you have no more than the Customs allowances and no prohibited, restricted, or commercial goods.

If you arrive by air and are transferring to a flight to another EU country, you do not collect your hold baggage until you reach your final destination. At the **transfer point**, you only have to declare goods in your cabin baggage. At your **final destination**, you must declare goods in your **hold baggage**.

This is usually the same if you are transferring to a UK domestic flight, but in some cases Customs must clear both your cabin baggage and your hold baggage at the transfer airport. The airline will tell you when this is necessary.

You may be arriving with goods for your personal use that you have bought and paid duty and tax on in another EU country. You will not have to pay any more duty or tax as long as you can show, if Customs ask you to, that you have paid duty and tax (by producing the receipt, for example) and that the goods are for your personal use.

The Customs allowance

For travellers arriving from outside the EU

200 cigarettes **or**
100 cigarillos **or**
50 cigars **or**
250g of tobacco

2 litres of still table wine

1 litre of spirits or strong liqueurs over 22% volume **or**

2 litres of fortified wine, sparkling wine, or other liqueurs

60cc/ml of perfume

250cc/ml of toilet water

£136 worth of all other goods including gifts and souvenirs

PEOPLE UNDER 17 CANNOT HAVE THE TOBACCO OR ALCOHOL ALLOWANCE

All other goods

If you bring something in worth more than the limit of £136, you will have to pay charges on the full value, not just on the value above £136.

If you are travelling as a family or group, you cannot pool your individual allowances towards an item worth more than the limit. You will have to pay charges on the **full** value of the item.

Prohibited and restricted goods from outside the EU

Certain goods are prohibited or restricted to protect health and the environment. We cannot list all the goods involved but we have listed some of them below.

Prohibited goods (that is, goods which are banned completely):
Unlicensed drugs, such as heroin, morphine, cocaine, cannabis, amphetamines, barbiturates, and LSD.
Offensive weapons, such as flick-knives, swordsticks, knuckledusters, and some martial arts equipment.
Obscene material, and indecent and obscene material featuring children, such as books, magazines, films, videotapes, laser discs, and computer software.
Counterfeit and copied goods such as watches, clothes, and CDs, also any goods with false marks of their origin.

Restricted goods (that is, goods which you cannot import without authority such as a licence):
Firearms, explosives, and ammunition, including electric shock devices (such as stunguns) and gas canisters. (Contact your advice centre - see page 4)
Dogs, cats, and other animals, including rabbits, mice, rats, and gerbils. You must not bring these in unless you have a British import (rabies) licence.
Live birds, including family pets, unless they are covered by a British health import licence.
Endangered species, including birds and plants, whether alive or dead, also such things as fur, ivory, or leather (or goods made from them) that have been taken from endangered species.
Meat, poultry, and most of their products including bacon, ham, sausages, pâté, eggs, milk, and cream. But you are allowed 1kg of meat per person as long as it is cooked and in airtight containers.
Certain plants and their produce. This includes trees, shrubs, potatoes, certain fruit, bulbs, and seeds.
Radio transmitters such as CB radios that are not approved for use in the UK.

Vocabulary

airliner	departure lounge	import duty	row
airside	departures board	interview/	safety
aisle	duty-free shop	interviewer	announcement
allowance	economy class	landing card	safety card
announcement	emergency exit	landside	scales
applicant	escalators	manually	seat-belt
autopilot	excess baggage	minibus	security check
baggage hall	fasten	obstruct	stow
board (vb)	flight crew	onward journey	taxi (vb)
briefing	fold away	oxygen mask	toggle
cabin crew	green channel	page (vb)	tray
candidate	ground steward	pilot	trolley
concourse	hand luggage (or	prohibited	unattended
conveyor belt	cabin baggage)	public address	upright
customs	immigration	system	vegetarian
declare	control	red channel	whistle
delayed	immigration	relief crew	
departure gate	officer	restricted	

6

Travel by sea and river – cruises and ferries

SECTION 1	**Cruise information**

Speaking

Types of water holiday

1 Have you ever been on a cruise, or spent a holiday on a ship or boat? What was it like?

2 What are the advantages and disadvantages of a holiday on the sea or on a river? Think about accommodation, activities, sights, food, and cost.

3 Look at this list of sea and river trips. Put them in two different orders: (a) the order in which you would most like to go on them, and (b) from most expensive to least expensive.

a	b	Sea and river trips
		Caribbean cruise
		Mediterranean cruise
		speedboat ride off the south coast of France
		round-the-world cruise on the QE2
		hovercraft trip across the English Channel
		rowing boat on a mountain lake
		sightseeing trip down the River Seine in Paris
		gondola ride in Venice
		canal holiday in the UK
		transatlantic voyage to New York
		white-water rafting trip
		River Nile cruise
		24-hour Baltic 'booze-cruise' (to buy duty-free goods, especially alcohol)

Discuss your opinions, first with a partner and then with another pair.

Reading

General information

1 You are going to read some general information from a cruise brochure. There are fourteen different items covered in the extract. Match the headings below with the paragraphs in the text.

a Currency
b Embarkation
c Entertainment
d Library
e Medical services
f On-board credit and credit cards
g Postcards/postal services
h Pregnancy
i Purchases on board
j Shore excursions
k The cruise includes
l Tipping
m Vaccination
n What to wear

1

An embarkation notice will be sent with your tickets approximately two weeks prior to your cruise departure date. Embarkation generally commences three hours before the ship sails and all passengers should be on board one hour before sailing. On arrival at the port, all passengers are requested to have all luggage labelled showing the passenger's name, ship, port of departure, and cabin number. Your luggage will be taken care of by porters who will arrange for it to be delivered to your cabin.

2

Full-board accommodation for the duration of the cruise. Meals on board (commencing with dinner on the day of embarkation) consist of early morning coffee or tea, the choice of continental breakfast in the cabin or full breakfast in the dining room, lunch, afternoon tea, and dinner. The last meal on board will be breakfast on the day of disembarkation. Coffee or tea with lunch and dinner is not included.

3

Optional shore excursions are available at most ports of call. Details will be sent with your tickets. Excursions can only be booked on board. Payment will be by the on-board credit card system.

4

Vaccinations are not compulsory for any cruises in this brochure. However, please check final vaccination requirements of each country you intend to visit with your doctor or travel agent at least eight weeks before departure.

5

There is a limited foreign exchange facility on board each ship where certain recognized foreign money and worldwide traveller's cheques may be exchanged. There is a charge for this service. The unit of currency on board is US dollars.

6

A 'No Cash' system operates on all cruises for bar, wine, and beverage purchases, as well as shore excursions and services provided in the beauty salons, spas, and hairdressers. This account is normally settled on the last evening of the cruise and payment can be made by credit card, traveller's cheques, or cash. Personal cheques and Eurocheques are not accepted on board. A service charge of 10% is added to all accounts.

7

A limited selection of postcards is available from the Information Office, which can also arrange to post your mail.

8

A qualified doctor and nurse are available on all cruise ships. Payment for treatment or medication should be made on board direct to the medical personnel.

9

Women up to their 28th week of pregnancy may travel as long as a doctor's certificate is provided.

10

Passengers may benefit from tax-free prices on a wide selection of goods. The attractive shopping galleries feature many top Italian designer products. Gift shops and boutiques have an extensive range of clothing, gifts, and souvenirs. Duty-free wines and spirits for consumption at home are only sold on the last day of the cruise.

11

This is not obligatory; however, passengers often ask us for guidance. The following scale is recommended: cabin steward – $3 per passenger per day, table steward – $3 per passenger per day, bus-boy – $1 per passenger per day.

12

The Cruise Director and staff arrange a comprehensive programme of activities and entertainment on board.

13

Casual and comfortable. For ship and shore, casual attire and swimwear is in order during the day. For days in port, comfortable clothes and walking shoes are a must. In the evening gentlemen require jacket and tie. For the Gala Nights, a bit more formality is requested – a cocktail dress for ladies, lounge suits for gentlemen. Formal evening wear is not essential.

14

Passengers will find a good selection of books available on loan, free of charge.

2 Imagine that you work for a travel agent or for the cruise company. How would you reply to the following questions from passengers who have booked one of the cruises? Use the information in the text on page 75 to find the answers.

1 How long before departure do I have to get to the ship?
2 How many meals a day are included?
3 Do I have to go on all the sightseeing trips?
4 Do I need any vaccinations?
5 How much cash do I need for daily expenses?
6 I'm pregnant – is it OK for me to go on a cruise?
7 Can I get duty-free goods whenever I want?
8 How much money would I need for gratuities on a seven-day cruise?
9 Do I need to pack a dinner jacket?
10 What leisure activities are there on board?

Language focus 1

The passive voice for giving information

1 Look at these examples from the brochure extract on page 75. All of them are in the passive voice. Note the position of the adverbs.

An embarkation notice will be sent with your tickets.
Excursions can only be booked on board.
Worldwide traveller's cheques may be exchanged.
This account is normally settled on the last evening.
Eurocheques are not accepted on board.
A service charge is added to all accounts.

The passive voice is commonly used in more formal written information, as in the text. If the information is in spoken form, it is more common to use the active voice – the passive voice is only used in formal or official situations.

Imagine you are giving this information to someone face-to-face. Transform these sentences into the active voice. Begin your sentences with *We …* or *You …*.

For example:
An embarkation notice will be sent with your tickets.
We will send you an embarkation notice with your tickets.

2 Find other examples of the passive in the text and transform them in a similar way.

3 Complete these sentences using either the active or passive form of the verbs in brackets. They are all in the present simple tense.

a Breakfast _____ (include) in the price.
b Cabaret _____ (take place) every evening in the cocktail lounge.
c Bed linen _____ (change) twice a week.
d Cocktails _____ (serve) before dinner.
e Passengers _____ (receive) a welcome basket of fruit in their room.
f English _____ (speak) by all crew members.
g The duty-free shop _____ (accept) credit cards.
h The sofa _____ (convert into) bunk beds at night.

Output task

Passenger information

1 **Writing**

Write some more sections for the 'General information' pages of the cruise brochure. The headings for eight sections are given below, together with some information in note form which you can include. Make sure you use the verb in brackets in the passive form.

Communications
telephone and fax available through ship's radio office
on-board contact for passengers also possible – only when ship at sea
(**contact**)

Electrical appliances
don't use in cabin – except razors
hair-dryers in cabins
ironing prohibited
(**use**)

Laundry service
special staff for laundry/pressing/ironing needs – small charge
(**attend to**)

Religious services
on-board chapel – Roman Catholic chaplain
(**hold**)

Dining reservations
specify preferred sitting on booking form – smoking/non-smoking, but can't guarantee confirmation at embarkation
(**give**)

Daily programme
news bulletin of next day's activities to cabin every evening
(**deliver**)

Disabled passengers
special cabins on all ships – to provide facilities for disabled
details on request
(**adapt**)

2 **Pair work**

In pairs, take turns to play the roles of a customer enquiring about cruise information, and a travel agent. The customer can ask about any of the topics. The travel agent has the information listed above and in the brochure extract on page 75.

Ticket information and itineraries

Greek ferries

Here is some information about ferries connecting the Greek mainland and islands in the central Aegean Sea.

1 Match the pictures with the descriptions of the different types of boat.

a **Car ferries** largest boats, reliable, operate on main routes from Piraeus, cars are usually on two or three decks with other decks for passengers; conditions vary, second class tickets include a cabin.

b **Landing craft ferries** large, single-platform boats with most of the deck used for carrying cars and other vehicles, operate in sheltered coastal waters only, passengers accommodated at stern.

c **Hydrofoils** skim fast over the water on 'legs', also known as 'dolphins'; twice as fast as ferries but only operate in calm sea, more expensive.

d **Catamarans** these boats have a flat deck, supported by two hulls, only a few in the Aegean, only operate in the high season.

e **Passenger boats** caiques, or local fishing boats, operating as 'taxi boats'.

2 Answer these questions using the map and the Ticket Information section.

1 Where can you buy tickets at the cheapest rate?
2 What is the cheapest class of ticket?
3 Can babies and children travel at a cheaper price?
4 What is the best way to pay for tickets?
5 Can you give or sell your ticket to another passenger?
6 How many direct ferries are there from Piraeus to Crete? Approximately how many journeys are there in a week?
7 How many times a week is there a ferry from Iraklion to Rhodes?
8 How many different islands can be reached from Paros in one journey?
9 What is the best way to get from Lesbos to Paros?
10 How many islands are connected by hydrofoil?

Ticket Information

- Tickets are available from ticket agents at ports or on the boats (in high season it is sometimes not possible to buy tickets on board). Ticket prices are regulated by the government.

- Three classes of ticket: first (luxury), second, and third (deck) – most people travel deck class. If you buy on board you will probably get a tourist class ticket (deck plus 20% surcharge).

- A return ticket usually means a 10% discount.

- Half-fare for children aged 4 to 10.

- Cash payment only (credit cards not usually accepted).

- Tickets are normally non-transferable.

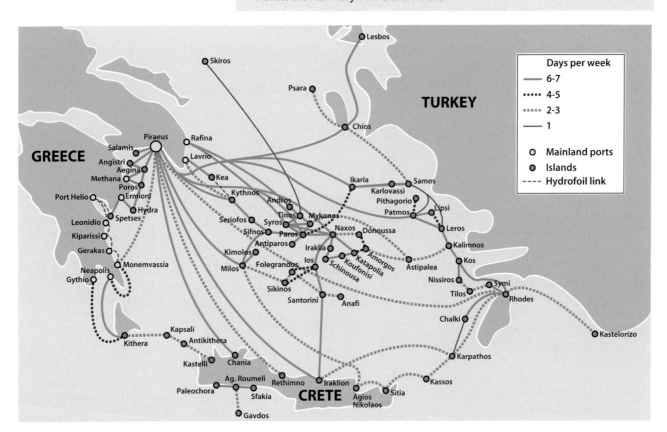

Speaking

In pairs, take turns to play the roles of a customer making enquiries about travelling by ferry, and an employee of the Greek ferry information service.

Customers   A

Customer **A** is travelling from Piraeus to Crete.
Customer **B** is travelling from Piraeus to the islands of Kalimnos, Kos, and Tilos.

Both customers need to decide what sort of group they are travelling with (e.g. a family, a group of friends, a couple), and to find out the following information about their chosen route:

– frequency of service
– type of boat
– different classes
– ticket arrangements and prices (including discounts)

Information officers   B

Both Information officers should use the Ticket Information and the map above to answer the customers' questions.

Reading and speaking

A trip down the Nile

1 Have you ever been to Egypt? If so, what was it like? If not, would you like to go there? Why? Why not? What famous tourist sights are there in Egypt?

2 You are going to read and ask questions about the itinerary of a Nile cruise.

1 Divide into two groups, **A** and **B**. **Group A** should read text A below. **Group B** should read text B on page 177. These are different versions of the same text, with different information missing. Decide what questions you need to ask in order to find out the missing information.

2 Work in pairs, one from each group. Ask each other questions to complete the information in your text. You may need to refer to the map for the place names.

Text A

THE MS RA

Recently built in ¹ _____, the MS Ra is a large purpose-built Nile cruiser that can accommodate up to 140 passengers. She is an excellently designed, sleek vessel offering all the benefits of modern high technology. Facilities on board include a large restaurant, lounge, bar, sun-viewing deck with swimming pool, jacuzzi, and a small health club. The cabin accommodation is bright and airy with large French-style windows which open to offer splendid views of the banks of the Nile. All the cabins are fully air-conditioned with private bathrooms.

THE NILE

Abydos · Denderah
Valley of The Kings
Western Thebes · El Karnak · Luxor
Western Desert · Esna · Eastern Desert
EGYPT · River Nile
Edfu
London · ASIA
AFRICA
Kom Ombo
N · W E · S
Kitchener Island · Aswan
Elephantine Island · Philae
Aswan High Dam
Abu Simbel ↓
25 miles

ITINERARY

DAY 1
London (Gatwick) – depart in the morning for Luxor. Arrive Luxor in the afternoon and drive to the first class MS Ra moored on the Nile at Luxor. Moor overnight in ² _____.

DAY 2
Sail at dawn to Denderah to visit the Temple of Hathor and drive across the ³ _____ to Abydos. Visit monuments, including the temples of Seti I and his son, Rameses II. Moor overnight in Denderah.

DAY 3
Cruise to Luxor, arriving at ⁴ _____. In the afternoon, visit the Great Temple of Karnak with the avenue of ram-headed sphinxes, and the Temple of Luxor, the Hypostyle Hall with its 134 columns, and the Obelisk of Queen Hatshepsut. Moor overnight in Luxor.

DAY 4
Excursion to the Valley of the Kings at Thebes to see the Royal Tombs of the New Kingdom. The tombs of 64 kings have been discovered, including the best known, that of ⁵ _____. Continue to the mortuary Temple of Rameses III at Medinet Habu, the Valley of the Queens, and the workmen's village of Deir ed Medina. Sail in the afternoon to Esna.

DAY 5
Sail to Edfu and visit the Ptolemaic Temple, one of the best preserved temples in Egypt. Sail in the evening to ⁶ _____ for an overnight.

DAY 6
Visit the temple dedicated to both Horus and Sobek at Kom Ombo, and sail to Aswan, arriving at lunchtime. Afternoon excursion to the High Dam and Philae Temple, dedicated to Isis and now rebuilt on an island between the two great dams. Moor overnight in Aswan.

DAY 7
Optional excursion by ⁷ _____ to Abu Simbel. Visits today are made by felucca and include Elephantine Island and Kitchener Island. We will also visit the Mausoleum of the Aga Khan which, being on top of a hill, affords marvellous views over ⁸ _____.

DAY 8
Depart Aswan in the morning by coach for Luxor airport. Fly from Luxor to London, departing in the early evening, and arrive at London Gatwick in the evening.

Language focus 2

Talking about future arrangements

1 Look at these sentences spoken by someone about to go on the Nile cruise.

a We're flying to Luxor to meet the boat.
b The boat leaves at dawn.
c We'll probably find it very hot.
d We're going to visit as many ancient sites as possible.
e This time next week I'll be lying by the pool on a boat floating down the Nile.

They all describe the future but they all use a different form. Which one

– makes a prediction about the future?
– expresses an intention?
– describes a definite future arrangement?
– describes a continuous activity in the future seen from a point in time?
– describes future timetabled events?

2 The following message was left on an answerphone. Use the correct future form of the verbs in brackets to complete the message.

'Hello. This is a message for Mr Osgood. This is Jane from Regency Travel here. We've got your final travel details now. I've put them in the post but I ____ (give) you a quick summary now. You ____ (fly) from Heathrow on Monday. The plane ____ (leave) at 10 a.m., but check-in ____ (start) two hours before. You ____ (travel) business class, and you ____ (arrive) in New York at 3 p.m. local time. When you arrive a taxi ____ (wait) to take you to your hotel. You ____ (stay) at the Plaza as arranged. I expect you ____ (want) a little rest, but remember you ____ (go) to the theatre that night – we've booked the ticket. Anyway, the details are in the post. I'm sure you ____ (have) a wonderful time. Oh, one last thing. We need to know if you ____ (pay) the balance by credit card or cheque. Could you let me know? Thank you. Bye.'

3 Look at this brief itinerary for someone who is travelling to Liverpool for a weekend conference. The person has added some of their own notes. Make sentences using the different forms and functions of the future identified in exercise 1. Try to include all five.

Group Conference and AGM

Saturday 11 February

Trains to Liverpool – 09.10, 10.10, 11.10, 12.10

from 13.00	Check-in at Royal Albert Hotel
14.00	Conference opens
14.15–17.00	Reports
19.00	Reception
19.30	Dinner
	(guest speaker Sir Arthur Dickens)
	– interesting man

Sunday 12 February

08.00	Breakfast
09.00–12.00	Workshops and Discussion Groups
	early start!
12.00–13.00	Free time
	– visit Albert Docks
	(Beatles Museum?)
13.00	Lunch
14.00	AGM – Resolutions and committee elections
16.00	Depart
	–probably later – trains at 16.30, 17.30, 18.30

Pronunciation focus

In longer sentences certain syllables are stressed more than others. The stresses give the sentence a rhythm, and help the listener to identify important information. Listen to these two examples.

            ●

Your daughter's catching the seven o'clock flight from Los

●   ●

Angeles which is due in New York at twelve.

    ●   ●

You have to be out of your room by eleven tomorrow.

a What happens to the other syllables in the sentences when you say the sentence quickly?

b How does the meaning change when different syllables or words are stressed (for example, *daughter* or *flight* in the first sentence, *you* or *room* in the second sentence)?

c Look back at exercise 1 at the start of **Language focus 2**. Decide where the main stresses fall in the example sentences (a–e). Then listen to see if you were correct.

Output task

Travel arrangements

Paula Houseman is Personal Assistant to Lindsay White, the Director of a large travel agency. Lindsay White is about to go on a familiarization trip to Egypt and the River Nile as part of a campaign to promote Nile cruises. Below are various notes and documents about the trip.

DON'T FORGET TO TAKE
- *formal evening wear*
- *business cards*
- *promotional material*
- *presents (typically British?)*
- *passport*

TRIDENT TRAVEL	Flight confirmation for Ms L White			
02 Nov	BA978	London – Cairo	dep. 10.30	arr. 19.15
12 Nov	BA979	Cairo – London	dep. 13.30	arr. 16.15

ALPHA TAXIS 081 673 7777

*Confirmed pick-up at 31 Eastlake Road
8.00 a.m. Friday 2/11*

TRIDENT TRAVEL
VOUCHER FOR HOTEL ACCOMMODATION

Name Ms L White **Hotel** Medina, Cairo

No. of nights 8 **Single**/double/twin

The Management of the

Hotel
MEDINA

*request the pleasure of
your company at a reception in
the Pyramid Lounge this evening
from 6 pm until 7.30 pm*

*Dress formal
Cocktails and canapés
will be served*

Writing

Paula has to write a briefing report for her boss about the trip. Using the notes and documents, continue the report. You can assume that the itinerary of the cruise is the same as the one on page 80, but you don't need to describe the whole itinerary.

> REPORT
> ....
>
> **Re: travel arrangements and itinerary for Lindsay White of Trident Travel, for trip to Egypt, 2–12 November.**
>
> Arrangements have now been finalized for your trip to Egypt next month. You'll be collected from home at 08.00 on 2 November, and taken to the airport …

Speaking

In pairs, role-play these two telephone conversations.

Conversation **1**

A

You are Lindsay White. You need detailed information about your forthcoming trip. Ask about: the taxi, the flight times, the hotel in Cairo, essential items to take.

B

You are Paula Houseman. Use the report you have written to give Lindsay White the information she needs. Remember to change from written to spoken register.

Conversation **2**

A

You are Paula Houseman. You have to give the same information to the company representative in Cairo, who will look after Lindsay White during the visit. Use the report you have written, but remember to change from written to spoken register. You also need to find out any additional information – especially about the people Lindsay White will meet on the cruise.

B

You are the company representative in Cairo. You need to find out when Lindsay White will be arriving, and the hotel arrangements. You also need to give Paula Houseman other information, especially who will be on the Nile cruise – directors of hotels in Cairo, the person responsible for organizing the guides, some of the lecturers, and so on.

SECTION 3

On-board information

Listening 1

International etiquette

Different countries and cultures have different ways of behaving. How much do you know about 'international etiquette'?

1 Which of these things would be socially unacceptable in your country?
   a wearing shorts in a religious building
   b wearing outdoor shoes in a religious building
   c topless bathing
   d crossing your legs in public
   e pointing with your forefinger
   f blowing your nose in public
   g kissing someone you're introduced to for the first time (man–man)
   h kissing someone you're introduced to for the first time (woman–woman)
   i using your left hand to eat with
   j asking for more food at a dinner party if you're still hungry
   k leaving food on your plate at a dinner party

2 Do you know any countries where these things would not be acceptable?

3 You are going to listen to part of a welcome talk to a group of passengers on a round-the-world cruise. Among the countries they will be visiting are Spain, Egypt and the Middle East, India, Singapore, Thailand, and Japan. Which kinds of behaviour in the list in exercise 1 do you think will be acceptable or unacceptable in these countries?

4 Listen to the cassette and fill in the table below. Where information is given, write ✓ for acceptable and ✗ for unacceptable.

	Spain	Egypt and the Middle East	India	Singapore	Thailand	Japan
a wearing shorts						
b wearing shoes						
c topless bathing						
d crossing legs						
e pointing						
f blowing nose						
g kissing (men)						
h kissing (women)						
i using left hand to eat						
j asking for more food						
k leaving food						

5 Write an entry for a tourist brochure, giving information and advice on local customs and social behaviour in your own country.

Think about the points discussed on the cassette – religious buildings, greetings and introductions, appropriate dress, posture and body language, eating and drinking. Include information about other areas, such as bargaining, tipping, queueing, attitudes to women, behaviour in business meetings, and so on.

Use expressions like:

It's a good idea (not) to …   *Never …/Always …*
Make sure you (don't) …   *Take care you (don't) …*
If possible, visitors should/shouldn't …   *Be careful (not) to …*

Vocabulary

Ships and cabins

1 What things do you find in a hotel but not on a cruise ship? What things do you find on a cruise ship but not in a hotel?

2 Some things are more or less the same in hotels and cruise ships, but are given different names – for example, a *room* is usually called a *cabin*.

Match the items in box **A** (hotels) with the nearest equivalent from box **B** (cruise ships).

A		B	
room	chain (of hotels)	cabin	embark
floor	double/twin room	porthole	cabin steward
check-in	window	two-berth cabin	crew
check-out	room service	deck	fleet
staff	waiter	table steward	passenger
guest		disembark	

3 Look at this list of items often found in a hotel room. Which of them would you also expect to find in a cabin on a luxury cruise ship?

bed – single, double	bidet	telephone
twin armchairs	jacuzzi	pillow
TV – colour, satellite	mini-bar	sheets
wardrobe	fridge	bathrobe
drawer/chest of drawers	balcony	trouser-press
mirror	sofa	hair-dryer
en suite facilities	coffee table	personal safe
bath	bedspread	multi-channel radio
shower	cushions	iron and ironing board
toilet	dressing table	verandah

4 Organize the vocabulary items into categories, depending on where you find them in the cabin:

a bathroom/toilet section   **c** living room section
b bedroom section   **d** outside the cabin

5 Use words from the list in exercise 3 to complete this extract from the Princess Caribbean Cruises brochure.

Space to call your own

UNLIKE some other cruise lines, Princess has never compromised on the spaciousness of its accommodation. We have the largest cabins in the Caribbean for ships of Princess class, many with the added bonus of a private ¹_____ – perfect for cocktails as the sun goes down.

Princess cabins have been crafted down to the last detail using coordinated fabrics in softly toning colours. Every room benefits from well-designed ²_____ with a shower or bath. Our cabins are also noted for their plentiful ³_____ and ⁴_____ space for putting your clothes.

Really comfortable beds promise rest-filled nights cradled between fresh white sheets. The majority of ⁵_____ can convert to doubles and a number of cabins are designed to accommodate a third or fourth person if required.

You'll also find offered as standard those touches which make all the difference between a good cruise and a truly luxurious one. Such as a ⁶_____ to wear after your shower and for your convenience during the cruise, and a luxury toiletries pack. Delicious petit-fours to welcome you to your cabin and a foil-wrapped chocolate on your ⁷_____ each night.

There's a ⁸_____ showing a selection of favourite films, programmes, and news around the clock. A ⁹_____ offering a choice of music and the BBC World Service when available. A ¹⁰_____ to connect you within the ship or to anywhere in the world. And in most rooms there's a ¹¹_____ for your valuables and a ¹²_____ to chill your drinks.

When you travel with Princess, you'll find it all seems like a home from home. But with a window on the world.

Cabin accommodation

Listen to this conversation between a travel agent and someone enquiring about a cruise. Below are some notes made by the customer about the questions she wanted to ask. As you listen, make a note of the answers.

1 Small cabins?
2 Share toilet and bathroom?
3 Room for three?
4 Facilities in the room?
5 Which cabin?

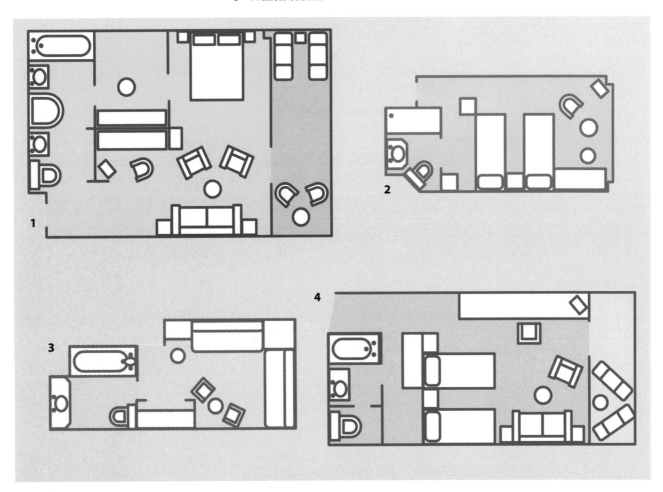

Output task

Designing and explaining cruise accommodation

1   In groups of three or four, design two cabins for your own imaginary cruise ship. One should be an economy cabin, the other a luxury cabin. Think carefully about the facilities and furniture you will include in each cabin.

2   When you have completed your plans, divide up into pairs with students from other groups and describe your cabins to each other. Discuss which are the best designs.

3   Write a brief description of the cabins like the description in 'Space to call your own' on page 85.

Cruise itinerary

Work in groups. You are going to plan a cruise trip of approximately seven to ten days. Choose an area of the world you know quite well.

1 Plan the details of your cruise.

1 Decide the approximate route your cruise will take, and note down possible ports of call and excursions.

2 Make a list of the main on-board facilities you will provide.

3 Plan an entertainment programme.

2 Produce a leaflet or brochure.

1 Write a general description of the cruise company, the area where you are cruising, and the places you will be visiting.

2 Describe the on-board facilities and entertainments (see page 75 for ideas).

3 Write a detailed itinerary. For example:

	port of call	arrive	depart	sights & visits
Day 1	Haifa	–	20.30	Jerusalem, Bethlehem
Day 2	Port Said	08.30	24.00	Cairo, the Pyramids
Day 3	Suez Canal	05.00	15.00	(in transit)
Day 4	Sarfaga	07.00	–	Luxor (overnight on board)

3 In groups, present your itinerary to the rest of the class, illustrating the talk with pictures if possible. Include a written handout of the itinerary.

Vocabulary

bathrobe	embark	monument	shore
bidet	embarkation	moor	speedboat
cabin steward	etiquette	mosque	stateroom
catamaran	evening gown	non-transferable	table steward
chest of drawers	fam trip	on board	temple
cramped	fridge	pillow	tomb
crew	gondola	port of call	trouser-press
crossing	hair-dryer	porthole	two-berth cabin
cushions	hydrofoil	pregnant	vaccination
deck	jacuzzi	purpose-built	verandah
dinner jacket	landing craft ferry	purser	wardrobe
disembark	lounge suit	round-the-world	
dressing table	mini-bar	cruise	

7

Travel by road and rail

SECTION 1	**The best way to travel?**

Speaking

Travel experiences

❶ Find out the answers to these questions by asking all the members of your class. Your teacher will give you one or more of the questions to ask. For each question ask an additional question (as indicated in brackets).

1 Who has travelled on a train most recently?
   (When and where?)
2 Who has spent the night on a train?
   (What were conditions like?)
3 Who has been on a long coach trip?
   (How long? Where to?)
4 Who has driven the greatest distance on any one day?
   (Where? How far?)
5 Who has stayed in a motel?
   (Where and when?)
6 Who has stayed in a motorhome or caravan?
   (Where and when?)
7 Where is the best place to sit on a train or a coach?
   (Why?)
8 Who prefers coach travel and who prefers train travel?
   (Why?)

❷ Now discuss the following questions.

1 Do you know where the longest train tunnel is?
2 Do you know where the longest road tunnel is?
3 Do you know which is the fastest train?
4 What are the advantages and disadvantages of travelling by coach and travelling by train?

Reading

A rail journey in India

❶ Look at this list of words to do with rail travel. Check that you know what they mean.

buffet	corridor	platform	sleeper
carriages	couchette	refreshments	station
compartment	engine	restaurant car	track

2 You are going to read someone's account of a train journey in India. What do you think it was like? Think about the stations, the facilities on the train, the scenery, and the other passengers.

3 Read the account to see if you were right. Complete the gaps with words from the list.

HEAT AND COAL-DUST

Across India by train

'I REMEMBER THE JOURNEY SO CLEARLY. THE ¹_____ IN Delhi was hot and crowded with thousands of people: taxi and rickshaw drivers, boys selling strange items of food, men selling carpets, and a million other things. The heat and the choking steam made us thirsty and hungry, so we found a sort of ²_____ and went inside for some ³_____. After a while, we returned to the heaving masses and stood on the ⁴_____ as the train pulled in. There was almost a fight to get on, but we managed to climb aboard one of the ⁵_____, fight our way down the narrow ⁶_____, and find a ⁷_____ which wasn't too crowded.

The journey was hot but exciting, with delicious smells from the open fires in the kitchens next to the ⁸_____ and fantastic scenery passing by as the ⁹_____ pulled us across the plains of India. We leaned out of the windows in search of fresher air. The ¹⁰_____ stretched before us – two metal lines running into an endless distance.

That evening we rested at Agra under the shadow of the Taj Mahal before boarding a ¹¹_____ for a night journey further south. We slept in a ¹²_____, the seats converting into narrow beds, and chatted to the early hours, our words full of the romance and excitement of our Indian adventure.'

4 Think about a train journey you have been on. In pairs, describe your journeys to each other. Make sure you include words from the list in exercise 1 – and any other train or rail vocabulary you can think of. Other useful vocabulary might be: *conductor, wagon-lit, express, luggage locker.*

A weekend break

1 Listen to this conversation in a travel agency between the travel agent and a couple who are trying to decide where to go for a weekend break.

1 Where do they decide to go?
2 What means of transport do they decide to take?

2 As you listen, note down the advantages and disadvantages of:

a a holiday in the city/a holiday in the country
b travelling by rail/travelling by coach/travelling by car

Language focus 1

Comparison, contrast, and reinforcement (spoken register)

Look at these sentences from the conversation.

Obviously if you stay for a week you get longer, but then you do have to pay a lot more.

Certainly the countryside is quieter and more relaxing. However, there's a lot more to do in the city.

On the one hand, you've got some fascinating buildings … On the other hand, it's also very relaxing.

The train is quicker, but it's much more expensive.

Despite the cost, I think we should go by train.

I do want to relax. Nevertheless, the idea was that this would be a cheap holiday.

You'd not only have more freedom, it would probably also be fairly cheap.

Which statements

a compare and contrast two different things?
b contrast negative and positive aspects of the same idea?
c reinforce two positive aspects of the same idea?

Comparison, contrast, and reinforcement (written register)

In written language a more formal structure is often used. In speech we tend to be less formal. Look at these examples. Decide which are written and which are spoken.

Contrasting two different things (the train is quick – the coach is cheap)

Although travelling by train is quick, travelling by coach is cheaper.

Travelling by train is quick. However, travelling by coach is cheaper.

Travelling by train is quick, whereas travelling by coach is cheap.

On the one hand, travelling by train is quick. On the other hand, it is not as cheap as travelling by coach.

Contrasting negative and positive aspects of the same idea (the train was expensive – we went by train)

In spite of the cost, we went by train.

Despite the cost, we went by train.

The train was expensive. Nevertheless, we went by train.

Even though it was expensive we went by train.

(*Although* and *however* can also be used to contrast negative and positive aspects.)

Reinforcing two positive aspects of same idea (the train is quick – the train is comfortable)

Not only is travelling by train quicker than travelling by coach, it is also more comfortable.

Travelling by train is quicker than travelling by coach. What's more, it's also more comfortable.

Travelling by train is quicker than travelling by coach. Moreover, it is also more comfortable.

Practice

In groups, discuss pros and cons of the following topics. When you have discussed them, write a report.

a travelling by plane/travelling by ship
b going on a package holiday/going on an independent holiday
c staying in a hotel/camping
d working in a travel agent's office/working in a holiday resort

London to Paris

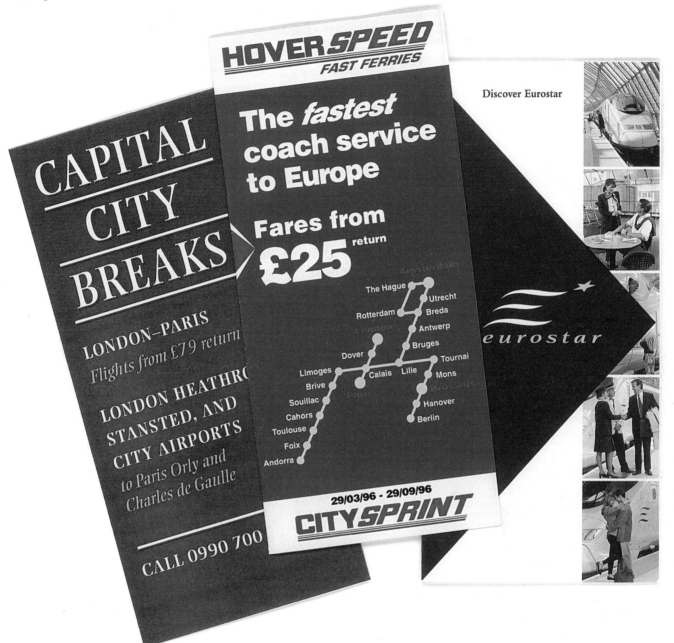

CAPITAL CITY BREAKS

LONDON–PARIS
Flights from £79 return

LONDON HEATHROW, STANSTED, AND CITY AIRPORTS
to Paris Orly and Charles de Gaulle

CALL 0990 700

HOVER SPEED FAST FERRIES

The *fastest* coach service to Europe

Fares from £25 return

29/03/96 - 29/09/96
CITY SPRINT

Discover Eurostar

eurostar

1 Work in three groups . Each group should look at one of the advertisements. Think about the advantages of travelling by the method suggested in the advertisement.

2 Divide into new groups of three with one person from each of the first groups. You are travelling as a group of three friends between London and Paris. Discuss which is the best way to travel – each person must argue in favour of the method they were given in their first groups.

3 Imagine you are a travel agent working in the corporate travel sector. You have to prepare a brief report on the various options for travel between Paris and London, and their advantages and disadvantages. Use some of the language you studied in the previous section.

Reading   **VIA Rail Canada**

① Imagine you are going on a holiday travelling across Canada by train. You want to enjoy the scenery and be comfortable. In pairs, discuss what facilities you would want on the train, and along the journey in general.

② Read the article 'VIA Rail Canada' and make a list of all the different facilities mentioned.

③ Read the text again and say whether the following statements are true or false.

1 There has been a railway across Canada for a long time.
2 Tea and coffee are free.
3 The best place to see the scenery is in the Mural Lounge.
4 The price includes breakfast, lunch, and dinner.
5 The internal design of the trains is in a modern style.
6 All 'roomettes' have their own washing facilities.
7 The beds in the 'section' are above each other.
8 The 'bedrooms' have private facilities.
9 All seats in coach class have foot rests.
10 Only first class passengers get meals served at their seats.
11 Young people under 24 receive a 10% discount on some journeys.
12 Children under 2 travel free.

④ Read the text again and find as many positive adjectives as possible (e.g. *unhurried* and *unspoilt* in the first line). You should be able to find at least twenty. Which adjectives are used to describe the following things?

– the journey
– the scenery
– the service
– the internal décor and carriages

⑤ Plan a similar rail holiday for a part of your country or an area you know well. Decide: the route, sights and scenery, the facilities on the train, meals and accommodation, different classes of passengers, discounts. Write out your plan in the form of a short article.

⑥ In pairs, take turns to role-play the conversation between a travel agent (selling the trip you planned above) and a customer (asking about the holiday – route, itinerary, and facilities).

VIA RAIL

AN UNHURRIED JOURNEY through unspoilt terrain or a fast, frequent service to cross the country – since the pioneer days, when the iron road first linked the eastern seaboard to the Canadian Pacific, the ideal way to see this great dominion has always been VIA Rail. Perfected now in VIA Rail, everything from a short journey to a transcontinental adventure is enjoyed in style, aboard transport that blends the comfort and technology of today's world with the romance and service of the past.

No long miles of driving behind you or parking problems ahead, just a leisurely journey on a sleek silver train, from the centre of one city to the heart of the next.

The Canadian

Travel across Canada from Toronto to Vancouver and enjoy the superlative Silver and Blue class service. Aboard the country's premier train you have exclusive access to three different salons, all serving complimentary tea and coffee throughout the day. There is the snug Bullet Lounge, the atmospheric Mural Lounge, and the Observation Dome, with its panoramic wrap-around windows. In addition, all meals are included. (Breakfast, lunch, and dinner – however, this does depend upon what time you join and depart from the train.) Silver and Blue class dining is a model of elegance and refinement: china, silverware, flowers, and linen adorn the dining car tables, which give you ample space: the menu matches the wine list in excellence and the service is friendly and efficient.

Corridor Service

On the shorter routes across central Canada VIA Rail's Corridor Service offers a convenient way to cross such a vast country.

Your accommodation

VIA Rail has refurbished some of its classic trains in all the rich fabrics, subtle colours, and polished wood of the art-deco era. Your choice of route and cabin accommodation is outlined below.

SLEEPING CARS: you have a choice of three levels of comfort. Roomette: ideal for one person, the little cabin has a comfy seat and turns into snug sleeping quarters at night (private facilities on western routes).

SECTION: semi-private with wide couch-style seats facing each other; these convert to bunk beds, with heavy curtains for privacy at night. Bedroom: ideal for two adults, by day a private living room with two armchairs and a picture window, by night this converts to lower and upper berths. The cabins have a sink and WC.

COACH CLASS: there is plenty of space to move around, comfortable reclining seats, and chair-side drinks and snacks service. On longer routes, Coach service seats are enhanced by foot rests and there's a café and glass-domed observation car.

VIA 1: VIA Rail's first class service and adds to the coach car comfort with exclusive lounges at Montreal, Toronto, and Ottawa, pre-boarding privileges, distinctive décor, a cellular phone on board, delicious meals served at your seat, complimentary drinks, and a choice of wine and liqueurs with your meal.

Discounted fares

VIA Rail offers discounted fares for the economy conscious. Senior (60 plus) and youth (up to 24 years) receive a 10% discount across the VIA network. Applicable at any time, on all VIA services. This can be combined with seasonal fares, giving a possible total 50% discount – to receive seasonal discounts, advance purchase may be necessary. Children aged 2–11 years are eligible for a 50% discount on Coach class, and FREE travel is available for each child under two years accompanied by one adult. (A second infant with just one adult pays 50% of Coach class fare.)

Enquiring about a motorhome

1 Have you ever stayed in a motorhome or a caravan? What was it like? What information does a motorhome hire company need to give its customers?

2 Listen to this telephone conversation between the representative of a motorhome hire company and an enquirer. Which of these things does the customer want?

– flush toilet   – TV   – cooker   – microwave   – double bed

3 Listen again and answer the following questions.
1 What is the age limit for drivers?
2 Is the motorhome available immediately on arrival?
3 What training is given?
4 Is petrol included in the price?
5 How much mileage is included in the price?
6 Do the motorhomes have flush toilets?
7 Which model would you recommend for the customer? (Look at the table on the next page.)

4 In the conversation the representative of the motorhome company has to explain a number of things. Listen to the conversation again and complete these sentences.
1 You have to be _____.
2 For safety reasons, we have a policy that _____.
3 We recommend you _____.
4 As far as mileage goes, we include _____.
5 There are full instructions in the manual on _____.
6 Most models can take _____.

5 In pairs, imagine you are going on a family motorhome holiday. Look at the information about different kinds of motorhomes and discuss which model you would choose.

Motorhome Facilities   Vehicle type

Vehicle specifications	MHC22	MHC24	MHC28	MHC31	MHB19	MHTC
Dash air-conditioning	●	●	●	●	●	●
Stove/sink	●	●	●	●	●	●
Shower	●	●	●	●		
Flush toilet	●	●	●	●		●
Three-way refrigeration	●	●	●	●	●	●
Microwave oven			●	●		
Freshwater tank	●	●	●	●	●	●
Dual batteries	●	●	●	●	●	
Automatic transmission	●	●	●	●	●	●
Power brakes	●	●	●	●	●	●

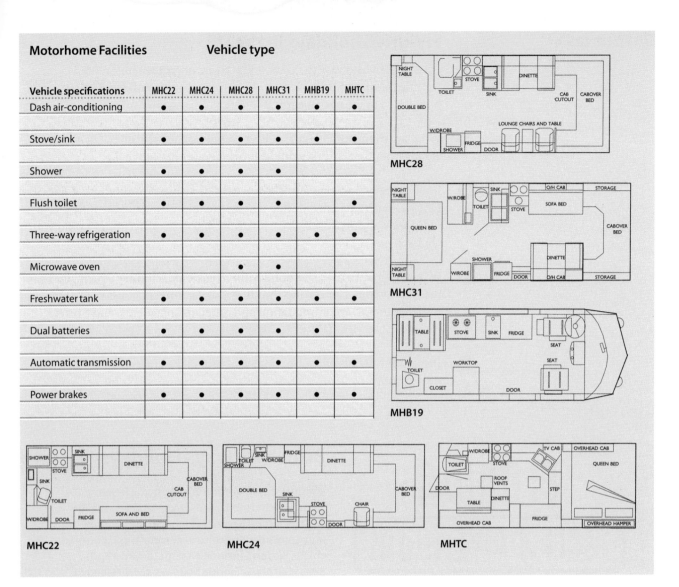

MHC28

MHC31

MHB19

MHC22

MHC24

MHTC

Reading and speaking

Explaining car-hire arrangements

In pairs, have a conversation on the phone like the conversation on motorhomes you listened to earlier. This time you have to talk about the details of a car-hire arrangement. Take turns to play the different roles.

The customer (**A**) should ask about the points below.
The car-hire representative (**B**) should look at the information on page 178.

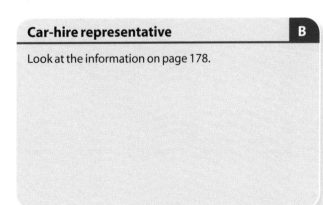

Customer   A

Ask about the following details (you can make up the exact details of your holiday group).

– suitable cars for different numbers of people
– cost per week and per day of different cars
– possibility of upgrading (and how much)
– what is not included

Make notes and make sure you understand the details.
At the end, choose a car which suits your needs.

Car-hire representative   B

Look at the information on page 178.

Output task

Fly-drive holidays in the US

On a fly-drive holiday the tourist flies to an airport where a rented car is waiting for him or her to use for the duration of the holiday. The car rental is included in the package price.

1 What are the advantages of such a holiday for the tourist? What arrangements and deals would a tour operator have to make?

2 Look at the extract on page 97 from a fly-drive brochure about holidays in Florida. With a partner, decide whether to take an independent fly-drive holiday or one of the self-drive tours. Which of the three tours would you choose?

3 In groups, plan a fly-drive holiday for a particular country which you know reasonably well. Each group should choose a different country. Include information on accommodation and other arrangements, and a brief itinerary.

4 Present the details of your holiday and itinerary to members of the other groups.

British Airways Holidays

The best way of getting around in the fabulous 'Sunshine State' is by self-drive car … you really can't go wrong because driving in the US is not only convenient but also very simple, and petrol is cheap. We have included a rental-free car with almost all of our Florida holidays, so travelling to and from the theme parks, superb beaches, and other exciting attractions couldn't be easier.

Choose an independent fly-drive holiday for complete flexibility and the freedom to travel at your own pace. Included is a flight to and from Miami or Orlando, plus a rental-free car. If you like, we can even arrange accommodation vouchers, giving you the opportunity to stay where you want, when you want, and for as long as you want.

If you prefer to leave the planning of your itinerary to someone else, why not select one of our self-drive tours? We will pre-book all your accommodation and give you the choice of three itineraries, each one allowing ample time at the start of your holiday to make the most of all that Orlando, the 'entertainment capital of the world', has to offer.

BEST OF FLORIDA

DAY 1 London Gatwick – Orlando
Fly direct to Orlando. On arrival pick up your self-drive car from the airport rental station and make your way to your chosen hotel.
Overnight: Holiday Inn Express (Orlando Marriott).

DAYS 2–5 Orlando
Four full days to enjoy the many attractions of the Orlando area.
Overnights: Holiday Inn Express (Orlando Marriott).

DAY 6 Orlando – St Pete Beach / Clearwater
A leisurely drive brings you to St Pete beach or Clearwater on Florida's Gulf Coast.
Overnight: Sandpiper (Sheraton Sandkey).

DAY 10 St Pete Beach / Clearwater – Sanibel / Captiva
Journey south to the beautiful islands of Sanibel and Captiva.
Overnight: West Wind Inn (Southseas Plantation).

DAY 13 Sanibel / Captiva – Miami Beach / Fort Lauderdale
Travel across Florida to the marinas and Atlantic beaches of Miami Beach and Fort Lauderdale.
Overnight: Quality Shawnee (Pier 66).

DAY 15 Miami Beach / Fort Lauderdale – Miami
At leisure until it's time to drive back to Miami Airport to drop off your self-drive car and check in for your flight home.

DAY 16 London Heathrow
Morning arrival.

COMPLETE FLORIDA

DAY 1 London Gatwick – Orlando
Fly direct to Orlando. On arrival pick up your self-drive car from the airport rental station and make your way to your chosen hotel.
Overnight: Gateway Inn (Travelodge).

DAYS 2–5 Orlando
Four full days to enjoy this 'Entertainment Capital' of the world.
Overnights: Gateway Inn (Travelodge).

DAY 6 Orlando – Hutchinson Island
A drive of about two hours brings you to Florida's east coast.
Overnight: Holiday Inn Oceanside (Indian River Plantation).

DAYS 7 & 8 Hutchinson Island
Relax on the beach.
Overnights: Holiday Inn Oceanside (Indian River Plantation).

DAY 9 Hutchinson Island – Fort Lauderdale
Journey south to the smart coastal resort of Fort Lauderdale.
Overnight: Sheraton Yankee Trader (Pier 66).

DAY 10 Fort Lauderdale
At leisure.
Overnight: Sheraton Yankee Trader (Pier 66).

DAY 11 Fort Lauderdale – Duck Key / Key Largo
Today's journey takes you to the Keys.
Overnight: Hawk's Cay (Sheraton Key Largo).

DAY 12 Duck Key / Key Largo – Key West
Travel along the sparkling Florida Keys to Key West.
Overnight: The Southernmost (Marriott's Casa Marina).

DAYS 13 & 14 Key West
At leisure.
Overnights: The Southernmost (Marriott's Casa Marina).

DAY 15 Key West – Miami
Drive back to Miami to drop off your self-drive car at the airport and check in for your return flight.

DAY 16 London Heathrow
Morning arrival.

ULTIMATE FLORIDA

DAY 1 London Gatwick – Orlando
Fly direct to Orlando. On arrival pick up your self-drive car from the airport rental station and make your way to your chosen hotel.
Overnight: Howard Johnson Park Square (Orlando Marriott).

DAYS 1–4 Orlando
Three full days to enjoy the many attractions in and around Orlando.
Overnights: Howard Johnson Park Square (Trade Winds).

DAY 5 Orlando – St Pete Beach
A drive of about 2 hours brings you to St Pete Beach on Florida's Gulf Coast.
Overnight: Sandpiper Beach Resort (TradeWinds).

DAYS 6 & 7 St Pete Beach
At leisure. Overnight: Sandpiper Beach Resort (TradeWinds).

DAY 8 St Pete Beach – Sanibel / Captiva
Continue south along the Florida's Gulf Coast to Sanibel Island or Captiva Island.
Overnight: West Wind Inn (South Seas Plantation).

DAYS 9 & 10 Sanibel Island / Captiva – Naples
At leisure.
Overnights: West Wind Inn (South Seas Plantation).

DAY 11 Sanibel / Captiva – Naples
Today, travel further south to Naples.
Overnight: Vanderbilt Inn (Edgewater Beach Hotel).

DAY 12 Naples
At leisure. Overnight: Vanderbilt Inn (Edgewater Beach Hotel).

DAY 13 Naples – Duck Key / Key Largo
Drive along Florida's 'Alligator Alley' to Duck Key or Key Largo.
Overnight: Hawk's Cay (Sheraton Key Largo).

DAY 14 Duck Key / Key Largo – Key West
Continue along the Florida Keys to Key West.
Overnight: The Southernmost (Marriott's Casa Marina).

DAYS 15 & 16 Key West
At leisure.
Overnights: The Southernmost (Marriott's Casa Marina)

DAY 17 Key West – Fort Lauderdale
Drive north to Fort Lauderdale.
Overnight: Sheraton Yankee Trader (Pier 66).

DAY 18 Fort Lauderdale
At leisure.
Overnight: Sheraton Yankee Trader (Pier 66).

DAY 19 Fort Lauderdale – Hutchinson Island
Travel north to Hutchinson Island.
Overnight: Holiday Inn Oceanside (Indian River Plantation).

DAYS 20 & 21 Hutchinson Island
Two full days of relaxation on the beach.
Overnights: Holiday Inn Oceanside (Indian River Plantation).

DAY 22 Hutchinson Island – Orlando
Drive back to Orlando Airport to drop off your self-drive car and check in for your flight home.

DAY 23 London Gatwick
Morning arrival.

Coach tours – dream or disaster?

A coach tour of Europe

1 You are going to read the itinerary of a European coach tour. Before you read, look at the map of Europe and discuss the best order in which to visit these places. The tour starts from London. How long do you think it will take?

2 Read the itinerary quickly and see if you guessed the order and time correctly.

3 Read the itinerary again in detail and find out where you can do the following things.

a ride in a gondola

b visit a diamond factory

c have a wonderful view of the Alps

d go on a canal cruise

e see a forum

f watch glassblowers

g visit a cathedral

h go on a river cruise

i buy some leather goods

j go on a 'magic' ride

7

Travel by road and rail

DAY 1

London–Channel Crossing–Amsterdam

You can join your tour by travelling on our complimentary feeder services from London. You will travel to the Channel port for your short ferry crossing and join your tour on the continent where you will be met by your Cosmos escort. From here your coach sets off to Amsterdam for overnight at Hotel Inntel at Zaandam or Grand Amstelveen ****. pf

DAY 2

Amsterdam–The Rhineland

A morning to enjoy Holland's busy metropolis. After your included visit to a famous diamond factory it's time for optional morning sightseeing; visit the Rijksmuseum with its collection of Dutch masters, then a drive with a local guide pointing out the city highlights, finally a canal cruise to see Amsterdam at water level. In the afternoon travel southwards to the Rhineland area for overnight at Hotel Kripp** at Coblenz . B, D, pf

DAY 3

The Rhineland–Innsbruck

A choice today of the included scenic drive along the shores of the Rhine or, even more thrilling, the optional Rhine cruise with vistas of the Lorelei Rock, hill-top castles, half-timbered wine villages, and terraced vineyards. In the afternoon drive along the comfortable autobahn to Austria. Overnight at Hotel Dollinger ***. B, D, pf

DAY 4

Innsbruck–Venice area

A morning to enjoy the sights of the Tyrol's capital city. Your included orientation drive will show you the Maria Theresien Strasse and the legendary Golden Roof. In the afternoon use the fast and comfortable motorway to reach the Venice area for overnight at the Colombo *** at Marghera. B,D,pf

DAY 5

Venice–Florence area

It's really more like a marvellous film-set than a real live city, with its criss-crossing canals, gondolas and water buses, arched bridges, palaces, and little quiet piazzas. The included tour starts with a boat ride and is followed by highlights such as a visit to St Mark's Basilica and a chance to watch Venetian glass-blowers fashion their delicate objects as they did centuries ago. This afternoon journey across the Apennines into the gentle hilly countryside of Tuscany. Overnight in the Florence area at Hotel Delta at Calenzano **** or Europa *** in Signa. B,D,pf

DAY 6

Florence area–Rome

Your orientation drive will make a stop in Piazzale Michelangelo to enjoy one of the best views of the city stretching across the river Arno. Later visit one of Florence's leather shops and then time to wander on your own. In the afternoon travel south on the autostrada. Pass the sunlit valleys of Chianti country and savour the timeless landscape of rounded hills, mellow medieval towns, and silvery olive groves broken by columns of dark cypress. Reach Rome well in time to enjoy your first evening in this great capital city. Overnights at Pineta Palace **** or American Palace ***. B,pf

DAY 7

Rome

The Eternal City and hub of the ancient civilized world is a sightseer's dream. Your included sightseeing takes in Piazza Venezia, the Monument to the Unknown Soldier, a view of the Roman Forum, and the Colosseum. Then, by way of the Circus Maximus, you reach the top of the Gianicolo hill to enjoy a full view of Rome and its seven hills. B,pf

DAY 8

Rome–Lugano

Take the 'Highway of the Sun' and motor northwards all day. Through more of Tuscany and into the flat and fertile plains of the Po Valley. Glimpses of the pre-Alps will make you aware that you're not far from Lake Lugano. Overnight in Lugano which will be an introduction to tomorrow's grand alpine scenery. Hotel Beha or Post Simplon ***. B,D,pf

DAY 9

Lugano–Lake Maggiore–Lausanne

A stupendous drive today going at first to Stresa on Lake Maggiore for a short stop before climbing to the summit of the Simplon Pass to enjoy a quite spectacular view of the surrounding alpine peaks. More mountain scenery as you motor through the Rhone Valley by way of Sion and Martigny to the shores of Lake Geneva. Overnight in Lausanne, the lively capital of Canton Vaud, at the Hotel City or Alpha ***. B,D,pf

DAY 10

Lausanne–Paris

Vistas of famous vineyards on the way to Beaune. Visit the medieval Burgundian town, known the world over for its wine production. Later via the fast and comfortable autoroute to Paris. Tonight maybe an optional cabaret show. Hotel Latitudes Paris Seine ***. B,pf

DAY 11

Paris

A full day in which to explore the city that's known throughout the world for its fashions, art and museums, delicious food, and joie de vivre. Optional sightseeing with a local expert starts with an inside visit to Notre Dame cathedral. Then many of the best-known Parisian sights: La Sorbonne, Boulevard St Germain, the Eiffel Tower, Opéra, Champs Elysées, and Rue de Rivoli. In the afternoon you have the option of visiting Versailles. B,pf

DAY 12

Paris–Included visit to Disneyland® Paris.

39 years of Disney magic, imagination, and expertise have gone into making this self-contained world of fun and fantasy by far the greatest and most dazzling amusement centre in Europe. Once inside Disneyland® Paris you can look forward to exhilarating non-stop fun and entertainment on a vast scale. Following the magic kingdom's tradition, all rides are included in your entrance ticket so you can have unlimited access to the Theme Park's facilities and enjoy them to your heart's content. B,pf

DAY 13

Paris–Channel crossing–UK

Leave Paris and travel north to the Channel port where your tour ends. After the short Channel crossing join the appropriate feeder service to London. B

Listening 3

A disastrous tour

❶ Look at this promotional leaflet about an imaginary coach tour in Europe.

Sunsearcher Tours—
why we're the ones for you

Our coaches...
- spacious, modern, and reliable
- air-conditioning on all coaches
- on-board toilet facilities
- comfortable reclining seats
- panoramic windows
- daily seat rotation

Our staff...
- highly-trained and courteous drivers
- efficient and knowledgeable escorts
- local English-speaking guides in all cities

Our accommodation ...
- good quality three-star hotels
- convenient central locations
- all rooms have private facilities
- breakfast included

SUNSEARCHER TOURS

With Sunsearcher Tours —
the pleasure's yours

Which of the advertised features of the tour could these negative adjectives be associated with?

broken down	dirty	out of date	rusty
cramped	ignorant	overbooked	steamed up
crowded	incomprehensible	rude	unhelpful

❷ Now listen to a conversation between two friends, one of whom was on the coach tour. As you listen, identify which of the advertised features were problematic. Note down the details of exactly what was wrong.

Features	Details of problem

❸ Look back at the language of complaining and responding to complaints in **Unit 4**. Imagine you were on the coach tour. Choose one or two of the problems and act out the conversation between a passenger and the tour company representative, after the tour is over.

Language focus 2

Dealing with problems – sympathizing

1 Look at these sentences from the listening section. In each case, Lucy is responding to her friend's problems by sympathizing with her.

Oh dear!
Oh dear. That must have been awful!
Oh no! That's the last thing you want.
It sounds terrible!
Poor you! You'll have to complain.

2 These expressions are being used between friends. Would any of them be used in a professional context – for example by a travel agent responding to a customer's complaints?

Dealing with problems – calming

1 When faced with someone with a problem who may be upset we might offer sympathy. We will probably also try to calm them down, using expressions like these.

Just calm down.
Don't worry.
There's nothing to worry about.
Try to relax.
I'm sure it'll be all right.
Take it easy.

2 If we can do something about the problem we will also suggest an 'action plan'. In the following mini-dialogues match each problem with a calming phrase and an appropriate action plan response.

Problems

1 I can't find my handbag! It's got my credit cards and all my money in it.
2 It's my daughter – she's missing!
3 Oh no! That's the last train! How am I going to get home now?
4 They've left all our luggage at the hotel.
5 It's very bumpy. Are we going to crash?

Calming down

a Just calm down.
b Don't worry.
c Try to relax.
d Take it easy.
e There's nothing to worry about.

Action plan/suggestion

i There's a night bus that leaves from just over there.
ii Are you sure you didn't leave it in the bathroom?
iii We'll send a van to collect it.
iv It's just a little pocket of turbulence.
v Let's go to the Information Desk and ask if anyone's seen her.

Practice

In pairs, choose some of the situations which Jude describes in exercise 1 – for example, the broken air-conditioning, the rude driver, the local guides. Act out the conversations that the passengers had with the tour representative.

Change roles and think of other problems that might occur on a different coach (or rail) tour.

Pronunciation focus 2

1 Listen again to the expressions Lucy uses and note how her intonation helps her to sound sympathetic.

2 Practise the expressions yourself. Make sure you exaggerate the intonation pattern to get maximum effect.

Output task

Faxes to head office

On the coach tour, the escort had to contact her head office to inform them of the problems she was having.

1 Look at her first fax and note the standard layout of the headings. The message is mixed up. Put the sentences in the right order.

Hotel La Plaza
Barcelona

Fax message

To Sunsearcher Tours Head Office
Attention Operations Manager
From Jane Dancaster
Date 15 August
Pages 1

Re: Tour ET612 : European Delights

a Yesterday the air-conditioning also broke down.
b Please reply a.s.a.p.
c I am writing to let you know we have had one or two problems with the coach.
d I have therefore had to restrict its use.
e Firstly, the toilet is not operating correctly.
f If not, could you authorize me to have an emergency service at the next convenient place?
g The temperature is now nearly 40 degrees Celsius and obviously it is very uncomfortable.
h Although I have tried to keep it clean, this has not been possible.
i Is there any chance of a replacement coach?

Regards,

Jane
Jane

---

2 Here are notes for Jane's second fax. Write the complete fax, including headings. She is now staying at the Hotel Majestica in Seville.

- pity you couldn't send replacement coach
- managed to get air-con to work a little
- must complain about driver
   rude and uncooperative
   argument with me yesterday
   swore at passenger this morning
   left luggage at hotel and refused to go back for it
   (eventually persuaded him)
- request advice

3 Now write a third fax concerning the incident with the lost passengers.

Vocabulary

broken down	cramped	model	track
buffet	crowded	out of date	transcontinental
bunk beds	driving licence	platform	tunnel
carriage	escort	refreshments	uncooperative
compartment	express	reliable	unhelpful
complimentary	ignorant	replacement	unhurried
condensation	incomprehensible	restaurant car	unspoilt
conductor	knowledgeable	rusty	wagon-lit
corridor	leisurely	sleeper	
couchette	luggage locker	spacious	
courteous	mileage	steamed up	

ACTIVITY

The Road and Rail Game

Divide into teams (two players in a team) and play against another team. You will need a dice and some counters. Toss a coin to see which team is the train and which team is the coach. The rules of the game are explained below.

How to play

The aim of the game is to collect as many Attraction Points as possible. You collect Attraction Points at the towns/cities and also along the way by picking up Chance cards and answering Language questions.

Throw the dice and move your counter forward along the road or railway track.

When you reach a town/city (you do not have to throw the exact number) you must wait there for the other player to arrive. Both players must stay there for at least one turn.

While you are there you can visit attractions, and gain Attraction Points by throwing the dice. The number of Attraction Points you gain is the same as the number on the dice. As soon as one player departs, the other must depart as well.

Chance cards if you land on a square marked with a **?**, take a card and follow the instructions on it.

Language questions the other team can ask you any question from the **Vocabulary** or **Language focus** sections of this unit (or other units if you agree). You get two extra attraction points for a correct answer and lose one attraction point for a wrong answer.

Trains travel faster than coaches so trains have more chance to collect Attraction Points in the towns/cities, but coaches will have more opportunity to collect points along the route.

The game ends when both players reach the final destination. The winner is the one with the most Attraction Points.

The Road and Rail Game

Beautiful scenery
2 points

Scenic village
2 points

Historic house
2 points

Optional visit to mountain village—if one player goes, the other must go.

ZOO

FARM

CIRCUS

THEATRE

Lovely restaurant
2 points

Scenic village
2 points

Beautiful scenery
2 points

Historic house
2 points

FINISH

AIRPORT

PARK

104

8

Tickets, reservations, and insurance

Facts and figures

Reading and vocabulary

Travel documents

1 Look at these seven items. What are they? Who would have them (e.g. an air passenger, a hotel guest)? Who would issue them?

item	picture	Who has it?	Who issues it?
air ticket			
money-off voucher			
hotel key card			
hotel bill			
receipt			
train ticket			
boarding pass			

② Look at the seven items in more detail. Can you think of questions that might be asked (in a tourism situation) to give these answers? The first one is done for you.

1	Room 418	*Can you tell me which room Mr Harding is staying in?*
2	9 November	_____
3	01904 45 99 88	_____
4	MON 2974	_____
5	28F	_____
6	13.35	_____
7	No, £6.40	_____
8	Fifty pounds	_____

Reading

Prices and facilities at Hotel King Solomon's Palace

① What is the difference between (a) *half-board* and *full-board*, and (b) *bed and breakfast* (*B&B*) and *room only*? What is an *all-inclusive* holiday?

② What is a *supplement*? What might a guest have to pay a supplement for when staying in a hotel?

③ A *discount* is a reduction in the price. It could be for booking early, for booking a large group, and so on. Holiday companies offer other discounts and saver arrangements. What other savers and special offers could be offered by a hotel in a Wintersun resort?

④ Read the brochure description of the Hotel King Solomon's Palace in Israel.

1 What facilities are there in the room?
2 What special offers are there?
3 What is the cheapest time of year to travel?
4 What is the most expensive time of year to travel?

⑤ Read the extract again and decide if these statements are true or false.

1 The walk to the beach takes five minutes.
2 There are four main restaurants.
3 There is a floodlit tennis court at the hotel.
4 Entrance to the health club is free.
5 All the rooms have air-conditioning.
6 All the rooms overlook the pool.
7 Prices are based on half-board.
8 Taxi transfers can be arranged.

Hotel King Solomon's Palace *****

EILAT

King Solomon's Palace dominates both the landscape and skyline of Eilat's North Beach lagoon. Unique in its design features, the hotel is renowned for its extensive range of well-organized sports and entertainments, giving it a lively atmosphere and effectively creating a self-contained resort-within-a-resort. Should you ever wish to leave the Palace, the beach is just a very pleasant five-minute stroll.

Isrotel

- Two popular swimming pools (one heated) with sun terraces, *Oasis* poolside snack bar
- Excellent range of dining choices: *Solomon's Table* (buffet style) with Chinese and Italian sections, *Café Royal* dairy restaurant, *French Brasserie* à la carte, *Off The Wharf* fish restaurant, Yacht pub bar.
- Main entertainments lounge
- Extensive sports facilities include floodlit tennis (at the nearby Isrotel Tennis Centre), daily aerobics, water sports at the Red Sea Sports Centre, and a Health Club (fee payable).

Rooms

Prices are based on two adults sharing a room with two beds, bathroom, air-conditioning, satellite TV, mini-bar, and balcony. Rooms with pool-view are available at a supplement.

Bed & breakfast

12 floors, 421 rooms, Telephone: 00 9727 334111

Sunworld savers

- **Save £60** on adult 14-night holidays departing 5, 16–22 Sept, 24 Nov–7 Dec and 12–26 Jan.
- **3 Free meals** for guests on Bed and Breakfast for departures 8–15 Dec, 5–18 Jan, and 12–26 May.
- **Save £70** on adult 7-night holidays departing 2 Jan.
- **Save £30** on adult 7-night holidays departing 5, 16–22 Sept.

Please note only one of the above applies per booking.

Accommodation	King Solomon's Palace					
Holiday Code	T80H01					
Accom./pers. share	Twin room					
No. of nights	7 nights		10/11 nights		14 nights	
	Adult	Child	Adult	Child	Adult	Child
5 Sept–30 Sept	519	309	659	335	769	349
1 Oct–17 Oct	519	305	659	329	759	349
18 Oct–31 Oct	509	299	649	325	749	339
1 Nov–14 Nov	489	279	659	325	719	319
15 Nov–28 Nov	429	269	589	315	669	325
29 Nov–11 Dec	439	265	579	299	659	305
12 Dec–18 Dec	449	265	699	399	989	479
19 Dec–25 Dec	899	525	1099	585	1329	619
26 Dec–31 Dec	849	495	1095	535	1119	555
1 Jan–22 Jan	475	259	609	295	669	295
23 Jan–9 Feb	459	275	599	319	679	309
10 Feb–17 Feb	519	289	729	325	849	329
18 Feb–16 Mar	579	295	779	329	899	339
17 Mar–23 Mar	595	299	859	365	1069	439
24 Mar–27 Mar	799	415	999	449	1169	479
28 Mar–31 Mar	729	295	765	319	949	349
1 Apr–16 Apr	579	299	949	345	949	355
17 Apr–4 May	729	425	–	–	999	489
5 May–14 May	499	269	–	–	729	309
15 May–29 May	469	269	–	–	699	285
Reduction per night	3rd adult £11.80					
Supplements per person per night	**Half-board** £14.40 (£20.80) **Single room** £27.30 (£45.00) **Pool view** £6.10 (£9.00) Taxi transfer available.					

Departures/Extra Weeks commencing

Bracketed figures apply for nights 22 Dec–4 Jan, 27 Mar–2 Apr & 21–30 Apr except Neptune 26 Dec–1 Jan & 21–27 Apr.

---

⑥ Calculate the price for the following customers, using the price grid in the brochure. Don't forget to include any necessary supplements and any savers which apply.

1. Two adults staying for seven nights and departing on 29 September. They want bed and breakfast.
2. One adult staying in a single room for fourteen nights with bed and breakfast, departing 2 October.
3. Two adults with one child staying for seven nights, departing 2 November. They want a pool view and half-board.
4. Two adults and two children, staying for seven nights, half-board, departing 22 December.
5. Two adults staying for fourteen nights with bed and breakfast, departing 25 November.
6. Two adults staying for ten nights with bed and breakfast, departing 25 November.

Language focus 1

Calculating and quoting prices

1 Look at these calculations for two of the parties travelling to the Hotel King Solomon's Palace in exercise 6 on page 107. Note the language which the travel agent uses to describe the calculation.

a 2 x £519 = £1038

Two adults at/times five hundred and nineteen pounds each **comes to/makes/equals** *one thousand and thirty-eight pounds.*

b 1 x £759   = £ 759.00
  supp. £27.30 x 14 = £ 382.20
  total   = £1141.20

One adult at seven hundred and fifty-nine pounds, plus the single room supplement of twenty-seven pounds thirty for fourteen nights, which **comes to/makes / equals** *three hundred and eighty-two pounds and twenty pence. That* **gives/comes to/makes a total of** *one thousand one hundred and forty-one pounds and twenty pence.*

2 We often use *if*-clauses when suggesting variations to the basic price.

If you travel on 22 September, you'll get a discount of £60.
If you have half-board, there'll be a supplement of £14.40 per night.

Practice

Look back at the calculations you made in exercise 6 on page 107. In pairs, take turns to talk your partner through the calculations you made, using the language from exercises 1 and 2. For each one, include a suggestion to help your partner get a cheaper price. (Your teacher can provide you with more calculations for other tourist parties if you need more practice.)

Pronunciation focus

1 Note the difference in pronunciation between *fourteen* and *forty* – /iː/versus/ɪ/, plus main stress difference. Read one number from either column **A** or **B** to your partner. Your partner must say whether it is **A** or **B**. Take turns and practise until you are both guessing correctly.

A	B
13	30
14	40
15	50
16	60
17	70
18	80
19	90

2 Stress is used in numbers to identify a particular digit, such as when correcting someone who has said the wrong figure. For example:

Did you say the single room supplement was £26.70?
No, it's £27.60.

Is the code for Eilat 9728?
No, it's 9727.

In pairs, practise using this shifting stress by giving your partner information from the Hotel King Solomon's Palace price grid with one number incorrect. Your partner must correct you.

Finding out about prices and facilities

In pairs, take turns to ask and answer questions about facilities and prices for two different holidays. **Student A** should look at the information below. **Student B** should turn to the information on page 179.

A

Holiday 1 You are going to ask about a holiday at the Gateway Inn in Florida for your family. You can use your own or an imaginary family group. Think about how many people are in the party and what they like doing. Choose your own departure dates (November to April) and the length of your stay.

Ask about:
- facilities for children   – room facilities
- pools and sports facilities – meal plan
- transport to local sights   – any supplements

Find out the total cost.

Holiday 2 When you have finished, take the role of travel agent and give information about facilities and prices at the Villa Coral in Cuba.

B

Look at the information on page 179.

GOLDEN TULIP HOTELS
Villa Coral ✳✳
SUPERIOR

Santa Lucia

Enjoying a perfect location, with its grounds resting directly upon the white sandy beach, the Villa Coral is an excellent choice for a value-for-money Caribbean holiday. Rooms are simply furnished and the accommodation is spread throughout the grounds in low-rise, red-roofed and white-walled buildings with lawns, shrubs, and trees all around. Water sports available from the nearby Hotel Tararaco include catamarans, jet-bikes, and snorkelling. To round off your day you can enjoy the excellent range of evening entertainment taking place nightly at the Villa Coral, or just relax over a drink in the thatched pool bar, which stays open until the early hours of the warm Cuban evenings.

- Good-sized irregularly shaped swimming pool.
- Large surrounding, furnished sun terrace.
- Main buffet restaurant (air-conditioned) with Cuban-style décor and lots of greenery; Parrillada Grill serves meat specialities.
- Thatched pool bar open till 1 a.m.; Los

Delfines beach bar serves snacks and drinks; El Paradiso jetty bar serves seafood specialities.
- 24-hour reception area with comfortable seating.
- Daily entertainment programme with free daytime activities including water-aerobics, volleyball, dancing classes, Spanish lessons in the evening, cabaret, games, live music from 11.00 p.m. and disco at weekends up to 11.30 p.m.

Child prices in Goa, Sri Lanka, Egypt, and Cuba
In all properties in Goa, Sri Lanka, and Cuba, the first child will receive a 25% reduction off the adult price. On properties that can accommodate a second child, the reduction will be £60 off the adult price.

Accommodation	Villa Coral Half-board
Holiday Code	J50H02
Accom/pers. share	Twin room
No. of nights	**14 nights** Adult
9 Oct–22 Oct	629
23 Oct–5 Nov	619
6 Nov–19 Nov	619
20 Nov–3 Dec	589
4 Dec–17 Dec	535
18 Dec–31 Dec	929
1 Jan–14 Jan	679
15 Jan–28 Jan	589
29 Jan–11 Feb	589
12 Feb–25 Feb	625
26 Feb–11 Mar	629
12 Mar–25 Mar	629
26 Mar–8 Apr	689
9 Apr–22 Apr	629
23 Apr–23 Apr	679
Reduction per night	3rd & 4th adult £3.00
Supplements per person per night	Single room £8.50

(Departures/Extra Weeks commencing)

Bookings and reservations

Listening 1

Stages in booking a holiday

For the travel agent there are many different stages involved in the booking of a holiday for a client – from handling the initial enquiry to carrying out follow-up and feedback.

❶ Here are the stages typically followed by one particular travel agent. Can you put them in the right order?

a take initial payment/deposit
b create computer file for client (personal details, etc.) – or add to existing 'client history' if a previous customer
c enter details of this particular booking
d deal with initial enquiry
e issue 'Welcome Home' feedback letter
f tickets checked against computer system
g confirm booking on computer system – booking links directly to tour operator system
h offer insurance and other services
i tickets collected (or sent to client)
j tickets sent out by tour operator to travel agent
k notify client that tickets are ready
l produce printed booking form (booking authorization form)

❷ Now listen to Sharon Kett from the Thomas Cook travel agency explaining the stages they go through. See if the order you chose was correct.

Reading

Travel agency documents

❶ Look at these extracts from travel agency computer screens and printouts which are related to some of the stages mentioned in **Section 1** of this unit.

Which is from

– the booking authorization form?
– the booking details (new transaction) screen?
– the printout from the payment history screen?
– the printout from the document history screen?

1

> I have read and understood the general information pages and booking conditions of Airtours (Tour Operator), as contained within their brochure and accept them on behalf of myself and every member of my party. I am over 18 years of age.
>
> Further, I authorize Thomas Cook Group Limited (Travel Agency) to make the booking detailed above, and as per the attached printout, on my behalf and that of my party.
>
> Signed . . . .(Client)
>
> Date . . . .

8

Tickets, reservations, and insurance

2

DOC Type	Description	Ref	Transact
PAY	Receipt No: 012165 for £403.04	AV	08/MAR
LET	Automated Insurance Indemnity Letter produced	AV	08/MAR
DOC	FIN No: LC024110 from AIR for Inclusive Tour	PE	14/MAR
LET	Final Invoice Letter	PE	14/MAR
DOC	Tickets Received from AIR for Inclusive Tour	PE	28/MAR
LET	Tickets Awaiting Collection Letter	PE	15/APR
LET	First Balance Due Letter	JV	15/APR
PAY	Receipt No: 012957 for £103.50	GB	19/APR
DOC	Tickets Collected for Inclusive Tour with AIR	JV	19/APR
DOC	Tickets Received from HCH for Car Hire	JV	19/APR

3

Tran type	Oper	Receipt number	Payment value	Payment mode	type	Ref	Date of payment	Travel receipt
IT	AIR	012165	164.16	PS	DEP	AV	08MAR	01248
IT	AIR	012165	238.88	VI	BAL	AV	08MAR	01248
CARH	HCH	012957	21.96	PS	DEP	GB	15APR	01333
CARH	HCH	012957	81.54	PQ	BAL	GB	15APR	01333

IT=inclusive tour   PQ = personal cheque

VI = visa   PS = staff point (discount)

4

Operator		AIR Airtours	Package Holiday
Date	20 APR	6 nights	
Dept.	LGW London Gatwick	Hotel Name	Corralejo
Dest.	FUE Fuerteventura	Accom. Type	self-catering
Htl.	OFU745		
Flt.	IH475		
Outbound	12.40 16.50 Flt. No. AIH475		
Inbound	17.40 21.40 Flt. No. AIH476		
Book. Ref.	LC024110		

2   Using the information on the computer screen and printout extracts, how would you answer these questions from a customer in your travel agency?

1 Which tour operator are we going with?
2 What am I signing here?
3 What's the flight number of the return flight?
4 What time does the flight get back?
5 What's the hotel called?
6 How much is the visa payment? I'm not sure I've got enough on my credit card.
7 What's the total cost of the holiday, including car hire?
8 What's the basic cost without the car hire?
9 I thought receipt number 012165 was for the car hire?
10 When will I be able to collect the tickets?

Travel agency letters

Travel agents use a number of standard letters when dealing with clients' reservations and ticketing arrangements. Below are twelve paragraphs which come from three different standard letters (four from each).

1 a confirmation of a travel booking
2 an accompanying letter sent out with tickets and travel documents (and offering other services)
3 an acknowledgement of a complaining letter

Decide which paragraph is from which letter and then put them in the right order.

a Passport and visas in order? Just a final reminder for you to check that your passports and any visas are valid.

b I am investigating the points raised in your letter and will reply to you as soon as possible.

c I am delighted to enclose the travel documentation for your holiday, and as your holiday approaches could I just remind you of some of the services we are able to offer you?

d I am pleased to confirm your forthcoming travel arrangements with Airtours to Fuerteventura, commencing on 20 April.

e If you have any questions relating to your travel arrangements please do not hesitate to call in and see me, or telephone me on 0181 889 8919.

f Are you driving to the airport? If so, and you need airport car parking or an overnight hotel, let us book it for you. We can provide these services at competitive rates.

g Thank you once again for writing to me.

h Please find enclosed a receipt, recording your payments, and providing you with current details of your travel arrangements and their costs.

i Thank you for your recent letter, the contents of which have been noted and are receiving my attention.

j Have you bought your holiday money?
If not, there are two ways in which we can help you. You can either order your money by ringing us on 0181 889 8919 and we will prepare the order for you to collect on a date convenient to you, or simply call in and buy your money in the shop. Whatever your preference we do recommend you take a combination of traveller's cheques and currency. All major foreign currencies are instantly available – others just take a day or two longer.

k Your final balance payment is due on or before 31 March. This may be paid by credit card, cash, or cheque made payable to JBC Travel. As explained at the time of booking your holiday a service charge will be levied for all credit card transactions.

l I am extremely sorry that not all the arrangements made on your behalf ran smoothly. Please accept my sincere apologies.

Listening 2

Selling an air ticket

1 What information would you need to get from a customer who wants to buy an air ticket? Complete the list.

– destination
– preferred date of travel
_____
_____
_____
_____
_____

2 Listen to this conversation in the Flight Reservations department of a large London travel agency.

1 Note down the information you listed in exercise 1. For example: destination – San Francisco.

2 Look at these screens from the travel agent's computer monitor and the explanation key underneath.

Screen 1 (outgoing flights)

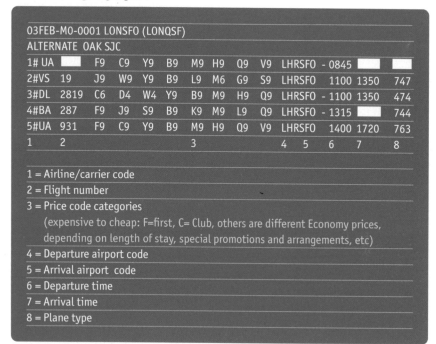

03FEB-M0-0001 LONSFO (LONQSF)												
ALTERNATE OAK SJC												
1# UA	☐	F9	C9	Y9	B9	M9	H9	Q9	V9	LHRSFO	- 0845	☐	☐
2#VS	19	J9	W9	Y9	B9	L9	M6	G9	S9	LHRSFO	1100	1350	747
3#DL	2819	C6	D4	W4	Y9	B9	M9	H9	Q9	LHRSFO	- 1100	1350	474
4#BA	287	F9	J9	S9	B9	K9	M9	L9	Q9	LHRSFO	- 1315	☐	744
5#UA	931	F9	C9	Y9	B9	M9	H9	Q9	V9	LHRSFO	1400	1720	763
1	2				3			4	5	6	7		8

1 = Airline/carrier code
2 = Flight number
3 = Price code categories
(expensive to cheap: F=first, C= Club, others are different Economy prices, depending on length of stay, special promotions and arrangements, etc)
4 = Departure airport code
5 = Arrival airport code
6 = Departure time
7 = Arrival time
8 = Plane type

Screen 2 (return flights)

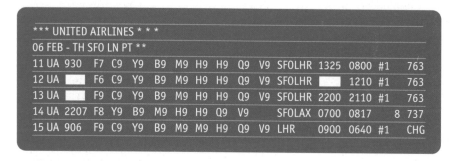

*** UNITED AIRLINES * * *														
06 FEB - TH SFO LN PT **														
11 UA	930	F7	C9	Y9	B9	M9	H9	H9	Q9	V9	SFOLHR	1325	0800 #1	763
12 UA	☐	F6	C9	Y9	B9	M9	H9	H9	Q9	V9	SFOLHR	☐	1210 #1	763
13 UA	☐	F9	C9	Y9	B9	M9	H9	H9	Q9	V9	SFOLHR	2200	2110 #1	763
14 UA	2207	F8	Y9	B9	M9	H9	H9	Q9	V9		SFOLAX	0700	0817	8 737
15 UA	906	F9	C9	Y9	B9	M9	M9	H9	Q9	V9	LHR	0900	0640 #1	CHG

Screen 3 (price details)

BF GBP	TX GBP	TX GBP	TX GBP	TOTAL GBP
		GB TAX	XA TAX	XT TAX
001– ☐		10.00	7.70	0.50 ☐

3 Listen to the conversation again and fill in the missing information.

④ Look at this selection menu from the bottom of screen 1 on page 113. Can you explain what each of the selections are and what information they would give? Which is the one that produced screen 2 on page 113?

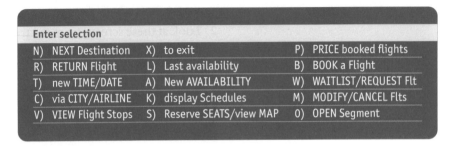

Enter selection					
N)	NEXT Destination	X)	to exit	P)	PRICE booked flights
R)	RETURN Flight	L)	Last availability	B)	BOOK a Flight
T)	new TIME/DATE	A)	New AVAILABILITY	W)	WAITLIST/REQUEST Flt
C)	via CITY/AIRLINE	K)	display Schedules	M)	MODIFY/CANCEL Flts
V)	VIEW Flight Stops	S)	Reserve SEATS/view MAP	O)	OPEN Segment

Output task

Making flight reservations

In pairs, act out similar conversations between a travel agent and a customer, using the information and notes below. Travel agents (**A**) should look at the information below. Customers (**B**) should turn to the information on page 180. Change roles for the second conversation.

Conversation 1

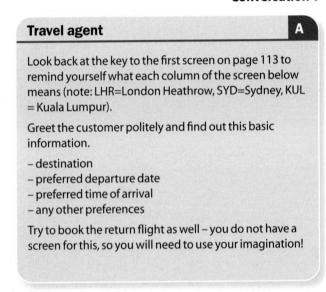

Travel agent   **A**

Look back at the key to the first screen on page 113 to remind yourself what each column of the screen below means (note: LHR=London Heathrow, SYD=Sydney, KUL = Kuala Lumpur).

Greet the customer politely and find out this basic information.

– destination
– preferred departure date
– preferred time of arrival
– any other preferences

Try to book the return flight as well – you do not have a screen for this, so you will need to use your imagination!

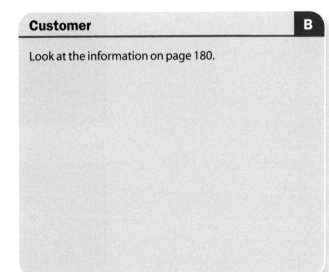

Customer   **B**

Look at the information on page 180.

10 FEB - MON - LONDON-SYDNEY								
1 QF 746	LHRSYD	1215	2045	#1	744	MM1	QANTAS
2 BA 990	LHRSYD	2145	0620	#2	744	MM1	BRITISH AIRWAYS
3 MH 503	LHRKUL	1050	0715		744	MM0	MALAYSIAN
4 AN 833	SYD	0935	2020	#1	744	DD0	ANSETT
5 VS 133	LHRKUL	1050	0715		744	MM0	VIRGIN ATLANTIC
6 MH 221	SYD	0935	2020	#1	744	MM0	MALAYSIAN

Conversation 2

<table>
<tr><td>Travel agent</td><td>A</td><td>Customer</td><td>B</td></tr>
</table>

Travel agent **A**

Look back at the key to the first screen on page113 to remind yourself what each column in the screens below means (note: YYZ is the destination code for Toronto; F in the price code categories means first class).

Greet the customer politely and find out the basic information (destination, return flights, dates, etc.). Book the most suitable flights using the information on the screens.

Customer **B**

Look at the information on page 180.

Screen 1

01 JUN - FRI - LONDON-TORONTO							
1 AC 869	J7	LHRYYZ	0740	1035	767	DD0	AIR CANADA
2 CP 87	J7	LHRYYZ	0855	1140	763	BB0	CANADIAN AIR
3 BA 89	F9	LHRYYZ	1050	1340	744	MM0	BRITISH AIRWAYS
4 AI 181	F2	LHRYYZ	1200	1455	747	0	AIR INDIA
5 AC 857	J7	LHRYYZ	1300	1535	744	DD0	AIR CANADA
6 BA 93	F9	LHRYYZ	1505	1755	747	MM0	BRITISH AIRWAYS
7 AC 863	J7	LHRYYZ	1645	1940	763	DD0	AIR CANADA
8 CP 89	J7	LHRYYZ	2100	2345	763	DD0	CANADIAN AIR

Screen 2

20 JUN - WED - TORONTO-LONDON							
1 AC 868	J7	YYZLHR	0900	2100	767	DD0	AIR CANADA
2 CP 86	J7	YYZLHR	1855	0650	763	DD0	CANADIAN AIR
3 AC 856	J7	YYZLHR	1915	0650	747	DD0	AIR CANADA
4 BA 92	F9	YYZLHR	2000	0805	747	MM0	BRITISH AIRWAYS
5 AI 188	F2	YYZLHR	2200	0940	747	0	AIR INDIA
6 CP 88	J7	YYZLHR	2200	0955	763	DD0	CANADIAN AIR
7 AC 862	J7	YYZLHR	2215	1005	747	DD0	AIR CANADA
8 BA 88	F9	YYZLHR	2255	1100	747	MM0	BRITISH AIRWAYS

When things go wrong

Travel insurance

1. Have you ever taken out a travel insurance policy? If so, have you ever had to make a claim? What items would you expect to be covered on a typical travel insurance policy?

2. In pairs, discuss whether you would expect a tourist or traveller to be covered for the following situations. What compensation would they be entitled to?

   a Their suitcase wasn't at the airport when they arrived at their holiday destination. It turned up two days later.

   b Someone stole their passport and wallet on the beach.

   c They had a bad attack of flu and had to stay in their hotel room for two days.

   d Their car broke down on the way to the airport and they missed their flight.

   e The alarm clock didn't go off and they overslept and missed the flight.

   f They broke a leg and had to go to hospital. They weren't able to travel home for a week later than planned.

   g They had to cancel the holiday at the last minute because one of the party had an accident.

   h They had to cancel the holiday at the last minute because they discovered their best friend was getting married at the same time.

   i Because of bad weather the flight was held up for twelve hours.

   j They were involved in a serious road accident. The hire car they were driving and the car they crashed into were both written off. One of the party was also permanently injured and unable to work again.

3. You are going to read a leaflet giving brief details of a travel insurance scheme. Match these headings with the paragraphs in the text.

   a Curtailment
   b Delayed baggage
   c Loss of deposit or cancellation
   d Loss of passport
   e Medical and other expenses
   f Medical inconvenience benefit
   g Missed departure
   h Personal accident
   i Personal baggage
   j Personal liability
   k Personal money
   l Travel delay

Our Premium Travel Insurance Plan provides:

1 _____

Sometimes your journey may have to be cancelled for reasons beyond your control. If this happens, you are eligible to make a claim.

2 _____

If you have to cut short your trip because of injury or illness, we'll repay a proportionate amount of your prepaid expenses.

3 _____

If an accident permanently prevents you from working or results in you losing an eye or a limb you will be paid £40,000. Should you die as a result of an accident your beneficiaries will be paid £25,000. These benefits are reduced if you are under 16 years of age.

4 _____

Our Premium Travel Insurance Plan covers medical costs and certain other expenses that may be incurred outside the UK.

5 _____

If you are sick or injured and have to spend time in hospital or confined to your hotel bed, you'll receive a payment for every complete day.

6 _____

We provide cover for any loss of personal property. There is a maximum payment for single articles and a maximum value for valuables and photographic equipment. Please ensure that this is sufficient for your needs.

7 _____

Loss of personal money, traveller's cheques, and travel tickets are covered under this section.

8 _____

You can claim for expenses incurred in obtaining a replacement passport.

9 _____

If your baggage is mislaid, we'll pay up to £100 for emergency purchases and compensation for the inconvenience.

10 _____

You are covered for legal liability for accidental injury to a third party or accidental damage to their property by an indemnity of up to £2.5 million.

11 _____

If you cannot reach your international point of departure in time, due to public transport failure, an accident, or mechanical failure involving the car you're travelling in, up to £1,200 will be paid to help you reach your scheduled destination.

12 _____

If your aircraft or boat is delayed for more than 12 hours, a compensation payment will automatically be made.

4 Read the text again and check to see if the answers you gave to the situations in exercise 2 are correct.

Vocabulary focus

Match the phrasal verbs and idiomatic expressions in column **A** with their definitions in column **B**.

A	B
break down	cancel
call off	have mechanical failure
cut short	appear
turn up	reach
write off	delay
go off	curtail
hold up	completely destroy (especially a car)
get to	make a sudden loud noise

Holiday disasters

1 Before you listen to three people talking about their holiday disasters, discuss the following questions.

1 What things can go wrong on a holiday?
2 Where do you think are the most dangerous places to travel to? Think about things like illness, accidents, theft, and violence.

2 A consumer magazine recently carried out a survey on holiday hazards. Here is some of the information they found out.

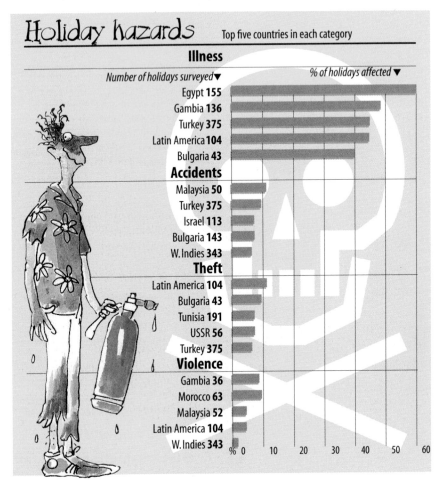

Holiday hazards — Top five countries in each category

Illness

Number of holidays surveyed ▼	% of holidays affected ▼
Egypt **155**	
Gambia **136**	
Turkey **375**	
Latin America **104**	
Bulgaria **43**	

Accidents

Malaysia **50**	
Turkey **375**	
Israel **113**	
Bulgaria **143**	
W. Indies **343**	

Theft

Latin America **104**	
Bulgaria **43**	
Tunisia **191**	
USSR **56**	
Turkey **375**	

Violence

Gambia **36**	
Morocco **63**	
Malaysia **52**	
Latin America **104**	
W. Indies **343**	

% 0   10   20   30   40   50   60

1 Does any of the information surprise you?

2 What actual incidents could occur under each of the hazard headings? For example, an 'illness' could be malaria, or food-poisoning, or sickness from drinking contaminated water.

3 How safe is your country for tourists and travellers?

4 What advice would you give to travellers going to a potentially dangerous country?

3 Listen to three people describing incidents that happened to them on holiday.

As you listen, make notes in the table.

	Alberta	Brian	Colin
Holiday location			
What happened?			
What were they doing at the time?			
What did they do after?			

4 Which of the dialogues is with

– a newspaper reporter?
– a travel agent?
– a friend?

5 Imagine the three people had taken out a recommended travel insurance policy. Look back to the leaflet on page 117. Can they claim anything? Under which sections can they claim?

Language focus 2

Describing events in the past

1 Look at these sentences from the story of the hotel explosion in San Francisco. In particular, notice how the past continuous tense is used to describe the incident of the explosion.

We were staying at the Plaza.
(Background information to the whole story – past continuous tense.)

We'd (we had) been to the movies.
(Event before the incident – the 'past in the past' – past perfect tense.)

We were just coming out of the elevator.
(Activity at the time of the incident – past continuous tense.)

The whole corridor seemed to burst into flames.
(The incident/event – simple past tense.)

I rushed through the smoke and grabbed it (the fire extinguisher).
(Events after the incident – simple past tense.)

2 Make a similar series of sentences for the other two stories – look back at the notes you made in exercise 1.

Checking and clarifying information

1 Look at these sentences from the three stories, and listen to them on the cassette. Note the way the information given by the speakers is checked and clarified. In particular, note the highlighted expressions.

***So you were** both on the same bike, **were you**?*

***Are you saying** you left poor Tony all on his own in that state?*

***Let me see if I've got this right** – you were actually on the floor where the explosion took place?*

***So what you're saying is that** you got the people out single-handed?*

***Let me just go over this again** – you were in the restaurant, and a young boy came up to you and snatched your jacket?*

*You were confined to your room for two days, **you said**?*

2 In pairs, retell the three stories. Take turns to be the tourist, while the other person is either the travel agent, the reporter, or the friend. As you listen, keep interrupting to check and clarify the information.

Output task

Insurance report forms

Imagine you are a resort representative. You have to write reports for your tour operator on any unfortunate incidents that happen to tourists in your resort. These reports may be used for future insurance claims or for handling complaints, so it is important to be accurate. Choose two of the incidents you heard about in **Listening 3**. Write the report, including a statement by the person involved.

Incident report form

Resort

Name of resort representative

Date of incident

Name of client

Summary of incident

Statement by client

Signature

ACTIVITY

Tourist budgets

① Look at the budget guide to prices in Sydney, Australia on the next page. The prices are in Australian dollars.

Find out the exchange rate of Aus$ with your own currency (you can check in a newspaper). Do any of the prices surprise you?

② Divide into groups.

1 Think about your own interests. Plan a day out in Sydney

   – for less than Aus$50 per person
   – for between Aus$50 and Aus$100
   – for more than Aus$100.

2 Plan a day out for other real or imaginary groups – for example, your family or your teachers.

Plan a weekend's accommodation and entertainment for the same people. Plan three weekends – one cheap, one medium-priced, and one expensive.

3 Prepare a similar budget guide for visitors to your own city/country.

Budget Guide

This list should be used as a guide only. Prices vary from city to city and state to state. Those given here are in Australian dollars, and are subject to change.

Services	Cost
Motorcoach	$20 half-day
Sightseeing tour	$65 full-day
Cruise on Sydney harbour	$16–$80
Theatre ticket	$25 and up, depending on seats
Concert ticket	$35 and up, depending on seats
Opera or ballet ticket	$60 and up, depending on seats
Rock concert ticket	$50 and up, depending on seats
Ticket to a movie	$12
Entrance to a museum or art gallery	Free–$8
Ticket to a sporting event	$7–$40
Accommodation per day (single)	$170–$350 deluxe
	$110–$240 premier
	$80–$180 moderate
	$55–$85 budget
	$12–$16 hostel
	$120–$200 serviced apartment
Breakfast in a coffee shop	$8 and up per person
Lunch at a café or bistro	$12 and up per person
Dinner at a fine restaurant	$40 per person (without wine)
Bottle of Australian wine	$11 and up
Glass of beer at a pub	$2.20 (10 oz. glass)
Cocktail	$9 and up

Vocabulary

all-inclusive	curtailment	hold up	snorkelling
break down	cut short	honeymoon	special offer
budget	deposit	key card	sun terrace
calculation	deserted	liability	supplement
call off	elevator	lobby	turn up
cheque	evacuate	meal plan	wallet
claim	floodlit	mislaid	watersports
Club class	food poisoning	money off	write off
contaminated	full payment	outgoing flight	
credit card	go off	quote	
currency	hazard	receipt	

9

Tourist information

Tourist attractions and facilities

Vocabulary

Tourist attractions

1 In groups, think of as many types of tourist attractions and facilities as possible. For example – museum, cathedral, park, hotel.

2 Find out which group has the biggest list. Which ones are *attractions* (places which tourists want to see and visit) and which ones are *facilities* (places which tourists need to use)?

3 Do you know what these attractions and facilities are? What happens there? What can you see or do?

amusement park	downtown (US)
marina	public conveniences (UK)
botanical gardens	theme park
shopping mall (US)	gallery
flea market	harbour

Listening 1

Enquiries at a tourist information centre

1 Listen to these enquiries made at a tourist information centre in Sydney. In column 1 note down what the enquirer is looking for.

	1 What the enquirer is looking for	2 Where to go in Sydney	3 TIC reply	4 Where to go in your country
1				
2				
3				
4				
5				
6				
7				
8				
9				
10				

2 Now look at this list of Sydney's top fifteen tourist attractions. They are numbered from west to east across the city. Where do you think would be the best place to suggest for each of the enquirers to visit? Write your answer in column 2 of the table in exercise 1.

Sydney's top fifteen tourist attractions	
1 National Maritime Museum	9 Sydney Tower
2 Aquarium	10 Sydney Opera House
3 Chinese Garden and Chinatown	11 Sydney Harbour
4 Sydney Observatory	12 Royal Botanical Gardens
5 Sydney Harbour Bridge	13 Art Gallery of New South Wales
6 Luna Amusement Park	14 Taronga Zoo
7 Museum of Contemporary Art	15 Bondi Beach
8 Queen Victoria Building	

3 Listen to the second part of the tape and in each case note down which place the Sydney Tourist Information Centre is recommending. Write the number in column 3 of the table.

4 How would you answer the same enquiries for your own town or city? Write the names of places for your town or city in column 4 of the table.

5 With a partner, role-play short conversations in the tourist information centre of your town or city, using the information in the table. Change roles so that you both get a chance to take the role of the tourist information officer.

Reading

Information on Bangkok

1 On the next page is a tourist information leaflet about the city of Bangkok. Before you read it, make a list of things you know – or think you know – about Bangkok. Think about location, size, climate, attractions, night-life, food, culture, and religion. Make a list of the facilities and attractions you would expect to find there.

2 Read the leaflet quickly to find out if you were correct. Scan the text for a general understanding – don't try to read every word.

BANÇKOK WHERE EAST MEETS WEST

SITUATED between the 'secret' countries of Burma, Laos, and Cambodia, Thailand remains a curious mixture of eastern and western influences. Nowhere is this more evident than in its capital, Bangkok. Bangkok is a city of contrasts. A modern city of ten million inhabitants, it is growing at breathtaking speed. Sometimes when the midday heat and the noise and traffic are at their worst, it feels a little too busy. But Bangkok is also a city with an ancient heritage. Take a ride on the Chao Phraya river and its connecting canals, and you'll find a city and a way of life that is not very different from that seen by the first Europeans to arrive there. Then there are the temples (known as 'wats'), the numerous statues of Buddha, and of course the splendour of the Grand Palace. But Bangkok is not just about monuments, it is vibrant, alive, and full of hope. It gives the visitor a feeling that anything might be possible – and it usually is.

Temples

No trip to Bangkok is complete without a visit to at least one of the Buddhist temples, and there are so many in the city that it's difficult to avoid them. Bangkok has the greatest concentration of Buddhist temples in the world. The most renowned is the Wat Phra Keo, which is also called the Temple of the Emerald Buddha, containing the mysterious Emerald Buddha statue, a Thai national symbol. Established in 1782, adjoining the Grand Palace, it is the ceremonial temple of the Thai Kings. If you're looking for Buddhist statues, then go to Wat Pho, the oldest and largest wat in Bangkok, containing the largest collection of Buddha images in Thailand. Of course, don't miss Wat Arun, the 'Temple of Dawn'. Despite the surrounding

skyscrapers, at over 100 metres high the glittering tower is still a breathtaking sight as you approach it up the river.

The Grand Palace and other sights

Once a city within a city and surrounded by 2 km of perimeter walls, the Grand Palace is a must for any visitor to Bangkok. It contains some of the finest examples of eastern architecture and art in the world. Among other delights, you can see the harem, the Chapel Royal, and the audience hall of Amarinda where kings are crowned. There is also the Grand Palace Museum which explains the 200-year history of the Palace.

There are so many places to visit in Bangkok that it is impossible to list them all. But two other places well worth visiting are the National Museum, a treasure trove of Thai art and culture, and the Wimanmek Palace, or 'Palace in the Clouds', the world's largest structure made entirely of golden teak.

After all this sightseeing you might like to take a rest. Try Lumphini Park, a pleasant green park at the meeting of the port and downtown areas. But be careful at night, when the park can be a little dangerous.

The river and canals

You can't leave Bangkok without going on a river trip to see the fascinating bustling life of the city. Bangkok has been called 'the Venice of the Orient' and any trip down the numerous canals will reveal a picturesque range of glittering wats and cool palms. Don't miss the Thonburi floating market, which despite recent commercialization still possesses a unique and fascinating character.

Shopping

Whether you are shopping in the colourful, lively, but sweleringly hot markets, or the ultra-modern department stores, one thing is clear – Bangkok is a city for shoppers, and you're sure to find something you want. Markets are everywhere, selling anything from artificial flowers to barber's scissors. If you're souvenir-hunting, why not buy some Thai wood-carving, some local jewellery, or a brightly-coloured sarong?

Food

Bangkok is a gourmet's paradise. Thai food can be extremely spicy and hot, but it's

delicious. Try the shophouse restaurants where you can get simple fried noodles with soy sauce at a very cheap price. Or the Thai delicacy of freshwater crab in one of the more up-market restaurants. There are numerous street food stalls which turn Bangkok into one huge open-air restaurant at night. The Thais enjoy wandering around to find out what's cooking in the next street.

Night-life

Since the days of the Vietnam War when American soldiers came to Bangkok for 'rest and recreation' Bangkok has had a reputation for rather sordid night-life. But this is changing fast. Of course, the red-light district is still there, but you'll also find more conventional clubs and discos, with a variety of jazz, rock, reggae, and Latin music. There are no licensing laws, so if you want an alcoholic drink it's not a problem. Try Saeng Thip, a rum-like local spirit. You can also find more traditional Thai entertainment – dancing and drama – at places like the National Theatre and the Cultural Centre.

This is just a glimpse of what Bangkok has to offer. For more information please visit the Tourism Authority office in Ratchadamnoen Nok Avenue.

☎ (02) 282 1143.

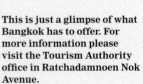

3 Divide into two groups, **A** and **B**. You are going to read part of the text again in more detail.

Group A

1 Read the sections on 'Temples', 'The Grand Palace and other sights', and 'The river and canals' in more detail, making notes. Be prepared to answer questions about them.

2 Think about the topics 'Shopping', 'Food', and 'Night-life', but do not read these sections. Prepare some questions that you would want to ask if you were a tourist in Bangkok.

Group B

1 Read the sections on 'Shopping', 'Food', and 'Night-life' in more detail, making notes. Be prepared to answer questions about them.

2 Think about the topics 'Temples', 'Grand Palace and other sights', and 'The river and canals', but do not read these sections. Prepare some questions that you would want to ask if you were a tourist in Bangkok.

4 In pairs, using your notes, act out a conversation in the Bangkok Tourist Information Office. Do not look at the original text.

Language focus 1

Advice and suggestions (written register)

Look at these examples from the text which all give advice or make suggestions for tourists visiting Bangkok. Can you find any others in the text?

No trip to Bangkok is complete without a visit to at least one of the Buddhist temples.

If you're looking for Buddhist statues, then go to Wat Pho.

... don't miss Wat Arun.

... the Grand Palace is a must for any visitor to Bangkok.

... two other places well worth visiting are the National Museum ... and the Wimanmek Palace.

After all this sightseeing you might like to take a rest. Try Lumphini Park ...

Be careful at night, when the park can be a little dangerous.

You can't leave Bangkok without going on a river trip.

Don't miss the Thonburi floating market.

If you're souvenir-hunting, why not buy some Thai wood-carving ... ?

Try the shophouse restaurants where you can get simple fried noodles ...

Practice

1 Use similar structures to produce sentences from a tourist leaflet about Sydney. Look back at the list of Sydney's attractions and facilities in **Section 1** to help you.

2 What are the spoken equivalents of the written advice and suggestions? Look at the tapescript of **Listening 1** on page 194 for some examples, and also at **Unit 3**, **Language focus 1** on page 33.

Output task

Writing a tourist information leaflet

1 Prepare a tourist information leaflet for your own city or local area, or a place you know very well. Follow the stages listed below.

1 Start by making a list of all the attractions and facilities.
2 Put them into groups to make the different sub-headings for the leaflet.
3 Write a general introductory paragraph.
4 For the sub-headings, follow the general example of the Bangkok leaflet.
5 Include as much practical information about each section as possible.

2 When you have finished your leaflet, show it to another member of the class and get them to ask you questions and make enquiries, as if they were a tourist visiting the tourist information office of your city.

Sydney – where to stay and what to see

Accommodation in Sydney

Most tourist information centres also help visitors with information on accommodation. On the next page is some basic information on a range of accommodation options in Sydney – moderately-priced and budget hotels.

1 Divide into two groups and take turns to role-play the part of tourist information offcer and tourist. **Group A** should look at the information below. **Group B** should turn to the information on page 180.

Group A

For the first stage of the role-play, you work in the Sydney Tourist Information Centre at the accommodation desk. Read the section on moderately-priced hotels and transfer the information to the accommodation information table below.

For the second stage of the role-play, you will be a tourist enquiring about budget hotels in Sydney. Decide what your particular needs are – refer to the headings in the table to help you.

Group B

Look at the information on page 180.

Accommodation Information

Moderately-priced hotels	central 1	quiet location 2	near famous sight 3	modern 4	historic building 5	views 6	restaurant 7	entertainment 8	swimming pool 9	family-owned 10	apartments (with kitchen) 11	laundry facilities 12	other
Castlereagh													
Manhattan													
Oakford													
Regents Court													
Savoy													
Victoria Court													
Budget hotels													
Cremorne Point Manor													
Kirketon													
Lodge Studios													
Manly Beach													
Traveller's Rest													
Thelellen Beach													

Sydney's accommodation

Sydney offers every category of accommodation – from backpackers' hostels to international standard five-star hotels (A$250 plus per person per night). There are also many economical self-catering serviced apartments, while reasonably-priced guest-houses and hostels are plentiful. Sydney's major hotel areas are The Rocks, the city centre, and round King's Cross.

The recommended accommodation in this section has been divided into two price categories.

moderate (££)
A$95–170

budget (£)
A$55–90

Prices are per room per night, regardless of single or double occupancy.

MODERATELY-PRICED HOTELS & APARTMENTS

Serviced apartments

Sydney offers many apartment-style hotels, which generally fall into the moderate price range. These serviced apartments vary from one to three bedrooms, with separate lounge/dining areas and kitchens or kitchenettes. The obvious advantage is that you can either go out to eat, or keep costs down by self-catering. Another bonus is that many of these apartments are large enough for families or those travelling in small groups.

The Castlereagh Inn (££)
Very centrally located and good value. The Castlereagh features a magnificently restored old-style dining room. All rooms have private facilities, and continental breakfast is included in the rates.
- → J6 (biv)
- 🏠 169 Castlereagh Street
- 📞 264 2281
- 🚉 Town Hall

Manhattan Hotel (££)
The long-established, friendly Manhattan is a short walk from King's Cross station. Recent upgrading and modernization have made this art deco property even better value.
- → L6
- 🏠 8 Greenknowe Avenue, Elizabeth Bay
- 📞 358 1288
- 🚉 Kings Cross

Oakford Apartments (££)
These comfortable self-contained apartments offer fully-equipped kitchens, private balconies, and water views. There is also an on-site swimming pool.
- → L5
- 🏠 Wylde Street, Potts Point
- ☎ 358 4544
- 🚉 King's Cross

Regents Court (££)
Another top-of-the-range, moderately-priced hotel, with spacious apartment-style suites, kitchens, and designer furnishings. This long-established, friendly hotel, in a quiet King's Cross street, is family owned.
- → L6
- 🏠 18 Springfield Avenue, Potts Point
- 📞 358 1533
- 🚉 King's Cross

Savoy Serviced Apartments (££)
Located near Darling Harbour, these comfortable one-bedroom serviced apartments feature kitchens, balconies, and separate lounge/dining rooms.
- → J6 (aii)
- 🏠 Corner of King and Kent Streets
- 📞 267 9211
- 🚉 Wynyard

Victoria Court (££)
This charming 1881 Victorian-style guest-house is a member of Historic Hotels of Australia. Very comfortable and atmospheric, and located in a leafy avenue.
- → L6 (div)
- 🏠 122 Victoria Street, Potts Point
- 📞 357 3200
- 🚉 King's Cross

BUDGET HOTELS & GUEST-HOUSES

Budget accommodation

In addition to these budget hotels, Sydney has dozens of backpackers' lodges. Prices start at A$10 per night and many establishments offer reduced rates for long stays. Accommodation varies from private rooms to dormitories, and the best backpacker areas are King's Cross, inner west Glebe, and beach suburbs like Bondi and Coogee. Another cheap accommodation option is staying in a 'hotel' – the Australian version of the local pub. More details can be obtained from the NSW Travel Centre (231 4444).

Cremorne Point Manor (£)
A few minutes by ferry from the city, this 30-room north shore manor house provides kitchens, a guest laundry service, and continental breakfasts on request.
- → L3
- 🏠 6 Cremorne Road, Cremorne Point
- 📞 9953 7899
- 🚉 Cremorne Point

Kirketon Hotel (£)
A true budget-priced hotel with a range of rooms, from those with private facilities to bunk rooms. Very close to King's Cross, with its own restaurant.
- → K6
- 🏠 229 Darlinghurst Road, King's Cross
- 📞 360 4333
- 🚉 King's Cross

The Lodge Studios (£)
Self-contained accommodation that is part of the Bayside Hotel (85). Studios include kitchenettes, air-conditioning, and a guest laundry.
- → L6
- 🏠 85 New South Head Road, Rushcutters Bay
- 📞 327 8511
- 🚉 King's Cross/Edgecliff

Manly Beach Resort (£)
This resort offers double, twin, and family rooms, a swimming pool and good facilities. Reached by a scenic ferry ride from the city.
- → Off map to north-east
- 🏠 6 Carlton Street, Manly
- 📞 9977 4188
- 🚉 Manly

Sydney Traveller's Rest Hotel (£)
Better-than-average budget accommodation near Darling Harbour. The hotel has a 24-hour reception service and a licensed restaurant and bar.
- → J7
- 🏠 37 Ultimo Road, Haymarket
- 📞 281 5555
- 🚉 Central

Thelellen Beach Inn
This 1930s hotel has a great location overlooking Bondi Beach. Friendly and family-run, the Thelellen isn't luxurious but represents good value.
- Off map to east
- 🏠 2 Campbell Parade, Bondi Beach
- 📞 30 5333
- 🚉 380, 382

Sydney Harbour Bridge

Listen to this recorded information on the Sydney Harbour Bridge and complete the Tourist Information Centre factsheet below.

Sydney Tourist Information Centre

Factsheet

5

Sydney Harbour Bridge

1   Nickname *'the coathanger'*
2   World's _____ long-span bridge
3   Built in _____
4   Took _____ years to build
5   Employed _____ men
6   Length _____
7   Width _____
8   Height _____
9   Water clearance _____
10 Railway lines _____
11 Road lanes _____
12 Average number of vehicles per day
    _____

13 Nearest station *Milson's Point*
14 Museum opening hours_____
15 Other information
    _____

    _____

Language focus 2

Giving factual information

1   Look at these sentences about the Sydney Harbour Bridge.

    It was completed in 1932.
    A workforce of up to 1,400 men was employed.
    A tunnel was opened in 1992.

    In each sentence the past passive is used. The past passive is commonly used when giving information, usually historical, about a monument or tourist attraction.

2   Complete these sentences using one of the verbs from the list.

bury	destroy
complete	discover
create	found
damage	open

    a Pompeii – completely – lava – 79AD
    b The Suez Canal – 1869
    c Tokyo – badly – earthquake – 1923
    d Oxford University – 12th century

    e Karl Marx – Highgate Cemetery
    f Chartres Cathedral – about 1240
    g America – Christopher Columbus – 1492
    h Mickey Mouse – Walt Disney

Measurement and dimension

1   Look at these sentences about Sydney Harbour Bridge.
    It is over 500 metres long.
    It is nearly 50 metres wide.
    It has a height of 134 metres.

    Note how both the adjective and the noun can be used to express dimension. For example:

    *The reservoir is 20 metres **deep**. (adjective)*
    *The reservoir has a **depth** of 20 metres. (noun)*

2   Transform the three example sentences in a similar way.

3   Find other examples of measurement and dimension sentences in the tapescript on page 194.

Pronunciation focus

1 Look at the pronunciation of these words. The vowel sounds are known as diphthongs.

/aɪ/	/eɪ/	/aʊ/	/əʊ/
wide	eight	thousand	road

2 Put the following words into the correct diphthong category, according to the vowel sound.

a how   d height   g house   j train
b high   e five   h nine   k low
c south   f lane   i most   l rail

3 Here are four other common diphthong sounds.

/ɔɪ/	/ɪə/	/eə/	/jʊə/
boy	near	hair	pure

Can you think of other words that contain the same diphthong as these?

Output task

Information on tourist sights

1 Use the information in the following factsheets on other bridges and monuments to produce a recorded information line like the one on the Sydney Harbour Bridge. If possible, record your information on cassette.

Eiffel Tower, Paris

World's tallest structure 100 years ago

Completed
1889

Height
300 metres

Material
iron

Humber Bridge, England

World's longest bridge span

Completed
1980 (took 8 years to build)

Cost
£96 million

Length of main span
1,410 metres

Length including side spans
2,220 metres

Height of towers
162.5 metres

Seto–Ohashi Road and Rail Bridge, Japan

Longest combined road and rail bridge in the world

Links Honshu with Shikoku

Opened
1988

Cost
£4.9 billion

Length
12,306 metres

2 Find out about other monuments in the place where you are studying and make similar recorded texts giving factual information.

Theme park holidays

Disneyland® Paris

① Discuss the following questions.

1 Have you ever been to a theme park or amusement park?
2 What kind of attractions and 'rides' did you find there?
3 What was your favourite?
4 What are
   – a ghost train?   – a haunted house?   – a white-knuckle ride?
   – a rollercoaster?   – a big wheel?

② Like most theme parks, Disneyland® Paris is divided into several different 'lands' with a mainly American theme.

   – Main Street USA   – Discoveryland   – Frontierland
   – Adventureland   – Fantasyland

③ What would you expect to find in each of these lands? Which one contains attractions concerned with the following?

a distant lands, a jungle, and a mysterious island
b fairy tales and magic castles
c shops and restaurants from America at the turn of the century
d space and technology
e cowboys and Indians

④ What do you think happens in each of the following rides and attractions – and which land would you find them in?

1 Space Mountain
2 Pirates of the Caribbean
3 Snow White
4 Big Thunder Mountain
5 Phantom Manor
6 Indiana Jones™ and the Temple of Peril
7 Star Tours
8 Sleeping Beauty's Castle

⑤ Now read the text to check your answers.

⑥ Where in the theme park would you advise these visitors to go – or not to go?

a a family with two children aged three and five
b someone interested in space and technology
c a pregnant mother and her three-year-old child
d two teenage friends
e a person with a heart condition
f the person sitting next to you
g a member of your own family
h your teacher

⑦ In pairs, act out the conversation between these visitors and the person at the Disneyland® Information Desk. Take turns to play the different roles. Refer back to the language of spoken recommendation in **Unit 3**, **Language focus 1** on page 33.

DISNEYLAND PARIS® Theme Park

MAIN STREET, U.S.A.

Pass through the gates of the Theme Park and enter another world with your first steps on Main Street, U.S.A. Antique automobiles and horse-drawn streetcars move up and down this busy street – and don't miss the spectacular daily parade!

The magic starts as soon as you enter **Main Street, U.S.A.**, every detail of the speciality shops and restaurants reflecting the charm of small-town America at the turn of the century. There's at least one fabulous **parade** every day of the year, with special themes and characters. Steam trains depart **Main Street Station** for a trip around the Park whilst at the far end of the Street is the **Central Plaza**, where all four lands come together. Which one will you explore first?

Opening Hours
09.00–23.00 (11 Jul–31 Aug)
09.00–20.00 (20 Dec 97–3 Jan 98, 20 Jun–10 Jul, 1–6 Sep)
09.00–18.00 (rest of year weekdays)
09.00–20.00 (rest of year weekends)

Occasionally certain rides and facilities may not operate due, for example, to routine maintenance, etc. Please note that some rides have a minimum height restriction and certain rides may also be unsuitable for pregnant women, or people with health problems.

Food & Drink in the Park

As well as the restaurants in the theme park (which serve everything from kid's menus at FF28 to full menus for adults from FF140), food stalls and carts on weekends and in school holidays serve snacks such as pizza baguettes from FF22; burgers are available from FF10 and many restaurants have simple set menus from around FF52, with a main course on its own from FF26.

DISCOVERYLAND

A celebration of space and vision! Disney's newest thrill, the incredible journey from the earth to the moon on Space Mountain … followed by a flight through space in the Star Tours simulator and a journey through time in Jules Verne's Visionarium.

Taking its theme from the Star Wars trilogy, the high-tech **Star Tours** intergalactic flight sets the pace for a whirl through space and time. At Videopolis you enjoy spectacular live stage shows and **Captain EO**, the extraordinary 3D musical space spectacular starring Michael Jackson. Jules Verne's extraordinary visions are explored to the full in **The Mysteries of the Nautilus** where his undersea world can be seen from Captain Nemo's submarine.

Space Mountain is Disney's £65 million white-knuckle ride which combines Jules Verne's imaginary world with a thrilling roller-coaster which catapults you to the moon! During the ride, you'll blast out of the great cannon, and dodge falling meteorites hurling through space in a breathtaking series of inversions – including a 360° sidewinder loop!

ADVENTURELAND

Pack your bags for distant lands and discover the mysterious Adventure Isle. Explore the jungle with Indiana Jones™ and set sail with the Pirates of the Caribbean!

Be prepared for a spot of swashbuckling with **Captain Hook** and **Peter Pan** aboard a magnificent pirate galleon. Just up ahead the Jolly Roger flies atop a menacing Spanish fortress – it's the **Pirates of the Caribbean!**

Indiana Jones™ & The Temple of Peril is a breathtaking rollercoaster chase. Trains career past ancient temple gods, teetering columns, and hidden perils, before climbing through a full gravity-defying loop! – not for the faint-hearted, this is one of the biggest thrills in the Theme Park!

FANTASYLAND

An enchanting land of fairy tales and make-believe. Sleeping Beauty's Castle forms the centrepiece of the Park and here your childhood memories become reality.

Especially popular with younger children, this fantasy land brings to life the stories of **Snow White** and **Alice in Wonderland**. Take a musical cruise around the globe with **It's a small world** and enjoy **The Voyages of Pinocchio**, **Peter Pan's Flight**, **Dumbo the Flying Elephant**, and the whirl of the **Mad Hatter's Tea Cups**. Ride through **Storybook Land** aboard **Casey Junior's Circus Train** or on the **Storybook Cruise** on the canal, taking in the scenes from **Peter and the Wolf**, **The Little Mermaid**, and **Beauty and the Beast**.

FRONTIERLAND

Relive the golden age of the American Frontier with cowboys, Indians, and rugged frontiersmen in this land of romance and excitement.

A chilling experience awaits you at haunted **Phantom Manor**, whilst children of all ages will enjoy the **Pocahontas Indian Village Playground** and live show and the small farm animals in **Critter Corral**. For sheer excitement, don't miss **Big Thunder Mountain**, one of Disney's most famous attractions and one of our favourites.

The runaway train takes you on a perilous plunge from rocky peaks to treacherous mine shafts. An explosive experience – hang on to your hats!

Reading and speaking

Accommodation options at Disneyland® Paris

Many visitors to Disneyland® Paris also stay on the site. There are a number of different types of accommodation, each with its own theme. You are going to read about some of these.

1 Divide into two groups, **A** and **B**. **Group A** should read the information below about the Hotel New York, the Sequoia Lodge, and the Hotel Santa Fe, and complete the table. **Group B** should read the information on page 180 about the Disneyland Hotel, the Newport Bay Club, and the Hotel Cheyenne, and complete the table.

Name of hotel			
Theme			
Facilities in the hotel			
Facilities in the room			
Restaurants			
Classification			
Price category			
Any other information			

Hotel New York

Prices from £228

The excitement of Manhattan comes to Paris! The architecture reflects the rich character of the Big Apple with midtown Skyscrapers, Brownstones, and Gramercy Park Rows.

Adjacent to the Festival Disney entertainment centre and five minutes' stroll from the theme park, the Hotel New York's luxury rooms have an art deco design. All are furnished with two large double beds, to sleep up to four people, private bathroom with hair-dryer, TV with international channels, mini-bar, private safe, and air-conditioning. The heated indoor and outdoor swimming pools are interconnected and there is a health club with sauna, jacuzzi, steam room, and gym (and at extra charge sunbed and massage), and two outdoor tennis courts.

The Parkside diner has all-day dining, breakfast from FF80, lunch from FF95, and dinner from FF175 (child menu FF55). The Manhattan Restaurant offers à la carte dining in a stylish setting: dinner from FF195 (child menu FF65). Enjoy a pre-dinner cocktail in the New York City Bar.

Room-only accommodation. Official classification four-star.

Sequoia Lodge

Prices from £185

Named after the giant American redwood trees, the Sequoia Lodge evokes the hunting retreats of a US National Park. Wood and stone together create a rustic ambience.

The Lodge lies on the east shore of the lake, with accommodation either in the main building itself or in one of the five other lodges. Decorated in hunting-lodge style, the rooms all have two large double beds to accommodate a family of four. Private bathrooms, TV with international channels, and air conditioning are standard throughout. There are ice machines on every floor and a coin operated laundry. The memorable indoor/outdoor pool has a slide, cascades, and jacuzzi. There is also a health club with sauna, jacuzzi, steam room, gym (and at extra charge a sunbed and massage) and a children's playground.

Guests can dine at Hunter's Grill restaurant: breakfast from FF60 (child FF40), dinner from FF175 , or the Beaver Creek Tavern – a BBQ grill (dinner from FF120) – and relax by the fireside in the Redwood Bar and Lounge.

Room-only accommodation. Official classification three-star.

Hotel Santa Fe

Prices from £167

The Hotel Santa Fe is spread among 42 pueblo-style buildings. Desert trails wind through the site which, with the trading post, New Mexico-style restaurant, and adobe architecture all evoke the American south-west.

Nestling on the banks of the Rio Grande river the Hotel Santa Fe's smart bedrooms incorporate Mexican styling. Each room has two large double beds to accommodate a family of four, private bathroom (bath and shower), TV with international channels, ceiling fan, and telephone. A laundrette is also available.

Tex-Mex specialities are offered at La Cantina restaurant with its attractively styled Mexican food market buffet: breakfast from FF45 (child FF35), dinner from FF110 (child menu FF55). The Rio Grande bar offers contemporary evening entertainment.

Room-only accommodation. Official classification two-star.

Guests may register credit card details on arrival to enable meals and purchases throughout the resort to be charged to their room.

2 In your groups, think about who the accommodation would be suitable for. Describe in detail three different groups of imaginary tourists for each accommodation type.

3 Work in pairs, one student from **Group A**, and one from **Group B**. Describe your three hotels to each other. Imagine the three groups of tourists you described for your own hotels have to choose one of the hotels described by your partner. Match each tourist group with one of your partner's hotels. Ask for more information if necessary.

Output task

Planning a theme park

© Disney

Epcot at Walt Disney World® in Florida is a theme park which consists of two parts: Future World, which explores the role of communications, transport, agriculture, and energy and also looks at the world of imagination, and World Showcase, which examines the world about us, recreating the sights and smells of such far apart places as Britain and Beijing.

1 **World Showcase**

In the World Showcase there are exhibitions on the following countries:

America (USA)	Germany	Morocco
Canada	Italy	Norway
China	Japan	United Kingdom
France	Mexico	

If you were designing your own World Showcase Theme Park what exhibits would you build for each of the countries? Discuss in groups. You can add other countries if you want.

To help you, here are some of the UK exhibits at the World Showcase.

red telephone boxes	warm beer in a traditional pub
half-timbered houses	a tea shop in a country cottage

2 **Other facilities**

Decide what your policy on other facilities and services would be. Here are some symbols. Write the instructions you would put on an information sheet in the theme park tourist information centre.

Tourism in Stratford-upon-Avon

Stratford-upon-Avon is a town in the centre of England, famous as the birthplace of William Shakespeare. It attracts a large number of tourists. What do you think are the advantages and disadvantages of tourism for the people who live and work in Stratford-upon-Avon?

1 Read the newspaper article, 'Town seeks refuge from tourism boom', and answer these questions. Record your answers in the survey report factsheet below.

   1 How many people took part in the survey?
   2 Did the majority of residents think tourism was a good thing or a bad thing for the town?
   3 What is the proportion of tourists to residents in the year?
   4 What other English town was also worried about the number of tourists?
   5 How many residents thought the number of visitors was too high?
   6 How many residents thought the number of visitors was too low?
   7 Which country do a lot of tourists to Stratford come from?
   8 Why has the number of visitors increased?
   9 What suggestions have been made for reducing traffic problems?
   10 How many jobs in the centre of Stratford depend on tourism? What type of jobs are they?

The effects of tourism in Stratford – a survey of residents
Survey carried out: 25 October

1 Sample size:

2

3

4

5

6

7

8

9

10

Other information:

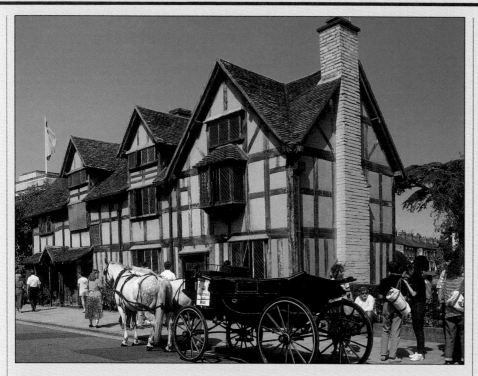

Town seeks refuge from tourism boom

**By David Nicholson-Lord
Consumer Affairs
Correspondent**

MORE tourists would not be welcome in Stratford-upon-Avon according to a survey of more than 2,000 of its residents. Visitor numbers have reached their limits and should be capped at existing levels.

The survey, thought to be the first of its kind in Britain, also showed that although slightly more than half the residents thought the benefits of tourism outweighed its drawbacks, a sizeable minority – 28 per cent – disagreed.

Stratford, with a population of 23,000 but about 2.5 million visitors a year, probably faces more pressure from tourists than any other English town and is the subject of the English Tourist Board's first three-year national pilot project on visitor management in historic towns.

The survey was carried out this summer after fears voiced by the English Historic Towns Forum that many historic centres are unable to cope with rising numbers of visitors. An 'environmental capacity' study of Chester showed that so many tourists were crowding into its centre that they were spoiling it for each other.

In Stratford, 57 per cent of residents thought that current tourist numbers were 'about right', 40 per cent thought they were too high, and only 3 per cent favoured an increase. However, the steady rise in numbers, which has brought a million more tourists to Stratford over the last 15 years, nearly half of them from North America, seems likely to continue.

Maureen Hicks, director of the visitor management project, said 'The message is that although we can just about manage as we are, we are reaching the point of severe congestion at peak times.'

The move out of recession, the increase in overseas visitors to Britain, and the popularity of Stratford meant some important decisions would 'have to be faced up to', she added.

The survey showed that 86 per cent of residents wanted an end to traffic congestion. However, they were divided about solutions. Park-and-ride schemes were the most popular but Mrs Hicks said that residents were 'petrified' of more permanent changes such as pedestrianization.

The 52 per cent who support tourism cited the jobs it brought, their 'civic pride' in the town's popularity, and the support tourism gave to town facilities. The 28 per cent who were opposed said tourism raised prices in shops and restaurants, caused congestion and environmental damage, and interfered with residents' enjoyment of the town.

About 28 per cent of the jobs in the town centre of Stratford depend on tourism. But despite the view that tourism was a major part of the local economy, most people viewed it as an industry of low-paid, seasonal, or part-time jobs.

② **Role-play/Debate**

The Stratford Tourist Information Centre has called a meeting to discuss what can be done and to make recommendations to the local government. Use the statistics and information in the Survey Report above to act out the following role-play and debate.

1 Divide into groups with a minimum of five in each. One person in each group is the co-ordinator from the Tourist Information Centre. The others should divide up as pro-tourism residents and anti-tourism residents.

Tourist Information Officer (Co-ordinator) A

Read the article again to identify the main problems and areas of concern. Set an agenda of discussion points. During the debate try to come to a conclusion in which everyone is reasonably happy. For example, turn someone's objection into a proposal. Think about how you as a Tourist Information Centre can help to improve the situation, by giving better information, introducing restrictions, etc. Make sure that by the end of the meeting you have a definite set of proposals to put to the local government.

Pro-tourism residents and local hoteliers B

You must argue for the advantages of tourism. What does tourism bring to the town? Read the article again to get some more ideas.

Anti-tourism residents C

Why are you opposed to tourism? What are the particular problems which tourism brings? What suggestions do you have for controlling and limiting it? Read the article again to get more ideas.

2 Hold the debate. When you have finished write down the list of proposals which you have agreed on as a group.

Vocabulary

amusement park	enchanting	magnificent	rides
antique	exhibition	moderate hotel	rollercoaster
apartment	fabulous	modernization	shopping centre
aquarium	flea market	mysterious	shopping mall
big wheel	found	palace	span
botanical gardens	fully-equipped	parade	spectacular
breathtaking	gallery	park-and-ride	statue
budget hotel	ghost train	pedestrianization	temple
canal	hands on	perilous	theatre
cathedral	harbour	popular	treacherous
chilling	incredible	public	white-knuckle ride
city centre	leaflet	conveniences	
downtown	luxury (hotel)	red-light district	

10

Guiding

Working as a tour guide

How to be a good guide

1 What does a tour guide have to do? What does the job involve?

Make two lists.

a the things a guide must do/is responsible for
b the personal and professional qualities needed

Compare your lists with another pair.

2 Jenny Townsend is a London 'Blue Badge' guide. Read the text on the next page. It gives Jenny's view of what the job involves and what people expect from a tour guide. Does she mention any of the things you listed? Add the extra items to your lists.

3 Read the text again and find words that match the following definitions.

a working for oneself, not for a particular company
b a description of action and moving events
c silly, not serious
d easy to talk to and ask questions of
e a planned travel route
f a person representing his or her country
g feeling tired and unwell as a result of air travel
h immediate medical help (after an accident, etc.)
i to advertise and publicize
j careful and skilful management of people and their problems
k treating someone like a child
l a very important person

4 Would you like to be a guide? In what ways do you think it would be a good job or a bad job?

'Most guides are freelance and are hired for particular jobs. Tour operators and other people employ guides mainly to inform tourists about the places they are visiting. Therefore a guide has to have a good sound knowledge not only of a particular place but also of other things which are generally relevant – for example, architecture, history, and local customs. During our training we intensively learn a vast amount of information about a whole range of subjects, and we have to be capable of jumping from one topic to another in the same sentence! But the way in which a person conveys this knowledge is the key: you have to be good at judging what your audience is interested in and you have to know how to keep their attention. These are not easy skills, I can tell you!

A guide's commentary should be interesting, lively, and above all, enthusiastic. It shouldn't be too academic and 'heavy', but neither should it be frivolous. A sense of humour is also important, but again one should only be humorous where appropriate. 'Getting the balance right' is the main skill of guiding and commentaries should vary according to each group. A group of schoolchildren and a group of architects require a very different approach.

Tourists ask a lot of questions and a guide should be friendly, helpful, and approachable. Guides shouldn't claim to know everything – we're not superhuman! If you don't know the answer, say so, but add 'I'll find out for you'.

Questions can vary. They can be practical ones; it's important to know where the toilets are situated as well as the date of a monument! When things go wrong – as they occasionally do – a guide should pause and calmly sort out the problem, and try to make sure that the original itinerary is kept to.

As a guide you really are an ambassador for your country and it is your job to promote it. For many people you are the only person from that country that they have any contact with. As an ambassador you also have to know about diplomacy and you are responsible for making sure everyone is happy.

You also have to be 'the boss' in order to ensure that the itinerary runs smoothly. You're often in charge of checking in and out of hotels, taking care of baggage, money, and so on. Efficiency is very important in all of this.

Above all as a guide you have to like people. You meet the world in this job, some great people and some awful ones, but you have to try to treat them all as equals. Don't be patronizing, but welcome everyone as if they were a VIP to your country. But most of all, enjoy it!'

How to be a
Good Guide

So you want to be a tour guide? Although I work mainly in London and England I'm sure the job's more or less the same wherever you do your guiding. So let me give you some advice ...

A guide takes on a number of roles for the tourist: teacher, entertainer, ambassador, nurse, and 'the boss'. As 'teacher' the guide is passing on information, as we've discussed. Most tour groups are on holiday so they want to enjoy themselves and want to be entertained to a certain extent. People also need looking after, so you sometimes have to be a nurse. Some people are jet-lagged or have minor illnesses (sometimes worse!). When we train, we do a basic first-aid course.

Answerphone messages

① Here are Jenny Townsend's diary pages for the 5th to the 18th of August. She already has some bookings.

AUGUST		AUGUST

5 MONDAY

6 TUESDAY

7 WEDNESDAY
Half-day London panoramic (a.m.)

8 THURSDAY
York city tour
8.30 a.m. pick-up – back late

9 FRIDAY

10 SATURDAY

11 SUNDAY

MONDAY 12

TUESDAY 13

WEDNESDAY 14

THURSDAY 15
York city tour
8.30 a.m. pick-up – back late

FRIDAY 16

SATURDAY 17
London Walking Tours–
evening pub crawl–8p.m.

SUNDAY 18
Lunch at mum's–no work

1 Listen to her answerphone messages. Note the dates of the jobs offered.

2 Look at her diary page and decide if she can do the jobs.

3 Listen again and make more detailed notes about the jobs and who she must contact. You may need to listen a third time.

Message	Date of job	Can do?	Details of job	Who to contact
1				
2				
3				
4				
5				
6				

Language focus 1

Telephone language – requests and responses

1 Listen again to parts of the answerphone messages and complete the sentences with the expressions used to ask if Jenny is available.

a I was _____ to do a half-day panoramic tour for us?

b Any _____ a repeat this year?

c Call us soon if _____.

d Do you _____ do another job for us?

e Would _____ ?

f I wanted to _____ do a Hampstead Sunday tour for us?

Which of the expressions are more formal?

Pronunciation focus 1

Listen again to the six sentences.

1 How many syllables are pronounced in each of the sections you filled in?
2 Which syllables are stressed?
3 Which syllables are weak?

Practice

Now Jenny has to confirm whether she can do the jobs or not. Use the information you have on her diary page, and the phrases below, to act out the conversations with a partner.

This is …
I'm returning your call.
I just wanted to confirm that I am available for …
I'd love to do the job on …
Could you give me some more information about …
I'm sorry, but I'm afraid I can't do …
I'm afraid I'm already booked.
Unfortunately, I'm doing a … on that day.

Vocabulary

Here are some words and expressions often used when booking a guide. Match them with the definitions below.

i pick-up point	vi incentive tour
ii voucher	vii hospitality desk
iii transfer	viii commission
iv gratuity ('grat')	ix panoramic tour
v pax	x rooming list

a abbreviation for 'passengers'
b place, usually at a hotel or conference, where visitors can get help and advice
c place where the guide and coach meet the passengers
d a percentage paid to someone for bringing customers to a shop or other service
e written details of which rooms visitors are staying in at a hotel
f a general sightseeing trip
g a ticket which a guide can use instead of cash to take a group into a famous place
h a trip offered to a group of employees as a reward for good work
i taking a group of visitors from their place of arrival to their hotel
j money given to someone to say 'thank you' for good service

Output task

Booking a guide

Use the language in the previous section to act out the following role-play. Divide into pairs. One of you is a tour operator, the other is a guide.

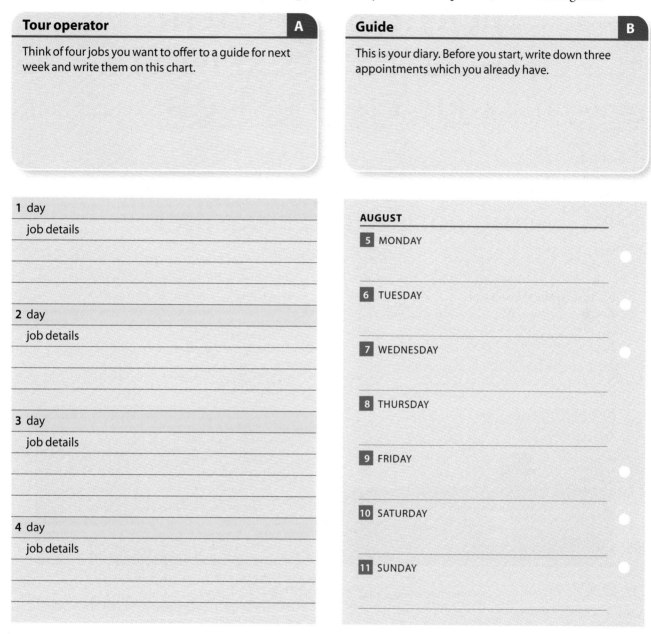

Tour operator	A
Think of four jobs you want to offer to a guide for next week and write them on this chart.	

Guide	B
This is your diary. Before you start, write down three appointments which you already have.	

1 day

job details

2 day

job details

3 day

job details

4 day

job details

AUGUST

5 MONDAY

6 TUESDAY

7 WEDNESDAY

8 THURSDAY

9 FRIDAY

10 SATURDAY

11 SUNDAY

If you are unable to make bookings with your partner try a different tour operator/guide.

SECTION 2

Information

Reading

A tour of Scotland

❶ You are going to read about a tour called 'Four-day tour of Scotland and the English Lakes'. Before you read, think about the title. What would you want to know about it (a) as a passenger thinking of going on the tour, and (b) as the guide working on the tour? Make a list.

FOUR-DAY TOUR OF SCOTLAND AND THE ENGLISH LAKES

OUR PRICE INCLUDES THE FOLLOWING FEATURES

- *Three nights' accommodation with breakfast in a four-star hotel in Edinburgh, Scotland's historic capital city.*
- *An evening of Scottish music and dancing with a traditional Scottish dinner.*
- *A guided sightseeing tour of Edinburgh.*
- *A visit to a whisky distillery (including a free tasting with instruction).*

- *A full-day excursion to the rugged Trossach mountains and the beautiful Loch Lomond – an optional cruise on the loch is available.*
- *A visit to a traditional tweed and woollen mill.*
- *A tour of the English Lake District.*
- *A scenic drive through Northumbria National Park.*

DAY 1

We travel to Edinburgh via Newcastle and the wild and charming scenery of the Northumbria National Park. We'll make a photo-stop at the Scottish border in the lovely Cheviot Hills. Passing through Jedburgh with its beautiful abbey, we'll arrive in Edinburgh in the early evening. After checking in at the hotel the rest of the evening is free for you to explore the city.

DAY 2

Morning sightseeing in Edinburgh. You'll see the elegant New Town and Princes Street, once described as 'the most beautiful street in the world', the Royal Mile, Holyrood House, and Edinburgh Castle. In the afternoon we have included visits to a whisky distillery, and a tweed and woollen mill.

DAY 3

Full day tour to the Trossach mountains and Scotland's largest and loveliest lake, Loch Lomond – an optional boat cruise is available on the loch. Returning to Edinburgh we stop for a photograph of the 100-year-old Forth railway bridge, a showpiece of Victorian engineering. Then it's back to the hotel for an evening of traditional Scottish entertainment with dinner included.

DAY 4

We'll see more stunning scenery today as we leave Edinburgh and travel south-west to Moffat, where we stop for coffee, and then on to England where we visit one of the most popular parts of the country, the Lake District. We stop for lunch in the village of Grasmere, home of the poet William Wordsworth. There'll be time to discover the many delights that Grasmere has to offer before boarding the coach for the final journey back to London.

3 Read the description again and answer these questions.

1 Which cities are visited?
2 How many nights' accommodation are included?
3 What is the accommodation like?
4 What meals are included?
5 Are there any special visits or excursions?
6 What attractions are there on the journey back?
7 Where and when is the pick-up point?
8 Are gratuities included in the price?

Listening 2

Guide instructions

1 Imagine you are going to be the guide on the tour. You have been sent the following guide instructions which give more detailed information about the various parts of the tour. Read them through once.

Guide Instructions Tour:

Scotland and the English Lakes   Sue Jameson is handling this group
Office tel. no. 0171 434 6370

Day 1   10 Jan (Friday)

08.00	Please depart to Victoria to check in group. Passenger list enclosed (43 pax) Coach Co. – London Coaching Services Ltd.
08.30	Depart London.
11.00	Arrive The George Hotel, Stamford for coffee stop. Served in Old Hall. Present voucher. Allow approx. 45 mins.
14.00	Stop en route for lunch (1 hour). Note: price of lunch not included.
16.00	Stop for photo at Scottish border. 15 mins.
18.30	On arrival in Edinburgh please point out notable sights and give information on local transport from hotel. On arrival at hotel assist with check-in. Rest of evening, pax at leisure. Please arrange porterage and alarm calls, and set up noticeboard in lobby. Pay driver £8 grat.

Day 2   11 Jan (Saturday)

08.00	Continental breakfast on first floor.
08.45	Liaise with driver and local guide.
09.00	Depart for city tour (approx. 3 hours).
12.00	Stop in city centre and give 1 hour free time for lunch.
13.00	Depart for Glenkinchie whisky distillery. A tour has been booked for our party at 13.45 – there are many groups there today so please be on time.
15.00	Depart Glenkinchie. En route back to Edinburgh visit Pringle woollen mill. Allow approx. 1½ hours for shopping. Pay driver £8 grat.
17.00	Arrive at hotel.
	Evening pax at leisure. Advise restaurant.

Day 3   12 Jan (Sunday)

08.00	Breakfast
09.00	Depart for full-day tour of Trossachs. Optional boat cruise on Loch Lomond booked for 12.00 – collect money from pax. (£4 per head); those who don't want to go can go for a walk or sit in Lomond Hotel.
13.00	Lunch: pax on own. Lomond Hotel know our group is coming.
14.00	Return to hotel. Must return by 17.00.
18.30	Depart for Scottish Evening at The George Hotel (doors open at 19.00). Present voucher.

Menu:
Scotch broth
Haggis and tatties
Tipsy laird
Coffee

Please ensure that jugs of iced water are placed on the tables. Give grat. (£10) to head waiter.

Day 4   13 Jan (Monday)

07.00	Bag pull. Make sure bags are outside rooms at 06.45.
07.30	Breakfast. Before departure pay porterage from your float.
08.30	Depart from hotel.
10.30	Stop for coffee at Moffat (30 mins.).
13.30	Arrive Grasmere in Lake District. Allow 2 hours free time for lunch and sightseeing.
15.30	Depart Grasmere.
17.30	Stop for tea en route to London (45 mins.).
19.30	Arrive London. Pay driver £8 grat.

---

2 Unfortunately there have been some last-minute alterations. Listen to the cassette and make the necessary changes to the instructions.

Output task

Additional arrangements

Work in pairs. The guide (**A**) should look at the information below. The representative (**B**) of the various companies and services used or visited on the tour should turn to the information on page 182.

Guide	**A**

You want to confirm the arrangements on your guide instructions and also find out additional information about the services offered.

The George Hotel, Stamford
1 Information on hotel
2 What's included?
3 Private room?

Loch Lomond Boat Tours
1 How long?
2 What will we see?
3 Commission?

Glenkinchie Distillery
1 Facts about distillery   2 Free tasting?

Customers	**B**

Look at the information on page 182.

Look at the information on page 182.

SECTION 3

On tour

Vocabulary

Describing cities, buildings, and people

1 *Rome is a nice city.* How many positive words can you think of to use instead of *nice* in this sentence? (e.g. *beautiful, exciting*). Make a list.

2 Complete this chart by ticking the boxes to indicate which adjectives can be used with which nouns.

	cities	buildings	people	night-life and entertainment
ancient				
elegant				
famous				
fine				
glorious				
important				
lovely				
magnificent				
powerful				
proud				
splendid				
superb				
wonderful				

Pronunciation focus 2

1 Mark the stress in each word (e.g. *beautiful, exciting*) and practise the pronunciation.

2 What is the effect of exaggerating the stress and intonation of a word?

Guide commentaries

1. Here are pictures of twelve famous places. Can you identify them and say which city or country they are in? Fill in the first two columns of the table.

	place	city/country	commentary	notes
a				
b				
c				
d				
e				
f				
g				
h				
i				
j				
k				
l				

2. You will hear seven guides each giving a commentary at one of the places. Can you identify which ones they are talking about? Write the numbers 1 to 7 in the third column of the table.

3. Listen to the cassette again and make notes about each of the places described.

4. When describing a place, a guide should make it sound interesting and exciting. In pairs, discuss how the guides on the cassette did this.

Guiding language

1 There are a number of different forms which occur frequently in guiding language.

Look at the language boxes below.

Indicating position

On your right is	the beautiful …
On your left is	the magnificent …
In front of you is	
We are now passing	
You can now see	

Superlatives

… is one of the	finest	buildings	in the world.
	most famous	sights	in Europe.
	most beautiful		

Passives

… was built	by (person)
… was painted	in (date)
… was designed	

… is said to	be haunted
	be the best example of …
	have lived here

Present perfect

| X | has stood | here | for (time period). |
| | has been standing | | since (date). |

Other expressions

Imagine, if you can, …
… without doubt …
… so the story goes …

2 Now use these models to expand the following notes into eight sentences to make a commentary about St Paul's Cathedral in London.

a on/left/beautiful/St Paul's Cathedral
b stood/over 300 years
c designed/Christopher Wren
d one/large/dome/world
e said/influenced/design/Capitol building/Washington
f Lord Nelson/buried/crypt
g Charles and Diana/married/1981
h imagine/how impressive/London/17th century

3 Think of two famous places you know. Make notes about them and produce a series of sentences like the ones for St Paul's Cathedral.

4 Describe one of the places to another student. Using the language you have studied in this unit, make your description sound interesting and exciting. When you have guessed each other's place, move on to another student and repeat the activity.

Output task

A guided tour of Seville

1 Imagine you are taking the following groups on a guided tour of a city. What things are they going to be interested in in general? Discuss with a partner.

a a group of businessmen   c a group of architecture students
b a group of elderly people   d a group of teenagers

2 Look at the extract from a guidebook to Seville. How suitable are each of the places mentioned for the four groups? Discuss and give each place a score from 0 to 5. (0 = not at all suitable, 5 = very suitable).

3 Using the map of Seville, plan a morning tour for each of the four groups, starting and finishing at the Tourist Office (1) and visiting at least three places.

4 Choose one of the tours and write what you would say at each of the sights. Then 'give' the tour to the others in the group or class.

Seville: what to see

Santa Cruz quarter

This quarter, part of which was the old Jewish neighbourhood, is cool and shady with narrow, twisting streets which are closed to cars, and delightful small squares full of flowers. Murillo was buried in the old church of Santa Cruz in 1682.

María Luisa Park

The María Luisa Park, with its majestic buildings built for the 1929 World Fair, is uniquely beautiful. Its eighteenth and nineteenth century surroundings overflow with geraniums and charm.

Cathedral

The gothic cathedral, which contains a vast wealth of artistic treasures, is one of the largest in Christendom, rivalling St Peter's in Rome and St Paul's in London. Columbus is buried here. Its tower, the Giralda, with a belfry and a huge bronze weather-vane in the form of a human figure, added in the sixteenth century, is the old minaret. The Orange Tree Patio was the site of the bazaar in Moorish times.

Alcázar

This is a fortified area containing an eleventh-century *mudéjar* palace which has undergone several reformations. The Hall of Ambassadors, the gardens, and the tilework generally are noteworthy. Open daily from 9 a.m. to 1 p.m. and from 3 p.m. to 5 p.m. Entrance on the Plaza del Triunfo s/n.

Archive of the Indies

In the Casa Lonja, Archivo de las Indias is an incredibly valuable repository of ancient documents relating to the discovery and conquest of the Americas. Not all of the documents have been fully studied yet: it is not open to the general public, only to scholars.

Bullring

The Real Maestranza bullring where, according to both Bizet's opera and to local legend, Carmen's former lover Don José stabbed her to death, is the most ornate in Spain.

Hospital de la Caridad

This Hospital (Plaza de Jurado), which houses one of Seville's most important collections of art, was founded to care for the poor and the sick and to bury the dead. Today it is an old people's home. It contains numerous artistic treasures, including paintings by Valdés Leal and Murillo. It was founded in the seventeenth century by a wealthy wastrel, Miguel de Manara (1629–79), after a bad binge in which he imagined men were coming to pick him up off the street and put him in a coffin.

Places to see

1. Tourist Office
2. University (former tobacco factory)
3. Cathedral and Giralda
4. Santa Cruz quarter
5. María Luisa Park
6. Alcázar
7. Casa Lonja and Archive of the Indies
8. Plaza de España
9. Real Maestranza Bullring
10. Hospital de la Caridad
11. Alameda de Hércules
12. Museum of Fine Arts
13. Archaeological Museum
14. Town Hall
15. Casa de Pilatos
16. Torre del Oro (Naval Museum)

Churches and convents

17. Basílica de la Macarena
18. Convento de Santa Clara
19. Monasterio de San Clemente
20. Iglesia de la Magdalena
21. Basílica de Jesús del Gran Poder

Stations

22. Bus Station
23. La Cádiz
24. Córdoba

The Guiding Game

Divide into groups of three or four in order to play The Guiding Game.

The Guiding Game

Rules

You will need a dice and counters. Your teacher will prepare the Chance cards.

Each player takes it in turn to be the guide and throw the dice. The other players are passengers until it is their turn to be the guide. They must listen carefully, but they can also interrupt and ask any questions they want.

The aim is to get to the end of the tour with the maximum number of Credit Points. You win Credit Points on the Commentary squares if the passengers decide you have given a good commentary. You can also win or lose points on the Chance squares. Keep a note of the points you score.

You can do as many laps of the Tour Circuit as you wish, depending on how much time you have, but all guides must finish.

Historic place – talk about the sight mentioned on the square for at least one minute.

General commentary – talk about some general aspect of your country as indicated on the square. (Good commentary = 5 points, OK commentary = 2 points, weak commentary = 0 points)

Blank – do nothing, the tour is continuing nicely.

Passenger question – one of the passengers can ask any question relevant to the tour. If you answer it well (according to the other passengers) you get two Credit Points.

Chance – take a card and follow the instruction – it could be anything!

Remember:
1 Practise the language learnt in the previous exercises.
2 A good guide is always interesting, friendly, and caring. Good luck!

Vocabulary

ambassador	diplomacy	horizon	pick-up point
ancient	distillery	hospitality desk	porterage
answerphone	dome	incentive	powerful
approachable	elegant	tour	proud
architecture	first-aid	marble	sculpture
bag pull	freelance	mausoleum	splendid
commentary	frivolous	open-top bus	superb
commission	gratuity	patronizing	
crypt	haunted	pax	

START

Art + Culture

Film Stars House

Education

Government

Palace

Monument to a War Hero

Castle

Art + Culture

Food + Drink

Church/Cathedral

History

Museum

Haunted House

FINISH

11

Promotion and marketing in tourism

SECTION 1	Selling a holiday

Reading and speaking

Types of advertising and promotion

1 Look at these slogans and extracts from advertisements connected with tourism (1–11). Match them with the destinations and services (a–k) listed on the next page.

1

Where the sunshine never goes on holiday

2

ANSWER THE CALL OF THE WILD

3

The surroundings may be your greatest handicap

4

Come fly the friendly skies

5

IT ONLY TAKES A TICK TO GET THERE

6

You drive – we'll take the car!

7

For the time of your life

8

The sun is smiling on you down under

9

It couldn't be easier. Step on in the heart of one capital city, three hours later step off in the heart of another.

10

LEADING THE WAY TO LATIN AMERICA

11

It's your last run of the day.
　Your legs are burning …
　Your back is killing you …
　What's the first thing you do when
　you reach the bottom?
Head straight for the lift!

a Eurostar train London to Paris
b holidays for people aged over 50
c Portugal
d brochure supply service for Australia and New Zealand
e Iberia group airline
f an American airline
g skiing in the Canadian Rockies
h Australia
i golf holidays in the US mountains
j African safaris
k car ferry company

2 The advertising slogans on the previous page are all from newspapers, magazines, and display posters. What other forms of tourism advertising and promotional activity can you think of? Make a list.

3 Here are some different ways of promoting a tourism product or service. What are the advantages and disadvantages of each? Are any of them particularly suitable for certain products and services?

a advertisement in magazine or newspaper
b leaflet given out in the street
c leaflet available in travel shops
d advertisement in theatre programme
e neon sign in city centre
f advertisement on billboard by roadside
g poster at railway station or airport
h television advertisement
i cinema advertisement
j press release
k sponsorship of a sporting event
l sales promotion, e.g. early booking discount
m personal selling, face-to-face or tele-sales
n direct mailing/mailshots
o web site on the Internet
p point-of-sale promotion (leaflet, poster)
q commission to selling agent

4 Which type of promotional activity do you think would be best for the following?

– cheap last-minute flights
– new caravan and camping site
– inclusive packages to see the next Olympic Games
– travel insurance
– new cut-price transatlantic air service
– trekking holidays in Nepal
– new children's theme park

'How to sell your product'

Travel agents are concerned with direct face-to-face promotion and selling. You are going to read an article, 'How to sell your product', which gives travel agents some information on the five stages of selling.

1 Before you read, what order do you think these five stages would be in?

a find out what the customer wants
b post-sales contact
c show product knowledge and expertise
d help the customer relax
e close the sale

2 Now read the article to identify the correct order and provide the five missing sub-headings.

How to sell your product

Competition in the travel agency business is tough. Businesses that want to survive must know how to gain customer confidence, present their products, and ultimately close the sale. Many books have been written on the art of successful selling, so here are some of the choicest tips in five simple stages.

1 _____

First impressions count. As Oscar Wilde said, 'Only the superficial cannot judge by appearances'. Whether or not you agree with him, there is no denying the fact that most people hope a visit to the travel agent will be a prelude to, if not the memory of a lifetime, then at least the high point of the year. A warm smile, a pleasant appearance, and good eye contact all help the would-be traveller to relax, safe in the knowledge that he or she is in the hands of a professional.

2 _____

The next stage is to identify the needs of the prospective client. This is done by asking questions about the composition of the group, the destination and duration of their trip, their preferred mode of travel, and their anticipated expenditure.

The problems encountered at this stage range from the client not having a very clear idea of what they want, to their being unrealistic about what it is going to cost. As soon as the salesperson has established the customer's requirements, he or she moves on to the next stage.

3 _____

Effective sales staff will demonstrate good product knowledge by pointing out not only the relevant features of a variety of travel packages, but also their advantages. Evidence shows that the agent who demonstrates intimate knowledge of the product that they are recommending is more likely to achieve a successful sale. However, it is impossible to be familiar with all aspects of each company's services. Therefore it is vitally important that the salesperson is able to access information quickly through use of the computer or the brochures provided by the tour operators.

Let's assume that the first package you draw to your customer's attention seems to meet with their approval. The sale does not stop here. It is now a good idea to show something else, if only to point out the comparative advantages of the first choice.

4 _____

That way, with luck, the salesperson may proceed with closing the sale – in other words the client makes a commitment of some kind. The ideal outcome is that the client makes a firm booking by paying a deposit. Yet the salesperson must make sure clients do not feel pressurized into deciding one way or another. If need be, the salesperson should offer to call them later or invite them back in.

5 _____

A good sales technique does not stop with a successful sale. Interest and care must still be shown to ensure customer satisfaction. It has become common practice in many travel agencies to maintain some form of post-sales contact through the use of a 'welcome home' card, both to instil customer loyalty and to encourage a high level of repeat business. The skill of selling successfully to a growing customer base requires human interest, dedication, and above all, hard work.

3 At which of the five stages might you hear someone say the following?

a I can really recommend this place – I was there myself last year.
b Please take a seat.
c Would you like me to make a definite reservation?
d Can I help you?
e We'll be sending next year's brochure to you in a few weeks.
f Do you know where you'd like to go?

g Let's see if we can find a similar package from another operator.

h That may be a bit beyond the price range you mentioned.

i Was everything satisfactory?

j Well, why don't you think about it and I'll give you a call in the morning?

4 What would you say in these situations? Discuss in groups.

a A customer is looking at a winter sports brochure.

b A young couple come in and start arguing about where to go.

c A young family tell you how much they would like to spend on a two-week holiday. The kind of holiday they want is twice as expensive but they do not know this yet.

d You are speaking on the phone to an important regular customer. Everyone else is busy. Suddenly someone comes in and starts complaining very loudly about the holiday they have just been on.

e A customer asks you a detailed question about a particular resort which you are unable to answer.

5 Now role-play one or more of these situations.

Language focus 1

Describing features

1 In advertising and promotion it is very important to use appropriate adjectives to describe features and facilities, so that they seem attractive. Here is a list of adjectives. Which nouns could they go with? Think of your own or choose from the list of nouns.

Adjectives

lively	traditional	secluded
panoramic	central	hearty
peaceful	well-stocked	relaxing
well-equipped	unspoilt	breathtaking
friendly	pretty	historic
delicious	interesting	

Nouns

rooms	view	cathedral
service	staff	hotel
village	facilities	setting
museum	location	restaurant
disco	mini-bar	beach
lunch	holiday	scenery

2 Which of these phrases might appeal to the following people?

a a honeymoon couple

b a company looking for a location for a conference

c a retired couple

d you

e your partner

f your teacher

Connotation

In advertising and promotion it is also important to present everything in a positive way. However, the same thing can often be described in different ways – either with a positive connotation or a negative connotation. For example, something which is described as 'luxury', might be interpreted from a negative point of view as 'expensive'.

1 Look at these adjectives, all of which have a positive connotation. Can you think of another way of describing the same thing but from a negative point of view?

a luxury	d simple	g lively
b popular	e relaxing	h remote
c cosy	f unspoilt	

2 Here are some words and phrases with possible negative connotation. Match them to the appropriate positive adjective.

i small	v crowded
ii impossible to get to	vi no facilities
iii expensive	vii nothing to do
iv noisy	viii boring

Pronunciation focus 1

1 As we saw in **Unit 10**, it is important to stress the correct syllable in an adjective. If the stress is strong and used with a high rise-fall tone, then the positive meaning of the adjective is also stressed.

●

For example: de – lic – ious

2 Mark the stressed syllable in all the adjectives listed in exercise 1 above. Practise saying the adjective-noun combinations you chose with exaggerated stress.

Output task

Selling a holiday

❶ Work in pairs. Fill in the chart below for a town or city that you know well, but that your partner doesn't. Make sure you include some negative points as well as positive ones (exaggerate if necessary – it is important that the place is not a perfect holiday destination!).

Name of place	
Type of resort	
Travel time (from where you are now)	
Climate	
Famous sights	
Places to visit	
Food/wine to try	
Accommodation	
Excursions	
Entertainment and night-life	
Possible inconveniences	
Languages spoken	
Need for a visa	
Cost of living	
Cultural and religious differences	
Other difficulties	
Disadvantages/reasons not to visit	

❷ When you have filled the forms in, exchange them with your partner. Look at the new form you have. You have to sell this holiday destination to your partner, so you will need to push and promote the positive aspects and disguise the disadvantages. Act out the role-play at the travel agency. Try to sell your partner's resort to your partner!

❸ Choose a few other tourist destinations and products which have obvious disadvantages and try to sell them to other members of the class. Here are some suggestions.

– a ski resort in the summer (when there's no snow)
– a beach resort in the winter (when it's cold and there's no sun)
– a cheap basic hotel with no facilities (to business people used to staying in luxury expenses-paid hotels)
– a plane ticket from London to New York via Moscow and Addis Ababa
– a broken-down caravan

Vocabulary and speaking

Specialist holidays

Holiday types and market segments

❶ Look at this list of specialist holiday types. What do they involve? What sort of customer are they likely to appeal to? Make notes.

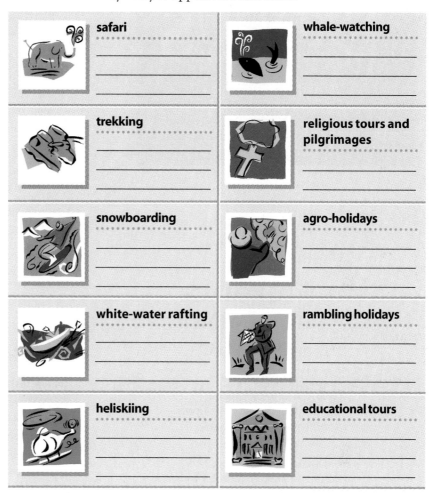

safari
_____
_____
_____

whale-watching
_____
_____
_____

trekking
_____
_____
_____

religious tours and pilgrimages
_____
_____
_____

snowboarding
_____
_____
_____

agro-holidays
_____
_____
_____

white-water rafting
_____
_____
_____

rambling holidays
_____
_____
_____

heliskiing
_____
_____
_____

educational tours
_____
_____
_____

❷ To market and promote these specialist holidays it is very important that the companies know who their market is likely to be. When identifying target markets, most organizations divide the total market into 'segments', or groups of customers who share similar characteristics.

There are several ways markets can be segmented or categorized.

a groups sharing a similar lifestyle (work patterns, social and leisure habits, etc.)
b age groups
c ethnic and culturally-distinct groups
d groups from the same country or region
e gender (male/female)
f socio-economic class (e.g. managers, professionals, semi-skilled and unskilled workers, etc.)

❸ In groups, choose three or four of the specialist holiday types listed in exercise 1. Analyse each one in terms of the six market segments in exercise 2. Compare your opinions with other groups. As a result of this discussion, how would you promote each of the holidays?

Holiday advertisements

1 Here are some advertisements for specialist holidays. Read them quickly and identify the type of holiday being advertised in each one.

11

Promotion and marketing in tourism

1

EXODUS
Discovery Holidays

Ring for Brochure
0181 673 0859 (24 hrs)

LEADERS IN SMALL-GROUP ADVENTUROUS
TRAVEL WORLDWIDE

2

Are you interested
in joining a group for a very
special religious walk?

THE PILGRIMAGE
OF THE CAMINO
DE SANTIAGO

A pilgrimage to the
tomb of St James the Apostle:
a 100-mile walk to the ancient religious
site in Santiago de Compostela
in north-west Spain.

Departing from Le Puy
in the French Auvergne late April,
and returning in late July.

Contact: Maureen O'Connor
on 976 2184

3

To India in
search of rhino

Our 18-day escorted tour takes you from Delhi,
Agra (and the Taj), to Darjeeling and Sikkim,
Shillong and Calcutta, tribal villages and
Buddhist monasteries, to Kaziranga and
elephant safaris to view rhino. Including first-
class hotels wherever possible and British
Airways' scheduled flights, that's unusually good
value at £2095.00 pp. For a free brochure call:

0171 487 9111 (24 hrs)
GREAVES TOURS

33 MARYLEBONE HIGH STREET LONDON W1M 3PF
FAX: 0171 486 0722

4

Leave the ordinary behind

You love to ski or snowboard but you are … tired of hard-packed runs, lift lines, and crowded slopes?

You have heliskied but you are … wondering if there is something beyond the experience of heliskiing with three or four groups using the same helicopter?

Yes … It is time to join us in British Columbia's Cariboo / Chilcotin mountains for Canada's extraordinary Helicopter Skiing experience.

Advanced to expert skiers and boarders will find lots of powder, diversified terrain, and challenging runs in a huge area!

Intermediate skiers and boarders will find our new Heli-Relax groups the perfect way to experience the most exciting skiing on earth!

All will find our exclusive service of skiing with only two groups per helicopter and our fantastic mountain lodge facility the perfect way to enjoy the most outstanding ski vacation ever.

Your powder paradise is located **62 miles** (100 km) north of Whistler Resort, British Columbia, Canada.

Tyax Lodge Heliskiing
PO Box 118, Vernon, BC V1T 6N4, Canada
Tel: 001 (250) 558-5379
Fax: 001 (250) 558-5389
e-mail: heliski@mindlink.bc.ca
Internet site: http//www.tlhheliskiing.com

5

Ocean Adventures
Journeys in search of wild places and wild nature
Antarctica
from £2150! also: Arctic Regions

Brochures: Two Jays, Kemple End, Stonyhurst, Lancashire BB7 9QY
Tel: 01254-826116 Fax: 01254-826780 ATOL 2937

EXCEPTIONAL SAFARIS-EXCEPTIONAL STANDARDS

THE EXCLUSIVE AND WORLD-RENOWNED MALA MALA PRIVATE GAME RESERVE PROVIDES THE DISCERNING TRAVELLER WITH A WILDLIFE AND BIG GAME EXPERIENCE SECOND TO NONE:

- 45,000 acres of privately owned, pristine bushveld situated on the banks of the Sand River with an unparalleled 37 kilometres of river frontage.

- Last year over 87% of guests who stayed two nights or more saw the big five – elephant, rhino, buffalo, lion, and leopard.

- Choice of three camps – Main Camp, Kirkman's Kamp and Cottage, and Harry's Camp.

- Mount Andersen Ranch lies in 20,000 acres in the Drakensberg Mountains and provides an exclusive haven for an unforgettable fishing and wildlife getaway.

- Limited to six guests.

- Accommodation and service of the highest standard.

- Excellent facilities for the wildlife enthusiast with safaris offered by horseback, vehicle, or on foot.

In addition, Safari Desk also represents other fine safari destinations including the unique Mashatu Game Reserve in Botswana and the legendary Ker and Downey camps in the enigmatic Okavango Delta.

For further information:

Safari Desk
86/87 Campden Street, Kensington, London W8 7EN
Tel no: 0171 229 1216
Fax no: 0171 229 1511

SAFARI DESK

2 Listen to these three conversations on the telephone. In each case the enquirer is asking for more details about one of the advertised holidays.

1 Which advertised holiday is being discussed?

Conversation 1 _____

Conversation 2 _____

Conversation 3 _____

2 In which of the holidays are these places and things mentioned?

– bed & breakfast
– Buddhist monasteries
– cathedral
– fiesta
– glaciers
– Himalayas
– library
– orchids
– penguins and seals
– plunge pool and sauna
– Pyrenees
– church halls
– Taj Mahal
– tigers
– whales

3 For each holiday, note down any information given about the following topics.

– location, scenery, etc.
– accommodation and facilities
– length of holidays and itineraries on offer
– what to do and see
– meal arrangements

Heliskiing holidays

1 Look again at the advertisement for the Tyax Lodge Heliskiing holiday on page 156. What type of people is it trying to appeal to?

  a experienced skiers or beginners
  b people who like to go to popular resorts and runs or people who like to go somewhere unspoilt and remote
  c people who like adventure and excitement or people who like relaxing lazy holidays
  d safety-conscious people or danger-loving people
  e people who like comfortable accommodation with good food and facilities or people who like to live simply and be close to nature
  f people who want cheap holidays or people who don't mind too much about the cost

2 Now read this extract from Tyax Lodge Heliskiing's online brochure.

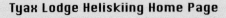

Tyax Lodge Heliskiing Home Page

ABOUT TYAX LODGE HELISKIING

Tyax Lodge Heliskiing offers two- to seven-day packages suitable for intermediate to expert skiers and snowboarders from its base at Tyax Mountain Lake Resort, a unique getaway just 100 km (62 miles) north of **Whistler Resort**. Skiers and snowboarders enjoy the convenience of having a helicopter at the service of a maximum of two groups.

This exclusive service allows skiers to set their own pace over a greater selection of untracked powder runs in three different mountain ranges. **Waiting times are virtually eliminated** and on average, eight to ten runs – selected by experienced mountain guides from more than **275 routes – are skied per day. A hearty lunch is served in the splendour of the mountains.**

Tyax Lodge is built on a plateau overlooking the frozen waters of **Tyaughton Lake**. The largest log building in western Canada, Tyax offers European and east coast cuisine **plus fresh-baked desserts and breads.** An outdoor jacuzzi features a panoramic view of the lake and mountains. Games, fitness rooms, and a sauna are additional features.

After skiing, enjoy a pleasant soak in the outdoor jacuzzi or a drink in the **Cowboy Bar**. After a fine dinner, you can relax in front of the **river-rock fireplace** or watch video footage of the day's adventures.

1 Have you changed your opinion about who they are trying to attract?

2 Find out information on the same categories referred to in **Listening 1**, exercise 3 on page 157. Make notes that will help you to pass the information on to someone enquiring about the holiday.

  a location, scenery, etc.
  b accommodation and facilities
  c length of holidays and itineraries on offer
  d what to do and see
  e meal arrangements

3 Another method of promoting a holiday or a resort and giving important information at the same time is to include a question and answer page. Here is the Tyax Lodge question and answer page from their online brochure. Match the questions with the answers.

a How good a skier should I be?
b Can I bring my snowboard?
c Why do skiers come to Tyax Lodge for heliskiing?
d How are the skiing groups chosen?
e What about physical conditioning?

Tyax Lodge Heliskiing Home Page

 # TYAX LODGE QUESTIONS AND ANSWERS

1 Our guests seek an incomparable powder skiing experience and want to enjoy it with old and new friends in an intimate setting. Our climate zone provides us with lots of snow and sunny weather. Add the more than 275 runs accessible in three different mountain ranges, and the exclusivity of skiing with only two groups per helicopter, and you have found the place for a superb heliskiing or heli-snowboarding vacation.

2 Our regular packages are well suited for advanced intermediate to expert skiers who are physically fit. Our new heli-relax packages are ideal for intermediate skiers and heliski connoisseurs who desire to ski at a more relaxed and less demanding pace. Our mountain guides are also ski instructors, trained to teach you the necessary skills as you may require.

3 Especially for our regular packages, your experience will be enhanced by being physically fit and prepared for your heliskiing vacation. For our new heli-relax

packages special conditioning is not necessary … but it certainly can't hurt!

4 Heliskiing at Tyax Lodge is an exclusive experience and we want it to stay that way. There are only two groups, each with a maximum of eleven skiers and a guide, per helicopter. Our heli-relax packages consist of a maximum of ten skiers and two guides. Groups are chosen based on the answers provided on the 'Skier Questionnaire' which is filled out upon your arrival at the Lodge. Please understand that groups travelling together may be split up into different groups according to their abilities. This is done in the interest of making the skiing as enjoyable as possible for all of our guests participating in a heliskiing holiday with us.

5 Of course! TLH is renowned in the inner circles of snowboarding as 'the place to go'. Snowboarders already account for nearly ⅓ of our total skier days. Please bring your own snowboard as we have no rental boards.

---

4 Look back at all the texts from Tyax Lodge. Make a list of all the positive adjectives used and note down what they are describing.

For example:
extraordinary (helicopter skiing experience)
challenging (runs)

Output task

Specialist holiday enquiries

1 In pairs, act out the conversation between an enquirer and the office of the company promoting Tyax Lodge, using the notes you made in the previous section.

2 For further practice, use the notes you made in **Listening 1**, exercise 3 on page 157 to act out similar conversations (but use your notes, not the tapescript!). Make sure that you each get an opportunity to be the person in the office.

3 Now choose another of the specialist holidays. It could be one of the other advertisements or one of your own.

1 Write down the details of the holiday, using the categories from **Listening 1**, exercise 3 on page 157.

– location, scenery, etc.   – what to do and see
– accommodation and facilities   – meal arrangements
– length of holidays, itineraries on offer

2 Divide into two groups. **Group A** are potential customers, **Group B** are representatives of different holiday companies promoting their particular holidays. The potential customers should visit each of the holiday companies and find out details about the holidays on offer. At the end, customers should decide which specialist holiday they are going to take.

3 Change roles so that **Group A** are now the company representatives and **Group B** the potential customers. Repeat the activity.

Promotion on the Internet

Reading

Promoting Georgia through the Internet

❶ What do you know about the American state of Georgia? Discuss these questions in groups.

1 Where exactly is Georgia located?

2 Which of these places are in the State of Georgia?

– Alberta   – Charleston   – Rome
– Atlanta   – Columbus   – Savannah
– Alabama   – Dallas

3 Do you know any songs or films associated with Georgia?

4 What type of holiday would visitors to Georgia have?

5 What do you think would be the aims and function of the Georgia Department of Industry, Trade, and Tourism?

❷ Georgia, like many other tourist boards, and travel companies and organizations in general, promotes itself through the Internet.

1 What do you know about the Internet? Discuss in groups.

2 Have you ever used the Internet – either for e-mail or to look at information on the World Wide Web?

3 What is meant by the following terms?

www   *to browse*   *to download*
website   *to click on something* *desktop*
home page   *to search*   *mouse*

4 What information would you expect to find out about Georgia through the Internet?

❸ Now look at the welcome page of Georgia's entry on the World Wide Web. Read it quickly and check your answers for exercise 1, question 5, and exercise 2, question 4.

❹ Look at the underlined parts of the text. When clicked on, they all give access to other pages in the Georgia website giving more information. What additional information would you expect to find for each of these underlined parts?

Welcome

The Georgia Department of Industry, Trade, and Tourism is Georgia's official state agency for developing new jobs and creating capital investment. The Department carries out this mission by encouraging business investment, expansion of existing industry, locating new markets for Georgia products, promoting tourism, and promoting the state as a location for film and videotape projects. For more information, visit the online office of the Georgia Department of Industry, Trade, and Tourism.

Economic Development

Information on Georgia's great business climate.

International Trade

Welcome to Georgia. We invite you to begin your tour with a message from Governor Zell Miller.

To assist you in identifying Georgia products available for export, we have compiled MADE IN GEORGIA USA.

For additional information on Georgia's growth contact

"trade@itt.state.ga.us" or call (404) 656 3571.

Tourism

Visit the host state of the 1996 Olympic Games. Browse a calendar of events or search by areas of interest.

Georgia Film

See Georgia's TV campaign across the Internet. Listen to Elton John's memorable theme for Georgia. Pattern your PC's desktop with lots of freely downloadable desktop images.

Registration

Request more information on State of Georgia and register in our guest book.

Photo gallery of Georgia images

USA GEORGIA ON MY MIND

Georgia Links allows you to search hundreds of web sites in the state. Visit the Georgia Research Alliance to learn about exciting projects GRA has started in partnership with our state's research universities and business.

Visit the Georgia Chambers of Commerce Directory

Visit Creative Services

5 Below are six extracts from other pages on the Georgia website. Match them with six of the underlined parts on the welcome page.

a
September 7 9 a.m.–6 p.m. 1st Saturday Arts & Crafts Festival, Savannah 912-234-0295

b
Georgia serves as the headquarters for dozens of major corporations. Many international companies also call Georgia home.

c
Georgia plays a vital role in the nation's economy in farm commodities and equipment and service.

d
Search: SAVANNAH – ATTRACTIONS Savannah Waterfront Association, River St. Address: PO Box 572, Savannah, Georgia 31402 Phone: 912 / 234-0295 Historic and scenic River St. First Saturday. Festivals – Dining – Shopping –Museums –Art

e
The State of Georgia contains a wide variety of tourist destinations. Our northern Georgia mountains feature white-water rafting and numerous outdoor activities. Our coastal region includes some of America's most interesting islands. The grandeur of the classic south and the gleaming towers of Atlanta are both symbolic of our state. To learn more about each of our regions simply click on your area of interest on the map.

f
The Georgia Film and Video Office helps make Georgia one of the most sought after locations for film production in America. Dozens of major motion pictures have been made in our state. From the rural vistas of *Deliverance* to the charming performances of *Driving Miss Daisy*, Georgia provides an excellent location for any story.

Superlative language

In order to sell and promote their product advertisers use 'superlative' language.

1 Look at the underlined words in these sentences from the 'Safari Desk' advertisement on page 157, and phrases from the heliskiing advertisement and the Georgia website.

*Mala Mala Private Game Reserve provides the discerning traveller with a wildlife and big game experience **second to none**.*

*Mount Andersen Ranch ... provides an exclusive haven for an **unforgettable** fishing and wildlife getaway.*

*Intermediate skiers and boarders will find our new Heli-Relax groups the perfect way to experience the **most exciting skiing on earth**.*

*All will find ... our fantastic mountain lodge facility the perfect way to enjoy **the most outstanding ski vacation ever**.*

*The Georgia Film and Video Office helps make Georgia **one of the most sought after** locations for film production in America.*

2 Can you find other examples of superlative words and phrases in any of the other texts in this unit?

3 Make similar sentences to the ones above to promote these features. For example:

– exclusive restaurant

You will find our exclusive restaurant the perfect way to enjoy a most romantic meal. or *Our exclusive restaurant provides one of the most romantic settings in the country.*

– historic hotel
– secluded beaches
– exciting night-life
– fascinating museum

Output task

Designing a website

Design a website for your region.

❶ Start with the welcome page. Would you have the same sections as the Georgia welcome page?

Which extra ones would you add to suit the attractions and facilities of your region?

Write the text for each section. Be brief – this is only the introduction!

What pictures would you include?

How would you lay out the page?

Decide which words to highlight or underline – to allow the reader to click on them and look at them.

❷ Make a complete list or map of all the pages you would include on your website. They will probably correspond with the underlined words on your welcome page.

❸ Design one or two of the other pages. For example:

a a page about a particular town or resort in your region
b a question and answer page like the one for Tyax Lodge on page 159

Planning a promotional campaign

Divide into groups. You are going to plan a campaign to promote tourism in the region where you are studying. These are your main aims.

– to promote the region in general as a destination for potential tourists
– to promote a particular annual event, such as a festival, a sporting tournament, or an anniversary of a local building or institution

You will need to research and plan your campaign very carefully. Follow the guidelines below.

1   Define exactly what it is that your region offers to tourists and visitors. Decide which annual event you are going to promote in particular (you can invent one if necessary).

2   Identify your target market and describe likely market segments. Who are your potential customers? What are their common characteristics?

3   Set detailed objectives for the campaign. Are you trying to attract new customers, maintain existing ones, raise awareness in general? What areas are you particularly aiming to increase?

4   Identify the best way to reach your target markets. Which promotional activities and methods are you going to use?

5   Identify the resources you will need to carry out your campaign.

6   Set a schedule for the next twelve months for both (a) the general campaign to promote your region, and (b) the promotion of the annual event you have chosen.

7   Prepare your opinions and plans in the form of a report that can be shown to the rest of the class.

Vocabulary

advertising	desktop	home page	press release
billboard	direct mailing	jacuzzi	print-run
agro-holiday	download	mailshot	rambling holiday
browse	expedition	market research	secluded
centenary	extraordinary	market segment	slogan
challenging	familiarization trip	mountain lodge	snowboarding
click on	fiesta	mouse	sponsorship
climate	game reserve	neon sign	target
cosy	glacier	online	tele-sales
cut-price	heliskiing	point-of-sale	well-stocked

12

Developments in tourism

SECTION 1 — The shape of things to come?

Speaking

Statements about travel and tourism

1 Look at the following statements made by tourists and travellers. In pairs, decide whether you agree or disagree. Give reasons. Afterwards, compare your opinions with another pair.

> ❝I would never go on holiday to a country whose politics I didn't agree with. ❞

> ❝It doesn't matter if you can't speak the language of the country you visit. ❞

> ❝Tourism is going to continue to expand. In fifty years' time more people will be working in tourism-related jobs than any other type of job. ❞

> ❝The best way to travel is alone. ❞

> ❝Space will provide a vast new frontier for the adventurous to explore. ❞

> ❝If you live in a tourist resort you need the tourists but you also resent them. ❞

> ❝Travelling makes you appreciate your home more. ❞

> ❝Tourism ultimately spoils a country. ❞

2 Two of these statements are making predictions about the future. In general terms, what do you think tourism will be like in fifty years' time?

Reading

Space hotel

1 Imagine a hotel in space. How would it be different from the hotels of today? Who would want to stay there? Discuss the following questions.

1 What will a space hotel look like? What shape will it be? How big will it be? How will it be built?

2 How might these types of traveller benefit from a space hotel: businessmen or women, elderly people, families with children, honeymoon couples?

3 What traditional hotel facilities will remain? How might they change? For example, think about cabins and showers/washing facilities.
4 Which sports and recreational activities will be possible in a space hotel?
5 What kind of food will travellers eat?
6 Staying in space will be expensive. How could tickets be made cheaper?

2 Read the article about the proposed NASA Space Hotel. It gives the answers to some of these questions. Compare them with your own answers and fill in the gaps in the advertisement below.

NASA to offer rooms with a view in orbiting hotel

By Edward Welsh

WELCOME to the ultimate penthouse suite: a hotel orbiting Earth. NASA, the American space agency, is sponsoring a project to build a space station for holidaymakers by 2012.

A firm of architects that specializes in hotels is drawing up designs. Wimberley Allison Tong & Goo, an American architectural practice based in Honolulu, Hawaii, envisages the hotel accommodating 100 people as it orbits the Earth. Passengers will be ferried to and from it by the next generation of space shuttles.

At present it costs about £5m to buy a ticket into space: two Japanese businessmen paid that amount to join a Russian space trip last year. But the project's backers believe prices will drop dramatically with the advent of new spacecraft.

They estimate it will cost less than £10,000 per head to check into the space hotel for three days of out-of-this-world views and the chance to experience weightlessness.

Buzz Aldrin, the former astronaut and second man to step on the moon, believes the opportunity to book a long weekend in a low-earth orbit would prove hugely popular. He is planning a lottery scheme that would reduce the cost of space travel for winners to a mere £50.

'The view from space is like having a globe on your desk', he said. 'It's a broadening experience after looking at parts of the Earth such as the Mediterranean or bits of America on maps and then to see them for real.'

A viewing deck designed as a glass bubble will have panels providing computer-aided images to help guests identify which part of the Earth they are looking at. The panels will also show relevant information such as weather conditions.

Guests will be served food grown hydroponically on board, and prevent their muscles from atrophying by playing ball games in zero gravity.

They will also get a chance to dock alongside and pay a visit to the planned international space station, which should be orbiting Earth by then. But with nowhere else to go, the only other day trips available would be spacewalks.

The plan envisages the hotel being divided between areas of zero and artificial gravity. This will allow guests to experience floating in space but also provide a refuge for the one in two passengers expected to suffer from space sickness. An area with artificial gravity will also help guests have a shower.

Howard Wolff, Vice-President of the architects, said the project had presented him with a completely different set of problems in comparison to his normal work designing holiday resorts. 'It's like developing a new, vast, and wonderful frontier', he said. 'But the point will be to strike a balance between creating an out-of-this-world experience and providing some creature comforts.'

The most exciting event in tourism this century!

The NASA Space Hotel

Opening in the year [1] _____ .

Accommodation for [2] _____ people at a cost of [3] _____ per person – but you can buy a ticket for only £50 in our special [4] _____ !

Special features include:

A chance to really watch the world go by from the [5] _____ .

Day trips to [6] _____ , and you can also go on a [7] _____ .

Zero gravity area and [8] _____ gravity area.

Designed by the architects [9] _____ , to give the perfect balance of an [10] _____ experience combined with some of the [11] _____ you naturally expect from a luxury hotel.

3 In groups, discuss the following questions.

1 How likely do you think these developments and predictions really are?
2 Would you like to visit the space hotel described in the article? What would you like or dislike about it?
3 What job opportunities would there be in such a hotel?

Future predictions

1 Look at these examples taken from the **Speaking** and **Reading** sections on pages 164 and 165.

Tourism is going to continue to expand.

In fifty years' time more people will be working in tourism-related jobs than any other type of job.

Space will provide a vast new frontier for the adventurous to explore.

Why are the different future forms used?

2 In the space hotel article, the writer mainly uses the *will* future form to make predictions. For example:

Passengers will be ferried to and from it by the next generation of space shuttles.

Find other examples in the text. Why is *will* used and not *going to*?

Personal opinions about the future

There are other ways of making predictions about the future, especially in spoken language. Look at these examples of people reacting to some of the opinions expressed in the space hotel article. In which one is the speaker more certain?

I expect there'll be hotels in space some time in the future.

It's bound to be a very expensive holiday.

It definitely won't happen in my lifetime.

They'll probably build a museum on the moon …

… and I wouldn't be surprised if they open a theme park on Mars!

There's a good chance that it'll happen in the next thirty years.

I doubt that I'll be able to afford to go.

Practice

In groups, respond to some of the predictions about hotels in space.

1 Adventurous travellers will be having holidays in space in the next thirty years.
2 Elderly people will enjoy staying in the space hotel.
3 Honeymoon couples will enjoy staying in the space hotel.
4 Hotel rooms will be fairly luxurious.
5 The holidays will not be cheap.

Output task

Predicting future trends in tourism

1 In groups, discuss likely future developments in world tourism.

1 In fifty years' time, where will the most popular tourist destinations be?
2 Which new countries will tourists come from in the next fifty years?
3 What kinds of holiday will these new tourists be looking for?
4 Will these new tourists be attracted to your country? What things will you need to develop in order to attract them?

2 Divide into groups of three or four. Choose one of the following topics.

– hotels (on earth!)
– air travel
– other forms of travel and transport (road, rail, sea, river)
– entertainment and recreational facilities
– holiday types
– tourist attractions and facilities in the town/city where you are studying

Discuss the possible developments in the topic area you have chosen over the next fifty years. Write down your main opinions and predictions and pass them to another group for discussion and reaction.

3 Produce an outline proposal for tourism development in your country over the next fifty years (for example, build a new airport, train more Chinese-speaking guides, etc.).

Speaking   The effects of tourism

New airport creates 1,000 jobs

The Tudor Café has closed. A new branch of

Fastburger

will be opening here soon.

HILL TRIBE TREKS

Three-day and five-day visits to remote hill tribe villages – an opportunity to witness a unique way of life that is fast disappearing.

STOP

FOOTPATH TO LOOK-OUT POINT CLOSED DUE TO EROSION

NO ENTRY

WANTED – suppliers of jewellery, ceramics, carvings, etc. for craft shop on popular tourist route. Guaranteed regular supply.

5 011472

Thank you. Your entrance fee has contributed to the upkeep of this historic monument.

1 Each of these items refers to a change or development due to tourism. Where would you find them? Discuss the probable impact of each one on the local area. Think about the benefits and the drawbacks.

2 Tourism brings both advantages and disadvantages. Here is a random list of 'pros' and 'cons'. Put them in the correct section of the chart below, and add any others you can think of.

  a creates jobs
  b leads to overuse of water and other natural resources
  c causes beach and cliff erosion
  d disrupts traditional work and employment patterns
  e preserves traditional arts and crafts (e.g. as tourist souvenirs)
  f helps people from different countries and cultures understand each other
  g creates a lot of pollution
  h brings money into a country (and to local people)
  i changes the real meaning of festivals to suit the needs of tourists
  j damages the environment
  k destroys the natural habitat of some animals and birds, as well as people
  l broadens people's knowledge of the world
  m encourages greed

	advantages	disadvantages
environmental		
economic		
social		
cultural		
other		

3 Which of the points in exercise 2 do you particularly agree or disagree with? Can you think of any real examples? For instance, the building of a new airport damages the environment and makes a lot of pollution, but also creates jobs and brings money into a country.

FUTURE SHOCK

Reproduced from Contours

When the tourists flew in

The Finance Minister said,
  'It will boost the economy,
  the dollars will flow in.'

The Minister of Interior said,
  'It will provide full
  and varied employment
  for all the indigenes.'

The Minister of Culture said,
  'It will enrich our life . . .
  contact with other cultures
  must surely
  improve the texture of living.'

The man from the hotel chain said,
  'We will make you
  a second Paradise;
  for you, it is the dawn
  of a glorious new beginning!'

When the tourists flew in
  our island people
  metamorphosed into
  a grotesque carnival
  – a two-week sideshow.

When the tourists flew in
  our men put aside
  their fishing nets
  to become waiters,
  our women became whores.

When the tourists flew in
  what culture we had
  flew out of the window,
  we traded our customs
  for sunglasses and pop,
  we turned sacred ceremonies
  into ten-cent peep shows.

When the tourists flew in
  local food became scarce,
  prices went up,
  but our wages stayed low.

When the tourists flew in
  we could no longer
  go down to our beaches.
  The hotel manager said,
  'Natives defile the sea-shore'.

When the tourists flew in
  the hunger and the squalor
  were preserved
  as a passing pageant
  for clicking cameras
  – a chic eyesore!

When the tourists flew in
  we were asked
  to be 'sidewalk ambassadors',
  to stay smiling and polite,
  to always guide the 'lost' visitor . . .
  Hell, if we could only tell them
  where we really want them to go!

The Bedouin of Petra

TOURISM is one of Jordan's major sources of foreign currency, and the government has decided to capitalize on the country's rich archaeological and biblical sites in order to attract large numbers of western tourists and Christian pilgrims. Most visitors come to Jordan as part of Holy Land tours. After visiting sites in Jordan they cross the King Hussein bridge to the West Bank.

Two sites in Jordan are always included: the Greco-Roman city of Gerasa (modern Jerash), 48 km north of the capital city of Amman, and Petra, the Nebatean capital, 262 km to the south.

Tourism in Petra has a long history, but it is only in the past thirty years or so that the area has witnessed rapid development for that purpose. Petra has been recognized by the central government as an important source of tourist revenue, and the benefits of tourism to the economic growth of the region and the nation have overshadowed consideration for the impact on the local tribes, especially the Bidul (Bedouin).

The Bidul used to raise gardens as well as herd flocks, but few young men are engaged in agriculture or pastoralism now. Most of the young Bidul families are supported by the tourist trade. Most try to sell souvenirs or to operate refreshment stands. Near the Roman theatre some six stands are located, operating in close competition. Only a few make much money, but the daily income is more than twice what they could make in agriculture. Where once dozens of gardens were found, only two remain today. Flocks have been given over to the women and children to watch.

The Bidul used to offer Bedouin hospitality to all visitors, even tourists. Being members of a poor tribe, they experienced hardship as a result of having to feed extra mouths. It was expected that the visitors would leave a gift, no matter how small, for their hosts. Tourist abuse of Bedouin hospitality has caused a change in this. Although hospitality is offered, Bidul expect to be paid in cash, any currency.

Tourism, and to a lesser degree archaeology, have been responsible for a number of changes in nearly every aspect of life in the Petra area. The region's importance to the national economy as a main attraction for foreign visitors has prompted rapid development. The local people have been caught up in the development process and have been forced to change in the manner dictated by it.   JOHN SHOUP

❶ Look at the cartoon on the previous page. What point is it trying to make? Which of the points listed in **Speaking**, exercise 2 are illustrated here?

❷ Read the article about the Bedouin of Petra in Jordan, and the poem, 'When the tourists flew in'.

    1 Which points listed in **Speaking**, exercise 2 are illustrated in the two texts?

    2 Make a list of the different effects tourism has had on the local people.

❸ Both the article and the poem present a very negative view of the impact of tourism. In groups, imagine you are responsible for the development of tourism in both of these regions.

    1 How can you put across a more positive message about the two situations?

    2 What changes and safeguards could you introduce in order to ensure that the impact of tourism was not so negative in those areas?

Listening 1

The independent traveller

❶

You are going to listen to a talk given by someone who has travelled extensively and who is concerned about the impact of tourism. Before you listen, discuss these questions.

1 What makes a 'good tourist'?

2 What do you understand by the term, a 'green tourist'?

3 What things would a 'good tourist' and a 'green tourist' be careful about, (a) when planning a trip abroad, and (b) when on holiday?

❷ The speaker mentions the following things. What advice do you think he gives about each of them?

    – local language
    – fast food chains
    – hiring a car
    – endangered species
    – photographs
    – hotel chains
    – souvenirs
    – complaining

❸ Listen to the cassette and see if you were right.

❹ The speaker advises people to ask their tour operator a lot of questions. Imagine you are a concerned tourist thinking about a foreign holiday. As you listen to the speaker, make notes of the questions you can ask your tour operator.

❺ Using your list of questions, take turns to role-play the conversation between the tourist and the tour operator/travel agent.

How to be a good tourist

1 The advice given by the speaker in the previous section is mainly about what to do when you are at your holiday destination. He also gives a few pieces of advice about what to do before you go. In pairs or groups, make more detailed lists of advice and suggestions for the concerned tourist under the following headings. Include the advice given by the independent traveller.

a Before you go – holiday preparation and planning
b Packing – what to take and what not to take
c Getting there – transport alternatives
d When you are there
e When you are home

2 Here is the opening paragraph of an article entitled 'How to be a good tourist'.

How to be a good tourist

A NEW BREED of greener, more enlightened traveller is emerging. The negative impact of mass tourism can no longer be ignored. Tourists, realizing that the things they set out to see are being spoiled by the way they see them, are keen to make amends. The following tips and suggestions may in themselves seem small things, but if everyone followed them the overall effect would be incredible.

(based on an article in the *Observer*, 31 March 1991)

Continue the article using the headings you discussed in exercise 1 above. If you need help with the language of advice and suggestion look at the tapescript on page 198. Are any of the structures specifically for spoken language, or could they also be used in a written leaflet of this kind?

Tourism and the environment

Listening 2

Sustainable tourism

1 You are going to listen to an interview in which Professor Roger Spencer from a British university talks about the principles of sustainable tourism. Before you listen, discuss what you think is meant by 'sustainable tourism'.

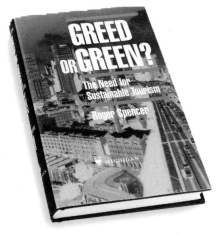

2 Here is a list of 'The Ten Principles of Sustainable Tourism' (from *Beyond the Green Horizon*, produced by Tourism Concern and the World Wide Fund for Nature). In pairs, discuss what is meant by each one. Can you think of any examples where the principles do or do not happen?

1 Using resources sustainably
2 Reducing over-consumption and waste
3 Maintaining diversity
4 Integrating tourism into planning
5 Supporting local economies
6 Involving local communities
7 Consulting stakeholders and the public
8 Training staff
9 Marketing tourism responsibly
10 Undertaking research

3 Now listen to the interview. Which three of the ten principles does Professor Spencer talk about?

4 Match the location in column **A** with the correct development or problem in column **B**.

A	B
Pattaya, Thailand	hotel construction and local ownership
Nepal	overuse of water
The Gambia	waste disposal
Costa Rica	brothels, sex shops, and strip clubs
Western Samoa	consultation with local groups
Philippines	destruction of religious sites
Hawaii	destruction of forests

5 Two of the examples are positive examples of sustainable tourism – which ones? What general recommendations does the professor make for achieving sustainable tourism?

Green Earth Travel

① Match the verbs in column **A** with the nouns and phrases in column **B** to form a suitable collocation. There may be more than one possibility.

A		B	
arrange	provide	local employment	activities
carry out	recruit	the use of …	research
encourage	support	the number of …	campaigns
listen to		detailed	our customers
monitor		information	

② Read this promotional statement by the tour operator, Green Earth Travel. For each of the points, decide which of the principles of sustainable tourism they could be connected with.

OUR PROMISE TO YOU …

Green Earth Travel is a responsible tour operator. We are committed to the principles of sustainable tourism. We aim to provide the traveller with a memorable and fascinating experience, but at the same time we are aware of the impact that mass tourism can have on the environment and on the culture and economy of a society. Like you, we are concerned, like you we want to do something about it.

In particular, we:

1 monitor the number of tourists visiting our chosen areas
2 keep in close contact with local conservationists and regularly discuss any environmental changes caused by tourism in the area
3 ensure that the type and scale of our tours is appropriate to local conditions
4 encourage the use of local materials and ensure that we only use hotels and accommodation options which blend in with the surroundings
5 recruit local employment rather than expatriate wherever possible
6 respect local customs and traditions
7 arrange activities and excursions which ensure genuine contact with local people
8 provide detailed information on the cultural traditions of the places our customers are visiting
9 carry out ongoing research into the impact of tourism
10 support campaigns to raise the level of environmental awareness in the industry
11 listen to our customers and welcome suggestions for improving standards

③ Which of the commitments listed above would be broken in the following situations? How would you respond to the comments (in brackets) made by the companies concerned?

a A hotel imports people to work as waiters and barpersons. ('There aren't enough local people with the right skills.')

b A tour operator tries to get as many people as possible to a resort, and builds extra hotels cheaply where necessary. ('If people want to go there, then we're only providing what they want.')

c An international hotel chain builds a fifteen-storey hotel on the beachfront. All the other hotels in the resort are four storeys or less. ('It takes up less ground space.')

d A tour company moves the date of a local festival so that it coincides with the peak season. ('That way more people get to see it and find out about the local people and their traditions.')

e A tour operator and travel agent doesn't bother to send out feedback questionnaires to its customers. ('We send them next year's brochure. We're not interested in the past, we just want them to buy next year's holiday.')

Output task

Responsibility in the tourism industry

1 Think about other sectors of the tourism industry. How could they help to be more 'green' and encourage sustainable tourism? In groups, list ideas for each of the following sectors.

Air travel
Road and rail travel
Cruises
Tourist information
Guiding
Promotion and marketing

2 Choose one of the sectors and prepare a statement of philosophy from a 'green' point of view, like the Green Earth Travel statement.

ACTIVITY

Simulation – the development of tourism in an imaginary country

Paradiso is an imaginary island. It is approximately 80 km long by 50 km wide. It is a former colony that recently gained independence, and has a democratically-elected government. There are only basic facilities, but the climate and geography are potentially good for tourism. At the moment only a few tourists visit the island, mainly independent travellers.

After a recent referendum, the government has decided to develop tourism. The referendum made it clear that any development needs to be on a sustainable basis, with proper concern for all aspects of the environment and the native culture.

Divide into groups of four or five. You are the government department which has been given responsibility for planning the development of tourism on Paradiso.

1 First you have to establish the details of Paradiso as it is now.

1 Draw a map of the island. Be sure to include geographical features like beaches, mountains, rivers and farmland, a port (or ports), a capital city and other settlements, and any other features you can think of.

2 Decide on other characteristics of the island.
– climate
– population
– location
– local food production and industry
– transport systems

2 Now think about your objectives.

What type of tourist destination do you want Paradiso to be?
What type of holidays can you offer?
What type of people do you want to attract, and where from?

3 Plan the first phase of development.

What things do you need to build immediately (e.g. roads, airport, hotels)? Where are the resorts going to be?

4 Plan more detailed development.

What type of accommodation are you going to provide?
What skills will you need? Will you train local people, or will you import workers?
What shops and facilities do you need?
What other services should you provide?

5 Plan your promotional campaign.

Where are you going to market Paradiso?
How are you going to market it?

Present your report in a clear and professional way, using diagrams and pictures if possible. Compare your plans with those of other groups. What similarities and differences are there?

Vocabulary			
altitude	elderly	module	safeguard
archaeology	environment	over-consumption	shellfish
brothel	environmentalist	overuse	solar panel
carnival	folk dance	pollution	souvenir
cliff erosion	gravity	recycling	stakeholder
conservation	greed	referendum	sustainable
conservationist	habitat	resources	tribe
craft	idyllic	responsible	waste disposal

B information
for Pair work and Group work

Unit 3	SECTION 3 Visas

Listening 3 — **Telephone conversations** (page 40)

1 Arranging an interview for a visa

Official   **B**

Appointments are fully booked for the next two weeks, although there may be a few cancellations.

2 Phoning a travel agent

Travel agent   **B**

You have one or two bargain-price late deals to the Caribbean (but it's the hurricane season!) and to Florida and Turkey (invent the details).

3 Asking for an upgrade

Travel agent   **B**

You have a special arrangement with a particular airline that guarantees upgrades. Unfortunately, it is not a very popular airline and the flight times are not always suitable.

Unit 4	SECTION 2 Negotiations

Pronunciation focus 1 — **Pair work** (page 50)

Tour operator   **B**

Before you talk to the travel agent, make a note of some appointments you have already made. You usually have to be at your office every day from 15.00 onwards, so you would prefer a meeting before that time.

Objectives

- review of last year's sales
- introduce new computer reservations system
- promote new Caribbean holidays
- any customer feedback from last year?

Negotiations with a hotel (page 51)

Hotel representatives   B

You would like a meeting at your hotel next week. Midweek and late morning is best for you (maybe over lunch?).

Your objectives are:
– set allocation – 60 rooms per night in high season?
– promote new self-catering villa complex
– limited credit period (account was settled very late last year)
– tell tour operator about new recreational facilities
– a more prominent display in the operator's brochure
– introduce a sell-on clause (sell the unsold rooms four weeks before date)

Which of these objectives do you want to set as agenda items?

Which objectives will be more difficult to achieve?

Think carefully about your tactics in the meeting. Read the article on negotiation techniques on page 48 again.

Unit 5   SECTION 3   Flight attendants

Output task

Cabin crew role-play (page 71)

Passengers   B

You and the other passengers are really airline inspectors travelling in secret. It is your job to see how new flight attendants cope with the pressures of the job. As a team, you have to work out the best way of testing each flight attendant. There are various ways in which this can be done. You can be frightened, worried, drunk, talkative, difficult to please, noisy, etc. No terrorists please!

It is very important that the flight attendants do not realize who you really are. Act like a 'normal' passenger at first. It is probably best if you save most of your extreme behaviour until Stage 2. Make notes in the table below before you start.

Stage 1	What to say and do
1 Greeting	
2 Seating	
3 Stowing baggage, fastening seat-belt, etc.	
4 Making safety announcement	

Stage 2	What to say and do
1 Drinks before lunch	
2 Lunch	
3 Tea and coffee	
4 Collect trays	
5 Duty-free goods	

Stage 3	What to say and do
1 Preparing for landing	
2 Goodbye	

A trip down the Nile (page 80)

Read the text and decide what questions you need to ask in order to find out the missing information.

Text B

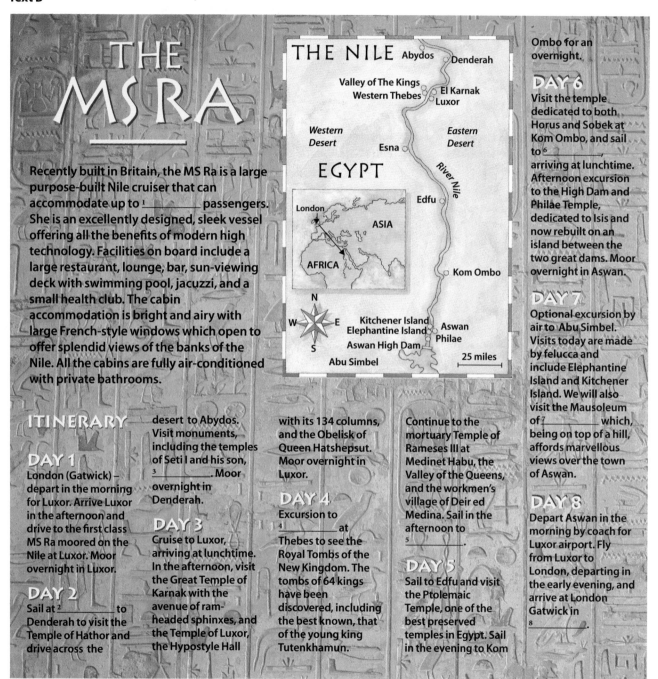

THE MS RA

Recently built in Britain, the MS Ra is a large purpose-built Nile cruiser that can accommodate up to [1] _____ passengers. She is an excellently designed, sleek vessel offering all the benefits of modern high technology. Facilities on board include a large restaurant, lounge, bar, sun-viewing deck with swimming pool, jacuzzi, and a small health club. The cabin accommodation is bright and airy with large French-style windows which open to offer splendid views of the banks of the Nile. All the cabins are fully air-conditioned with private bathrooms.

THE NILE

EGYPT

London, ASIA, AFRICA

Abydos, Denderah, Valley of The Kings, Western Thebes, El Karnak, Luxor, Western Desert, Eastern Desert, Esna, River Nile, Edfu, Kom Ombo, Kitchener Island, Elephantine Island, Aswan High Dam, Aswan, Philae, Abu Simbel

N, S, E, W

25 miles

ITINERARY

DAY 1
London (Gatwick) – depart in the morning for Luxor. Arrive Luxor in the afternoon and drive to the first class MS Ra moored on the Nile at Luxor. Moor overnight in Luxor.

DAY 2
Sail at [2] _____ to Denderah to visit the Temple of Hathor and drive across the desert to Abydos. Visit monuments, including the temples of Seti I and his son, [3] _____. Moor overnight in Denderah.

DAY 3
Cruise to Luxor, arriving at lunchtime. In the afternoon, visit the Great Temple of Karnak with the avenue of ram-headed sphinxes, and the Temple of Luxor, the Hypostyle Hall with its 134 columns, and the Obelisk of Queen Hatshepsut. Moor overnight in Luxor.

DAY 4
Excursion to [4] _____ at Thebes to see the Royal Tombs of the New Kingdom. The tombs of 64 kings have been discovered, including the best known, that of the young king Tutenkhamun. Continue to the mortuary Temple of Rameses III at Medinet Habu, the Valley of the Queens, and the workmen's village of Deir ed Medina. Sail in the afternoon to [5] _____.

DAY 5
Sail to Edfu and visit the Ptolemaic Temple, one of the best preserved temples in Egypt. Sail in the evening to Kom Ombo for an overnight.

DAY 6
Visit the temple dedicated to both Horus and Sobek at Kom Ombo, and sail to [6] _____, arriving at lunchtime. Afternoon excursion to the High Dam and Philae Temple, dedicated to Isis and now rebuilt on an island between the two great dams. Moor overnight in Aswan.

DAY 7
Optional excursion by air to Abu Simbel. Visits today are made by felucca and include Elephantine Island and Kitchener Island. We will also visit the Mausoleum of [7] _____ which, being on top of a hill, affords marvellous views over the town of Aswan.

DAY 8
Depart Aswan in the morning by coach for Luxor airport. Fly from Luxor to London, departing in the early evening, and arrive at London Gatwick in [8] _____.

B

B Information

SECTION 2 Independent travel overland

Explaining car hire arrangements (page 95)

Car-hire representative   B

Here is the information you need to answer your customer's questions. Make sure you give detailed answers and check that your customer has the correct information. At the end, suggest a car to suit your customer's needs.

ALAMO RENT-A- CAR PRICES

Vehicle Type	Vehicle Group	Season	Vehicle Price	
			Per week	**Per day**
Economy	E4	Low	75	25
		High	100	40
Compact	C4	Low	100	40
		High	140	60
Midsize	I4	Low	140	60
		High	180	90
Full size	S4	Low	180	80
		High	210	105
Luxury, Convertible, or Minivan	LC IS LX	Low	360	150
		High	420	200

Prices and supplements shown are in US$ per car. Prices are exclusive of gasoline, insurance, and taxes.

You will be allocated a vehicle according to the number of people in your party (see paragraph headed **Car allocation**). To upgrade to a larger vehicle, the supplement may be calculated by taking the difference between your allocated car group and the group you require: e.g. a party of three will be allocated a group E4 car. To upgrade to a group I4 the supplement will be $50 per week or $12 per day in low season.

Low Season
Departures on or between 01 Jan – 14 Jul and 21 Aug – 19 Dec

High Season
Departures on or between 15 Jul – 20 Aug and 20 Dec – 31 Dec

Your choice of cars	Car allocation *The number of people in your party determines the car type included in your flight price*		Suggested maximum capacity
Economy GEO Metro or similar	A party of up to two adults or two adults and two children will be allocated a two-door Economy car (EC).		
Compact Chevrolet Cavalier or similar	A party of up to three adults and one child will be allocated a two-door Compact car (CC). A party of four adults will be allocated a four-door Compact car (C4).		
Midsize Pontiac Grand Am or similar	A party of up to four adults and one child will be allocated a four-door Midsize car (I4). Parties larger than this will be allocated more than one car.		
Full size Oldsmobile Ciera or similar	Available for any party size subject to payment of a supplement to upgrade.		
Luxury Cadillac Sedan De Ville or similar	Available for any party size subject to payment of a supplement to upgrade.		
Convertible Pontiac Sunbird or similar	Available for any party size subject to payment of a supplement to upgrade.		
Luxury Minivan Chevrolet Astrovan or similar	Available for any party size subject to payment of a supplement to upgrade.		

Finding out about prices and facilities (page 109)

Holiday 1 You are the travel agent. You are going to give information on facilities and prices at the Gateway Inn, Florida.

Holiday 2 When you have finished, take the role of a potential customer asking about facilities and prices for your family at the Villa Coral in Cuba. You can use your own or an imaginary family group. Think about how many people are in the party and what they like doing. Choose your own departure dates (November to April) and the length of your stay.

Ask about:
- watersports   - room facilities
- entertainment   - meal plan
- facilities for children - any supplements.

Find out the total cost.

GATEWAY INN *** Superior International Drive Area

Drive Times

Disney 20 mins.

Sea World 10 mins.

Universal 5 mins.

We've added this to our line-up because it's an excellent place for families – in fact it's the sort of hotel with so much to do even our kids could probably keep out of serious mischief! The bars are designed like an old-fashioned saloon, complete with dance hall, and Country and Western dance lessons. We've found it incredibly welcoming, with a lobby bar where you can meet people and make friends over a drink and a chat to compare notes.

- Two pools, pool bar
- Cafe, restaurant, saloon bar
- Volleyball, basketball, miniature golf; video games room
- Free transport to Disney, Seaworld, and Universal Studios and the Beiz factory outlet shopping mall
- **For children**: kids under 12 eat free from breakfast, dinner buffet, kids' pool, kids' check-in, free gift bag

Rooms: Prices are based on two adults sharing a room with two double beds, air-conditioning, colour TV, telephone, and bathroom.

Room only: Child prices, age limit 19

Accommodation	Gateway Inn room only					
Holiday Code	U00H09					
Accom./pers. share	Double room					
No. of nights	**7 nights** Adult	Child	**14 nights** Adult	Child	**Extra wk.** Adult	Child
1 Nov–9 Nov	**439**	269	**499**	269	–	–
10 Nov–16 Nov	**429**	269	**489**	269	**99**	29
17 Nov–23 Nov	**425**	249	**459**	249	**99**	29
24 Nov–30 Nov	**419**	249	**439**	249	**99**	29
1 Dec–7 Dec	**399**	199	**425**	199	**99**	29
8 Dec–14 Dec	**385**	199	**649**	349	**105**	29
15 Dec–21 Dec	**699**	449	**819**	449	**209**	99
22 Dec–28 Dec	**745**	449	**835**	449	**295**	199
29 Dec–4 Jan	**449**	299	**515**	299	**199**	149
5 Jan–18 Jan	**349**	249	**419**	249	**105**	49
19 Jan–1 Feb	**379**	249	**425**	249	**105**	29
2 Feb–8 Feb	**389**	249	**465**	299	**109**	29
9 Feb–15 Feb	**499**	299	**599**	299	**169**	49
16 Feb–1 Mar	**455**	249	**569**	245	**149**	29
2 Mar–14 Mar	**465**	249	**575**	249	**149**	29
15 Mar–21 Mar	**485**	229	**659**	429	**149**	29
22 Mar–28 Mar	**635**	429	**849**	449	**245**	149
29 Mar–30 Mar	**735**	449	**829**	449	**265**	199
31 Mar–19 Apr	**515**	249	**609**	249	**129**	29
Reduction per night	3rd adult £10.00					
Supplements per person per night	Sole use of room £10.00					

(Left vertical label: Departures/Extra Weeks commencing)

Bracketed figures apply for nights 2 Feb–30 Apr.

SECTION 2 Bookings and reservations

Output task

Making flight reservations (page 114-5)

Conversation 1

Customer	B

You want

– to fly to Sydney on 10 February
– a direct flight
– to arrive in Sydney in the evening

Talk to the travel agent. Make a note of the flight you choose (flight number, departure and arrival times, etc.).

Conversation 2

Customer	B

You want

– to book a return flight to Toronto departing on 1 June and returning on 20 June
– to fly first class on the outward journey
– to fly with a Canadian or British airline
– to arrive in Toronto before lunch if possible
– to leave Toronto in the early evening

Unit 9

SECTION 2 Sydney – where to stay and what to see

Reading and speaking

Accommodation in Sydney (page 126)

Group	B

For the first stage of the role-play, you are a tourist enquiring about moderately-priced hotels in Sydney. Decide what your particular needs are – refer to the table on page 126 to help you.

For the second stage of the role-play, you work at the accommodation desk of the Sydney Tourist Information Centre. Read the section on budget hotels on page 127 and fill in the accommodation information table.

SECTION 3 Theme park holidays

Reading and speaking

Accommodation options at Disneyland® Paris (page 132)

Group	B

Read the information about the Disneyland® Hotel, the Newport Bay Club, and the Hotel Cheyenne. Complete the table on page 132 for each of the accommodation types you read about.

Disneyland® Hotel

Prices from £263

With a distinctly turn-of-the-century Victorian ambience, this elegant and luxurious hotel enjoys panoramic views of the resort and is located at the gateway to the theme park.

This superb hotel is right at the centre of this fabulous resort. The stylish bedrooms have private facilities, TV with international channels, mini-bar, hair-dryer, telephone, and air-conditioning. All rooms have two large double beds suitable for families of up to four people.

The hotel boasts a heated indoor pool and a health club with sauna, jacuzzi, steam room, and gym (and at extra charge sunbed and massage). The elegant California Grill has dinner from FF260 (child menu FF110), whilst Inventions is a buffet restaurant offering dinner from FF250 (child menu FF140), and the Café Fantasia (breakfast from FF90, child FF50) has décor inspired by the film of the same name.

Guests may register credit card details on arrival to enable meals and other purchases throughout the resort to be charged to their room.

Room-only accommodation. Official classification four-star.

Newport Bay Club

Prices from £191

Designed in the grand tradition of a New England seaside resort, the Newport Bay Club has a charming yacht club atmosphere with a glass-enclosed pool pavilion.

At the southern end of Lake Disney, the Newport Bay Club is within 10 minutes' walk of the theme park and Festival Disney entertainment centre.

The smart bedrooms have a nautical flavour and are furnished with two large double beds. They have private bathroom, TV with international channels, mini-bar and air-conditioning.

There are ice machines on each floor and a coin-operated laundry.

Leisure facilities include a glorious heated indoor/outdoor swimming pool pavilion; health club with sauna, jacuzzi, gym and steam room (and at extra charge sunbed and massage) plus a children's playground.

The Cape Cod offers an American buffet-style menu from FF145 (child menu FF55), whilst the Yacht Club is a speciality steak and seafood restaurant, breakfast from FF60 (child FF40), dinner from FF175 and Fisherman's Wharf has cocktails, piano music, and panoramic views. Guests may register credit card details on arrival to enable meals and purchases throughout the resort to be charged to their room.

Room-only accommodation. Official classification three-star.

Hotel Cheyenne

Prices from £174

Like a scene from a Wild West movie, the fourteen frontier-style buildings of the Hotel Cheyenne are grouped around a Main Street of wooden walkways and covered porches, behind which lie the Indian village and Fort Apache play area.

The Hotel Cheyenne stands on the left bank of the Rio Grande river. It is superbly themed and the Western styling runs right through to the bedrooms. They are especially suitable for families, with one double bed and two bunk beds in every room. In fact, the bunk beds are even large enough for adults who wish to share a room. They have private bathrooms (bath and shower), ceiling paddle fan, TV with international channels, and telephone.

You can eat at the Texas-style Chuckwagon Café with its BBQ specialities, breakfast from FF45 (child FF35), dinner from FF100 (child menu FF55), and enjoy country music at the Red Garter Saloon. There is a coin-operated guest laundry available within the hotel.

Room-only accommodation. Official classification two-star.

Output task

Additional arrangements (page 144)

Representative　B

Read the information about The George of Stamford, the Glenkinchie Distillery, and Loch Lomond Boat Tours. Answer the guide's questions. Also, find out the information from the guide so that you can fill in the chart below.

The George of Stamford

PERIOD CHARM and modern comfort come in equal measure at this delightful eighteenth-century coaching inn, where a gallows sign across the road offers a warning to any prospective highwaymen. Characterful public rooms include two inviting lounges, one conservatory-style with exotic plants, a stylish cocktail bar, and a cosy little beamed snug. The pretty walled garden is just the place for sitting in summer.

GROUPS CATERED FOR PRIVATELY

Try our NEW coffee shop! Fresh coffee and home-made biscuits

£1.50

Whisky made in the traditional way!

Glenkinchie

LOWLAND SINGLE MALT SCOTCH WHISKY

DISTILLERY TOURS

Enjoy a fascinating guided tour of GLENKINCHIE DISTILLERY and sample its unique single malt whisky. Our superb distillery museum is open through the year.

Guided tours Mon.–Fri. from 09.30–16.30 (other times by appointment)

❁Free tours ❁Visitor centre ❁Car parking ❁Shop ❁Distillery museum ❁Bowling green ❁Picnic site

NB For group visits please arrange in advance.

FREE TASTING!!

Loch Lomond Boat Tours

Why not bring your group on a romantic steamer cruise? Enjoy the scenic beauty of Loch Lomond, 'Queen of the Scottish Lakes', 24 miles long. See the haunting beauty of Lennox Castle! Gaze at the height of Ben Lomond!

The one-hour cruise costs £4.00, and we pay 10% commission on pre-booked groups of 20 or more.

	The George of Stamford	Glenkinchie Distillery	Loch Lomond Boat Tours
Name of group			
Date of arrival			
Time of arrival			
Service required			
Number of people			
Special notes			

Tapescripts

Listening 1   Unit 1
Personal experiences

1

JUAN MENACHO GONZÁLEZ I finished my studies at the School of Tourism in Spain last year and I've just started my first job in a travel agency. It's fun. I love helping people to decide which places to visit. I've always loved travelling myself. I've been to most parts of Europe and also to Egypt. I think Egypt is my favourite. I went there last year and had a wonderful time. I saw the Pyramids, the Sphinx, and the Valley of the Kings. I'm very interested in ancient civilizations. So maybe in the future I'd like to get a job in Egypt.

2

ULLA LINDSTRÖM I travel a lot on business, especially to Japan. I like travelling, but in fact I'm not very fond of flying – it gets very boring after a while, and I can't stand airline food. But I don't mind it most of the time – at least I get to see the world. I particularly like the Far East. I'm fascinated by the mixture of ancient and modern civilizations – things like ancient historic temples right next to sophisticated up-to-date technology. Last year, for the first time, I actually had a holiday in Japan, and it was so interesting. I hope that one day I'll be able to spend a whole year out there.

3

ANITA CLAYTON I haven't travelled a lot, but I really want to. I've been to Amsterdam, mainly because I love art galleries. I'm a real art freak! My favourite place in the world is the Van Gogh Museum. I went to Paris when I was a little girl, but I can't really remember much about it. I really want to see a bit more of Europe. I've just applied for a job as a tour rep in Greece. I hope I get it. My sister's a rep. She's spent the last three summers in Turkey and she loves it.

4

PAOLA GALLIZIA I travel a lot in my job, of course, and I've visited a lot of different places. I've been working mainly on long-haul flights to Central and South America for the past few months. Last month, for example, I spent a lot of time in Mexico City, but I think my favourite place is Rio – it's so full of life and excitement. I stayed there during the carnival and it was absolutely incredible! If you ever get the chance, you should go.

Pronunciation focus 2   Unit 1

destination	resort
brochure	excursion
charter	itinerary
festival	sightseeing
currency	visa
self-catering	museum
heritage	

Listening 2   Unit 1
Imnarja festival

Right, everyone, while we're driving along here I want to tell you about one of the local island festivals that is happening this weekend. This is the Imnarja festival or, as it's officially known, the Feast of St Peter and St Paul.

Let me start by saying that this is probably the most exciting festival on the island. It coincides with the end of the harvest and essentially it is a folk festival, where the crops are laid out on display and there is a lot of eating, drinking wine, and singing and dancing. The name 'Imnarja' comes from the Italian word *luminaria*, or illuminations, because in the old days torches and bonfires were lit on the ramparts of the city of Mdina on the night of the festival.

What happens is this. On the weekend closest to St John's day, the 24th of June – so that's this weekend – the festival is opened by a simple ceremony known as the Bandu. When you see this you'll see a procession with lots of people parading brightly-coloured banners which will later be given as prizes to winners of the horse races – the horse races are the main part of the festival and they take place on the last day.

You're probably wondering about the food and drink, and of course no festival is complete without a feast. On the evening before the races there's a big party in the Buskett Gardens. Vegetables, fruit, poultry, honey, and wine are laid out on display, and there are stalls which are set up selling delicious local cakes, pastries, and sweets. Everybody gathers round to cook the favourite Maltese dish of fried rabbit. And then there is a party which lasts all night, with music and dancing, and a lot of Maltese wine is drunk.

On the following day you have the climax of the festival, when the horse and donkey races are held along Rabat's Racecourse Street. Traditionally the animals are ridden bareback, and the jockeys have a stick in both hands to encourage the animals. At the end of the races the banners are handed out at the foot of the hill. In the old days it was from here that the Grand Masters and the other important people used to watch the races. Another interesting thing is that the winners take their banners to be displayed in their church for the rest of the year.

So, as you can see, it's well worth visiting. It's a very spectacular occasion, and we will be arranging special excursions. If you want to come along please reserve your place at hotel reception.

OK. Let's move on. Now we're coming to another interesting part of the island …

Listening 1   Unit 2

A passenger survey at an airport

Interview 1

INTERVIEWER Excuse me. Could I ask you a few questions? I'm doing a passenger survey on behalf of the Tourist Board and the airport to help plan our services.

WOMAN Right.

INTERVIEWER First of all, could you tell me where you're going?

WOMAN Yes, we're off to Corfu.

INTERVIEWER And what is the purpose of your visit?

WOMAN We're going on holiday. It's our first trip abroad, as a matter of fact.

INTERVIEWER You must be very excited. How long are you staying in Corfu?

MAN Two weeks.

INTERVIEWER Thank you. And this is your daughter? (Yes.) Is there anyone else in the party?

WOMAN No, just the three of us.

INTERVIEWER How did you get to the airport?

WOMAN On the train.

INTERVIEWER OK. We've nearly finished now. Could you tell me your occupation?

WOMAN I work part-time in a supermarket and my husband's a chef in a hotel.

INTERVIEWER Right. Finally, would you mind telling me how old you are?

WOMAN We're both twenty-nine and Sarah here's six.

INTERVIEWER Great. Thanks. Well, I hope you have a lovely holiday.

WOMAN Thank you. We'll try!

Interview 2

INTERVIEWER Excuse me, sir. Could I ask you some questions?

MAN Certainly, dear. I've got plenty of time – my flight doesn't leave for another hour. I got here a bit early – didn't want to be late, you know.

INTERVIEWER OK, first question. Where are you going?

MAN I'm off to Australia, to Melbourne. I'm going to see my sister and her family. I haven't seen her for twenty-five years. But I retired recently and I thought, well, I've got the money, so why not?

INTERVIEWER I think that's great! So how long are you planning to stay in Australia?

MAN Well, I've got a return ticket to come back in a month's time, but if all goes well I might stay a bit longer. It's a bit of a risk, you know. I don't really know what my sister's like any more – or her family. I've never seen her children and I've only met her husband once.

INTERVIEWER Yes, it's always a bit of an unknown. Anyway, just a couple more questions. How did you get to the airport?

MAN My son gave me a lift.

INTERVIEWER OK. And finally, would you mind telling me how old you are?

MAN Twenty-one, dear. No, I'm only joking. I'm sixty-five – sixty-six next month.

INTERVIEWER Thank you. I hope you have a wonderful time.

MAN Thank you. So do I!

Interview 3

INTERVIEWER Excuse me, madam. I wonder if you'd mind answering some questions?

WOMAN Er … OK. Will it take long?

INTERVIEWER No, just a few minutes. Could you tell me where you're travelling to?

WOMAN Frankfurt.

INTERVIEWER And are you travelling on business?

WOMAN Well, actually I'm going home. I've been here on business – at a meeting with our partners in the UK.

INTERVIEWER I see. So how long did you stay in the UK?

WOMAN For just two days.

INTERVIEWER Thank you. And could you tell me if you're travelling alone?

WOMAN Yes, I am.

INTERVIEWER OK, nearly finished. Can you tell me how you got to the airport?

WOMAN By taxi, from my hotel.

INTERVIEWER Good. Finally – occupation. I know you're in business.

WOMAN Yes, I'm a Marketing Manager for a company making pharmaceuticals.

INTERVIEWER And can I ask which of these age groups you're in?

WOMAN Here – thirty to thirty-nine.

INTERVIEWER Right. Thank you very much. Have a pleasant journey.

Interview 4

INTERVIEWER Excuse me. Do you have a few minutes to answer some questions?

YOUNG MAN Yes, I think so.

INTERVIEWER Thank you. I'm conducting a passenger survey.

YOUNG MAN Right.

INTERVIEWER Can you tell me where you're going to?

YOUNG MAN To St Petersburg.

INTERVIEWER St Petersburg – and what's the reason for the trip?

YOUNG MAN I'm going out to teach – to teach English. I've just qualified, so it's my first job abroad.

INTERVIEWER You must be excited.

YOUNG MAN Yes, excited, and a little bit apprehensive to be honest. It's a big commitment – I've signed a twelve-month contract.

INTERVIEWER So you're staying for a year?

YOUNG MAN That's the plan. If it all works out.

INTERVIEWER And are you travelling on your own?

YOUNG MAN Yes.

INTERVIEWER And can you tell me how you got to the airport?

YOUNG MAN I came on the coach – it's cheaper than the train.

INTERVIEWER Right, I think I've got everything. Just one last question – could you tell me your age?

YOUNG MAN I'm twenty-four.

INTERVIEWER Good, well thank you very much, and I hope it all goes well for you in Russia.

YOUNG MAN Thanks.

Pronunciation focus 1   Unit 2

a Could you tell me where you're going?
   Could you tell me where you're going?

b Would you mind filling in this form?
   Would you mind filling in this form?

c Could you tell me how old you are?
   Could you tell me how old you are?

d Could you possibly turn the radio down?
   Could you possibly turn the radio down?

Could you tell me where you're going?

Could you tell me where you're going?
Of course. I'm flying to Brussels.

Listening 2   Unit 2

Identifying jobs and situations

Conversation 1

RECEPTIONIST Is that a double or a single?

GUEST Double.

RECEPTIONIST And will you be requiring continental or cooked breakfast in the morning?

GUEST Continental, please.

RECEPTIONIST And newspapers?

GUEST No, thank you.

RECEPTIONIST OK. Can you sign here … ? Thank you. Right, here's your key. The lifts are over there on the left. If you leave your luggage here I'll get the porter to bring it up to you. Have a pleasant stay.

GUEST Thank you.

Conversation 2

CUSTOMER We were thinking of a city, but not too hot and crowded.

TRAVEL AGENT Have you thought of Paris? It's not too hot at this time of year. Or Scandinavia – you could always try Stockholm or Oslo.

CUSTOMER That's an idea. Could you give us some prices?

TRAVEL AGENT Right. Let's see what's available … there's a weekend break in Stockholm, two nights' accommodation, return flights for 379 pounds. No meals except breakfast, but there's a guided tour of the city included … .

Conversation 3

PASSENGER Could I possibly have a glass of water?

FLIGHT ATTENDANT Certainly, sir. Still or sparkling?

PASSENGER Oh, still, please. Could you hurry – I'm feeling a bit sick.

FLIGHT ATTENDANT Of course. Shall I get you a blanket as well?

PASSENGER No, I'm all right – just the water. It's just that it's a bit bumpy back here.

FLIGHT ATTENDANT Right, I'll get it straightaway. We'll be landing in about twenty minutes – I'm sure you'll be fine then.

Conversation 4

PASSENGER I really couldn't sleep a wink last night. The noise was terrible!

PURSER I'm sorry to hear that, sir. It was a bit stormy last night.

PASSENGER It wasn't the storm – it was the engines. Now, I insist you move me immediately.

PURSER Well, I don't think it would be very different in any of the other cabins – the lower decks are a bit noisier sometimes, I'm afraid.

PASSENGER What about the upper decks?

PURSER Well, there would be a supplement, and in any case I'm afraid they're fully booked.

PASSENGER I don't believe it! Well, if it's noisy again tonight I shall complain to the captain!

Conversation 5

A If you ask me, we need to be attracting more business clients. There's a lot of good conference facilities in the area.

B Yes, I agree. I had a meeting with some of the local hoteliers recently and they were very keen to bring in more conference business.

C You've got a point, but the problem is transport. We haven't got an airport nearby – we haven't even got a decent rail link.

B But there's the motorway, and it's only a two-hour drive from places like Birmingham and Manchester.

C Two hours! More like three or four! No, if you want my opinion, this region is always going to depend on the family holiday trade. Now, I think what we could do is promote more in certain European countries, like … .

Listening 1   Unit 3
Booking a holiday

TRAVEL AGENT Hello, can I help you?

CUSTOMER Yes, we're looking for a holiday in November, somewhere hot – you know, near a beach and all that, but not too far away if possible.

TRAVEL AGENT OK, well, what about going to the Canaries? They're warm throughout the year and they're very interesting.

CUSTOMER Yes, we thought that. In fact we saw this ad here for Tenerife – Playa de las Américas. It seemed very reasonable.

TRAVEL AGENT OK, I'll check availability for you … No, I'm sorry they've all gone. It was a special offer. There's plenty more choice in the Canaries, though. But, I wonder, have you thought of going to The Gambia? It's very reasonably priced and you're guaranteed sun.

CUSTOMER Yes, but it's a long flight, isn't it?

TRAVEL AGENT It is a six-hour flight, you're right. OK, let's stay with the Canaries. What type of accommodation are you looking for? Something with a bit of life or something more relaxing?

CUSTOMER We want somewhere quiet but with some facilities – restaurants and things like that.

TRAVEL AGENT How about La Gomera? It's a small island, very quiet but with things going on and very pretty. The only problem is that there are no direct flights, so you have to get a ferry from Tenerife.

CUSTOMER Mmmm. We've only got a week so we need somewhere with a direct flight.

TRAVEL AGENT You could try Lanzarote. There are some very peaceful parts. I think you'd like it. We often recommend Playa Blanca – there's a great hotel there called the Lanzarote Princess. All the usual facilities, near the beach, but very tastefully designed and built. Here's a picture – it's fairly cheap as well, as you can see.

CUSTOMER Mm. Sounds good.

TRAVEL AGENT I'll check availability for you … Would you want a twin room with a balcony?

CUSTOMER Yes.

TRAVEL AGENT Bed and breakfast or half-board?

CUSTOMER Er … I'm not sure.

TRAVEL AGENT If I were you, I'd choose B&B, then you can eat out in the restaurants at night. That way you'll see a bit of the local life.

CUSTOMER OK – bed and breakfast.

TRAVEL AGENT I'm sorry, did you say you wanted a balcony?

CUSTOMER Yes, we did.

TRAVEL AGENT OK. There's availablity on the 14th of November. Flight from Gatwick at 09.35 arriving 13.30 local time. Returning on the 21st of November, departing Lanzarote 15.00 and arriving at Gatwick at 19.00.

CUSTOMER That's good – no night flights.

TRAVEL AGENT Do you want to confirm it?

CUSTOMER Can we think about it?

TRAVEL AGENT Of course. I can put a 24-hour hold on your reservation, and you can let me know tomorrow.

CUSTOMER Yes, that's a good idea. We're not committed then, are we?

TRAVEL AGENT No, you're not. You can make your minds up in your own time. Can I just take some details? What name is it?

CUSTOMER John and Amanda Hollins.

TRAVEL AGENT That's H-O-L-L-I-N-S?

CUSTOMER Right.

TRAVEL AGENT And a daytime phone number?

CUSTOMER 340 0838.

TRAVEL AGENT OK. What I'll do is hold this for 24 hours. If you could phone us tomorrow and tell us if you want to confirm the booking we'll take some more details then. I'll just give you the booking reference number. It's 17583.

CUSTOMER 17583. Great, thanks. I'll call you tomorrow. Thanks for your help.

TRAVEL AGENT You're welcome. Goodbye.

Pronunciation focus 1   Unit 3

<u>Can</u> I help you?

OK, well, what <u>about</u> going <u>to</u> the Canaries?

Have you thought <u>of</u> going <u>to</u> The Gambia?

<u>Can</u> I just take <u>some</u> details?

Listening 2   Unit 3

The needs of the business traveller

INTERVIEWER Mark, your company specializes in corporate travel. What exactly does that mean?

MARK Well, we aim to look after all the needs of the business traveller. That includes booking flights and hotels, planning and arranging itineraries, advising on locations, sorting out conference venues, providing VIP services, arranging visas and insurance, and so on.

INTERVIEWER Quite a range.

MARK Yes. What we're doing really, is offering a complete package for the business traveller so that he or she can concentrate on the business while we look after the travel.

INTERVIEWER Do you find that the needs of the business traveller are different from the ordinary tourist?

MARK Yes, quite different. To start with, we don't usually deal directly with the person who's going to be using our services – it's more likely to be a secretary or an assistant who makes the arrangements. Also, for the ordinary tourist the arrangements for the flights, the hotel, the resort, or whatever are all part of the fun, and they want to spend time choosing them. But for the business traveller they're just a means to an end. First and foremost what the business traveller wants is speed and efficiency. One of the most common requests is a reservation at short notice, and we pride ourselves on being able to provide this.

INTERVIEWER Do you have any special ways of doing this?

MARK Well, we keep detailed records of a client's history, all their preferences and particular needs, so we know which airline they prefer to fly with, which class they want to fly, and so on. With corporate travel the secret is knowing your customer and being able to provide the full range of services for their needs. We take over the whole contract for a company's business travel arrangements. In return we can offer attractions like discounts and extended credit.

INTERVIEWER What exactly is extended credit?

MARK It means we can set up an account and give the client a longer period to pay, sometimes as much as ten weeks. The ordinary tourist usually has to settle up eight weeks before departure.

INTERVIEWER I see. And in general, what things are most important for business travellers?

MARK It's difficult to generalize, but it's probably flight times – they want to have a choice of times. That and a speedy transfer through the airport, so if we can ensure express check-in and check-out it's a bonus. Things like good food and free champagne aren't as important as some advertisers want you to think.

INTERVIEWER What about upgrades?

MARK Yes, they're quite important. Automatic upgrades, which some airlines offer, are especially important for the frequent traveller. We always make sure we know which airlines have special promotions on, because you often get good deals which can save the client money.

INTERVIEWER Could you tell me something about what the business traveller looks for in the hotel accommodation that you arrange?

MARK Number one is location – not far from the airport and not far from the city centre, or wherever they're doing business. That's assuming, of course, that the hotel has everything that we would regard as essential, such as en suite facilities, and access to fax and modem.

INTERVIEWER What about things like meeting rooms and business suites?

MARK Yes, well they can be important, depending on the purpose of the trip. But I would say that comfort is probably more important. You often find that particular clients are very loyal to certain hotel chains, partly because they can often get better deals through 'Priority Clubs' – you know, things like discounts, and express check-in and check-out – also because they like to know what to expect, a sort of home from home. So once again it pays to keep our client history records up to date.

INTERVIEWER Right, thanks, Mark. Good luck with the business.

MARK Thanks.

Listening 3   Unit 3

US visa requirements

This is the American Embassy visa information line. This service includes information on various types of visa and related matters.

A visa is not required for British citizens for most holidays and business visits of ninety days or less. In total citizens of twenty-five countries are able to travel to the US without a visa. You must be a citizen of one of the following countries: the United Kingdom, Andorra, Argentina, Australia, Austria, Belgium, Brunei, Denmark, Finland, France, Germany, Iceland, Ireland, Italy, Japan, Liechtenstein, Luxembourg, Monaco, the Netherlands, New Zealand, Norway, San Marino, Spain, Sweden, and Switzerland.

In addition to being a citizen of a qualifying visa-free travel country, you cannot stay in the US for longer than ninety days, you cannot perform productive work, and you are not allowed to accept paid or unpaid employment while in the US. If you are entering by air or sea (including ferry) you must hold a return ticket or an onward ticket, and you must enter on board an air or sea carrier that has agreed to participate in the programme. Please check with your airline to make sure they participate in the programme. If your onward ticket terminates in Canada, Mexico, Bermuda, or one of the Caribbean Islands, you must be a resident of that country of destination. You must carry an unexpired passport valid for more than ninety days. If you are entering the US overland from Canada or Mexico you don't need to have a visa. However, you need to complete a visa-waiver application form at the border crossing. Once you enter the US you may make side-trips to Canada, Mexico, and the Caribbean Islands and return without needing a visa.

If you are not a citizen of one of the countries named, or you plan to be in the US for longer than ninety days, you need a visa. A B1/B2 visitor's visa is the appropriate visa for holiday and business visits. You cannot perform productive work or accept paid or unpaid employment while in the US.

If you require a visa for travel to the US the embassy strongly recommends that you obtain a visa before purchasing your ticket. You may apply for a visa through the post. Unfortunately, because of the high demand, an appointment to apply in person at the embassy may not be available for several weeks. In addition, those who have been refused visas twice in the past six months are not eligible for further consideration.

Please note that applications by post take three weeks. To apply by post, please send a completed visa application form, your passport, a receipt showing payment of the visa application fee, a passport-sized colour photo, and a stamped self-addressed envelope to the following address: Visa Branch, US Embassy, 5 Upper Grosvenor Street, London W1A 2JB.

Pronunciation focus 2   Unit 3

Could you hold on a moment?
I'll just put you through.
Could you call back a little later?
I'll get back to you this afternoon.
He's really busy, so don't be surprised if he's late.

Listening 1   Unit 4

Travel agents and tour operators

The difference between a tour operator and a travel agent? Well, it's quite simple, really. Obviously there is a lot of overlap between the two roles, but basically, a tour operator buys the separate elements of transport, accommodation, and other services, and combines them into a package. A travel agent sells this product and other services to the public, and provides a convenient location, such as a shop or office, for the purchase of travel.

If you imagine how a car is made and sold, the tour operator is like the factory where the different pieces of the car are assembled. The travel agent is like the car showroom which sells the finished product.

So a tour operator will have to do things like decide what tours and holidays to organize – it might be inclusive tours, or independent holidays. They'll probably investigate and research new markets to find out what people actually want. Then, when they're putting together a tour, they'll have to negotiate with the various airline companies and hotels and other principals, as we call them, in order to get good bulk purchase deals. They'll probably charter aircraft, and later on they'll need to recruit and train staff to be resort representatives, guides, and so on. When that's all sorted out and they've signed contracts with the principals, they'll be able to concentrate more on promotion – designing and printing a brochure, and planning an advertising campaign. Once the tours are being sold, the tour operator deals more directly with the agent in accepting bookings. They have to continue to work with the principals – sending room lists, flight manifests, that sort of thing.

So a tour operator doesn't usually have so much direct contact with the customer. The travel agent, on the other hand, is in direct contact with the customer, advising on resorts, carriers, and travel facilities in general, helping to plan itineraries for customers, arranging corporate travel.

Then, when they're actually selling holidays, inclusive tours, air tickets, or whatever, they'll be involved in recording and confirming reservations, sending invoices to customers, and issuing tickets and vouchers. They're also involved in ancillary services like arranging car hire or selling insurance. And plenty of other things as well, from ordering stocks of brochures for rack display to making sure the windows are kept clean!

Listening 2   Unit 4

Preliminary negotiations

PETER Peter Nicholson.

CARLA Hello Peter. This is Carla Manson from Flights of Fancy.

PETER Oh, hello. We met last year, didn't we? How are things going?

CARLA Not too bad. We've had a pretty good year.

PETER That's good. I heard you sold all your allocation on our Far East routes. I've just been looking at the figures.

CARLA That's why I was calling, actually. I thought we ought to meet to discuss charter arrangements for next season.

PETER Yes, that's a good idea. Shall we fix a time now? I've got my diary here.

CARLA What about next week – say, Thursday?

PETER That's the 28th, isn't it? No, I'm sorry, I'm busy all day. Could you make the following Thursday – that's the 4th of April?

CARLA No, that's not very convenient. I could do the Friday, though.

PETER Yes, that looks good. Shall we say 10.30?

CARLA Fine. I'll come to your offices, shall I?

PETER If you don't mind. You remember where we are?

CARLA Yes. I thought it might be useful to sort out the basic agenda now, if that's all right with you. I'd rather know in advance what'll be coming up. Then we can both be prepared and get down to business quickly.

PETER Good point.

CARLA I think we should start with a review of last year.

PETER Yes, I agree. I've got most of the reports in. I can make sure I've got them all together by the 5th.

CARLA OK, I'll have our reports too. Then I suggest we look at the question of seat rates and the size of our booking next year. Obviously we're looking for a more favourable rate if we take a larger block of seats.

PETER Well, I understand what you're saying. We can certainly look at that. I think we'll have to take into account release dates and cancellation charges.

CARLA OK, point taken. My directors also wanted me to bring up the matter of time slots. We'd have preferred some better departure times last year – there was quite a lot of customer dissatisfaction with some of the departure and arrival times. We felt we got a bit of a raw deal to be honest.

PETER Well, maybe, but you've got to remember that on long-haul flights there's always going to be some inconvenience on timings, either when you leave or when you arrive.

CARLA I'm not so sure, but in any case we can discuss that at the meeting.

PETER Of course. Are there any other points you think we should discuss?

CARLA Just one other main one really. I thought it would be a good idea to look at the on-board extras – meals, drinks, movies, that sort of thing. We want to go a bit up-market this year, and stress the comfort and luxury of the whole package, including the flight. I'm sure you'll agree we can make the flight itself a selling point – especially with an airline with your reputation!

PETER Hmm, flattery won't get you anywhere! But sure, let's look at the whole flight package. So, is that everything?

CARLA I think so. We've got a pretty full agenda there.

PETER Yes. Will you be coming alone?

CARLA No, I'll probably bring my assistant, Jo Greenyer. She's new to the company and it'll be good experience for her.

PETER OK. It'll probably just be me on our side, although I'll make sure I have someone there to take minutes. I'll also bring along the proposed flight schedules so we can look at that question of time slots.

CARLA I'll bring our draft brochure for you to look at as well. And the reports I mentioned.

PETER Good, that all sounds fine. So I'll see you at 10.30 on the 5th of April.

CARLA OK, see you then. Bye.

PETER Bye.

Pronunciation focus 1   Unit 4

1 Not too bad. We've had a pretty good year.
2 I'd rather know in advance what'll be coming up.

3 We'd have preferred some better departure times.

4 I'm sure you'll agree we can make the flight itself a selling point.

Listening 3 — Unit 4

Three complaints

Conversation 1

TOUR REP Hello. Have you settled in OK? Is everything all right?

GUEST Well, seeing as you ask, no it's not. I'm afraid we're not very happy with the hotel so far. In fact, to be honest, it's a disgrace.

TOUR REP Oh dear, I'm sorry to hear that. What exactly is the problem?

GUEST The noise for a start. There was disco music until three o'clock this morning – right under our room! And then at eight o'clock the builders started with their drills. I didn't pay all this money to stay in a building site, and frankly I want to know what you're going to do about it! Your company certainly didn't mention anything about building work in their brochure.

TOUR REP OK, look, I'm really very sorry. Let me take some details. What room are you in?

GUEST 209.

TOUR REP Oh yes, it's Mr and Mrs Pratt, isn't it?

GUEST That's right. Now can you do anything or not?

TOUR REP Well, I'll see if I can sort it out. I know the hotel is very full at the moment, but I'll talk to the management and see if we can move you to a quieter room. There's a much quieter area over on the other side of the pool.

GUEST That would be something, I suppose.

TOUR REP If you wait here I'll go and talk to the manager right away. Perhaps you'd like a coffee on the house while you're waiting?

GUEST OK.

TOUR REP I'll be right back.

Conversation 2

PASSENGER Are you supposed to be in charge here?

AIRLINE REP Yes, madam. How can I help you?

PASSENGER I've just been told by that person over there that I can't check in. Some story about the flight being overbooked. She says I've got to wait until seven o'clock tonight!

AIRLINE REP I see. That sounds unfortunate.

PASSENGER Unfortunate! It's a disaster. I've got a meeting in Stockholm at eight o'clock tomorrow morning. I'll be exhausted – that's if I ever get there!

AIRLINE REP Let me see if I can help. I just need a few particulars. Were you booked on flight SA716?

PASSENGER Yes, I was.

AIRLINE REP Ah, well, I'm terribly sorry, but there has been a bit of a problem.

PASSENGER What do you mean?

AIRLINE REP If I could just explain – I'm afraid there was a technical fault on the plane you were meant to be on and we have had to replace it with another one, which unfortunately is not so big.

PASSENGER I don't believe it! So because of that I've got to wait another six hours?

AIRLINE REP I may be able to help. Just have a seat. This is what I'll do – I'll have a word with another airline and see if we can squeeze you onto an earlier flight.

Conversation 3

JOHN FRASER Hello.

MIKE STAKIS Hello, Mike Stakis here from the Opal Beach Hotel. Is that John Fraser?

JOHN FRASER Yes, it is. How are you, Mike?

MIKE STAKIS Fine. John, I'm sorry to trouble you but there seems to be a problem. Have you got a moment?

JOHN FRASER Sure. What's up?

MIKE STAKIS I've just been looking at your new brochure.

JOHN FRASER Oh yes, do you like it?

MIKE STAKIS It looks very nice, but I don't like the way you've featured the Opal Beach.

JOHN FRASER Really? I'm sorry to hear that. What do you mean exactly?

MIKE STAKIS I thought we'd agreed that you'd make us the main hotel for the resort, but in the brochure you've got the Coral Sands at the top – and with a bigger picture.

JOHN FRASER Mike, I'm sorry you feel like this, but I don't remember agreeing to anything like that – I remember proposing it, if we got a better room rate – but you said you couldn't bring the price down.

MIKE STAKIS John, you know me, I'm not one to complain, but I've got my notes here in front of me – you agreed to give us a special promotion anyway.

JOHN FRASER And my notes appear to say something different. Look, I don't want to argue about this. I'll tell you what I'll do. I'll change it for the next print run – we only did a small run this time in any case. I'll put you at the top, next to the Coral Sands. Unless of course you can reconsider that proposal about room rates – then you can have the top slot to yourself.

MIKE STAKIS You don't miss a trick! Well, I'll think about it … .

Listening 1 — Unit 5

Airport announcements

Announcement 1

Passengers are reminded that smoking is not permitted in any part of the terminal building.

Announcement 2

Will passenger Eckber from Miami please go to Airport Information where your tour leader is waiting. Passenger Eckber to Airport Information.

Announcement 3

This is a staff call. Will Roger Broom please go to the Baggage Hall immediately. Roger Broom to the Baggage Hall.

Announcement 4

This is the final call for flight IB763 to Madrid. Will any remaining passengers please proceed immediately to gate number 14 where the aircraft is about to depart.

Announcement 5

British Airways regret to announce the delay of flight BA008 to New York. Passengers should report with their boarding cards to the BA desk where vouchers for refreshments will be given. We would like to apologize for any inconvenience.

Announcement 6

This is a security announcement. Passengers are reminded not to leave baggage unattended at any time. Any unattended baggage will be removed and may be destroyed.

Pronunciation focus — Unit 5

1 It all starts with the pre-flight briefing when we go through the detailed arrangments for the whole flight.

2 The next stage is the briefing for take-off.

3 While all this is going on we're getting instructions from air traffic control.

4 Later on, the original crew take over control again and then we go through the briefing for landing.

5 The final stage is that we have to park the plane.

Output task, exercise 4   Unit 5
Passenger safety briefing

Ladies and gentlemen.

This announcement contains important safety information. Your hand baggage must not obstruct aisles or emergency exits, and must be placed under the seat in front of you or in the overhead locker.

In your seat area there is a safety card which contains details of escape routes, oxygen masks, and life-jackets. Please study it carefully.

Emergency exits are located on both sides of the aircraft. They are clearly marked and are being pointed out to you now.

In the unlikely event of having to use an escape slide, please leave all hand baggage behind, and ladies remove high-heeled shoes.

Please now ensure your table is folded away, your seat back upright with the armrests down, and your seat-belt fastened. The seat-belt is fastened and adjusted like this … and unfastened like this … Whenever the 'Fasten Seat-belt' signs are on you must return to your seat and fasten your belt securely.

If for any reason the air supply fails, oxygen will be provided. Masks like this … will appear automatically. When you see the masks, remain seated and quickly cover your mouth and nose like this … and breathe normally. Pulling the mask to your face opens the oxygen supply. Do not smoke when oxygen is in use.

Your life-jacket is stowed under your seat. When directed to do so by the crew, remove the life-jacket from its container and pull it over your head … Pull the tapes down, passing them around your waist and tying them securely in a double bow at the side … To inflate, pull the red toggle as shown … If necessary, the air can be topped up by using this mouthpiece … There is a whistle here … for attracting attention. Do not inflate your life-jacket until you are outside the aircraft. Junior life-jackets are carried for the use of small children.

Thank you for your attention.

Listening 2   Unit 5
At the check-in desk

Dialogue 1
CHECK-IN CLERK Good morning.
PASSENGER Good morning. Is this the check-in for BA113 to Paris?
CHECK-IN CLERK It is. Can I see your ticket?
PASSENGER Sure, here you are.
CHECK-IN CLERK Thank you. Can you put your suitcases on the baggage scales?
PASSENGER OK.
CHECK-IN CLERK Three cases. Hmmm. They're a bit heavy. You'll have to pay an excess baggage charge, I'm afraid.
PASSENGER Oh dear. What's the limit then?
CHECK-IN CLERK Thirty kilos on this flight. And you have nearly forty kilos.
PASSENGER How much do I have to pay then? Or can I take this one on as hand baggage?
CHECK-IN CLERK I suppose so – if you put your other bag inside it.
PASSENGER OK. Yes, it fits. Is that under thirty kilos now?
CHECK-IN CLERK Yes, just about.
PASSENGER Good, that's saved some money! Thank you very much indeed.
CHECK-IN CLERK Now, would you like an aisle seat or a window seat …?

Dialogue 2
CHECK-IN CLERK Unfortunately, I can't put you all together.
PASSENGER What!
CHECK-IN CLERK I can do two in row 6 and two in row 11.
PASSENGER Oh no! Can't you do anything else? It's an eight-hour flight to Orlando. We don't want to be separated for that length of time.
CHECK-IN CLERK Well, I don't think there's any other possibility, I'm afraid. As I said, I haven't got four seats together.
PASSENGER That isn't good enough. Isn't there something else you can do?
CHECK-IN CLERK Let me see. Well, what about two together in row 14 – an aisle seat and a middle seat – and two aisle seats in 13 and 15. At least you'd be able to talk to each other.
PASSENGER OK, I suppose that'll do if you've nothing better, but I would have thought that as we got here two hours before the flight we'd have been able to sit in the same row … .

Dialogue 3
CHECK-IN CLERK Would you like a window seat or an aisle seat?
PASSENGER Could I have an aisle seat, please?
CHECK-IN CLERK Of course. Seat 15C.
PASSENGER Good, because I want to keep my guitar with me.
CHECK-IN CLERK Oh, I'm sorry. You won't be able to put anything in the aisle.
PASSENGER Really? Yes, of course, I didn't really think. But what do I do with this guitar case?
CHECK-IN CLERK I'll have to check it in with your suitcase.
PASSENGER But I don't really want it to get damaged in the hold – it's very valuable to me personally.
CHECK-IN CLERK I'm sure it'll be safe.
PASSENGER Hmm, I don't know … .
CHECK-IN CLERK Well, what you could do is check it in with one of the ground staff just before you board the plane. They'll put it in a special place in the hold reserved for fragile items.
PASSENGER OK, I guess that's all right.
CHECK-IN CLERK Right, I'll just put this tag on.
PASSENGER Thank you.
CHECK-IN CLERK And here's your boarding pass … .

Listening 3   Unit 5
Could you be a flight attendant?

INTERVIEWER Right, let's look at what it takes to be a stewardess.
KIM Well, the first thing to say is that we don't use the term stewardess – or steward, or air hostess – any more. The proper term is flight attendant.
INTERVIEWER Of course, I'm sorry.
KIM I'm afraid that there's little hope for you if you're not in your twenties. Of course, some airlines will take you on, say, if you're nineteen, but practically no airline will look at you if you're over thirty. So, sort of 19 to 29 is about it.
INTERVIEWER What about the way you look?
KIM Companies do differ quite a bit when it comes to physical appearance. If you're under five feet two inches – that's about one metre 55 – your chances are slim, and also if you're over six feet two (about one metre 85) you're probably excluded. You should be of average build and your weight should be proportionate to your height. Some of the aisles are a bit narrow and it helps if you can squeeze past the drinks trolley without knocking a passenger's drink out of their hand!
INTERVIEWER Is it the same for men and women?
KIM Yes, more or less. Another thing is that you're on your feet for hours at a time, walking back and forth, so you've got to be in pretty good health. You don't need twenty-twenty vision but you've got to have fairly good eyesight. Naturally accidents can happen so just about all companies

insist on your being able to swim. Another important qualification is that you have completed secondary school. I think it's true to say that a lot of companies prefer to take on people with some college education too. It helps if you have a good grasp of geography – passengers sometimes like to know what countries they're flying over, and if a flight attendant doesn't know it doesn't exactly inspire confidence! A good memory also comes in handy when you consider that, on a 747 transatlantic flight for example, there are over 28,000 items loaded on every flight – and a flight attendant has to know every one of them!

INTERVIEWER Presumably a flight attendant also needs to know a language or two.

KIM Well, I'm afraid to say that airline companies based in English-speaking countries are a little bit guilty here. Some don't have any foreign language requirements at all. English is enough, I'm afraid. However, in other countries at least one foreign language is an absolute necessity, and it's usually English.

INTERVIEWER So let's say you've got the interview – they're interested in you. What's important now?

KIM First impressions are important. I think it's crucial to look smart, but there's no need to put on your most boring outfit. There's nothing wrong with wearing something fashionable – fashionable but smart. Try to come across as being friendly and confident. Some airlines try to test your poise by asking some difficult personal questions, or by making personal remarks about your appearance or your foreign languages. They want to see how you respond to pressure. Try to remain calm and poised is the best advice I can give. Finally, I should say it's surprising how many people don't actually think about what the job involves before they apply. For some companies you have to spend up to three weeks away from home at a time! So if you've just met the man or woman of your dreams, think twice before you send off that application form!

Pronunciation focus   Unit 6

Your daughter's catching the seven o'clock flight from Los Angeles which is due in New York at twelve.

You have to be out of your room by eleven tomorrow.

We're flying to Luxor to meet the boat.

The boat leaves at dawn.

We'll probably find it very hot.

We're going to visit as many ancient sites as possible.

This time next week I'll be lying by the pool on a boat floating down the Nile.

Listening 1   Unit 6
International etiquette

… OK everyone. On a round-the-world cruise you're obviously going to visit a lot of different countries and experience a lot of different cultures, and I just wanted to say a few words about what we call international etiquette – being aware of the appropriate way to behave socially, in public. We'll give you specific advice when you're going on particular shore excursions, but I thought a few general words of advice now wouldn't go amiss.

Really, it's all about respect. I'm sure a lot of you already know about visiting churches, mosques, and other religious buildings. It's important to wear appropriate clothes and cover up bare skin. Men should always wear shirts. Shorts are not a good idea for women – women should in general avoid showing bare shoulders, arms, or legs, and in mosques and temples you'll need to cover your head too. In fact, when we're in Egypt, the Middle East, and Asia you'll also need to take off your shoes before you enter any religious building – outdoor shoes are seen as carrying all the impurities of the world.

I wonder if any of you know about some other customs. For example, when we get to the Far East, from Singapore onwards, you should be particularly careful about your posture. The soles of your feet, for example, are considered to be the dirtiest part of your body, and you should never point your foot at someone – so crossing your legs in public is not a good idea when we're in Singapore and Thailand. Also, avoid pointing, certainly at people, but also at objects. In Japan and other Far Eastern countries, blowing your nose in public is also not really acceptable.

When it comes to greeting people in different countries there are a lot of differences. You'll find Egyptian and Middle Eastern men kissing each other. The Spanish and many southern Europeans also kiss each other on the cheeks – though not normally the men. In Japan they'll bow – and the extent of the bow depends on the respect due to that person. But for you, probably the safest way to greet someone, certainly outside Asia, is just with a firm handshake. Although you

must make sure it's your right hand: in a lot of countries, particularly African and Middle Eastern countries, the left hand is regarded as unclean, so you shouldn't give things to people, pass food, and so on, with your left hand.

Food and eating habits is probably the most interesting area of international etiquette, but you'll be eating in international restaurants most of the time – although I hope you can all handle chopsticks! You probably won't get invited to anyone's home on this trip but if you ever do, make sure you check out the way to behave first. There's lots of potential for unintentionally causing offence. For example, in Singapore you should always say no to a second helping of food (you'll probably get some anyway!), and it's polite to leave some food on your plate at the end, whereas in somewhere like Russia that would probably offend your host!

Well, perhaps that's enough on international etiquette for the moment. You'll find a lot more information in your welcome packs, and I'd like to suggest you have a good look at the section on tipping and bargaining in particular.

Now I'll hand over to Julia who's going to tell you about the entertainment programme on board …

Listening 2   Unit 6
Cabin accommodation

CUSTOMER We're interested in going on a Caribbean cruise, but we're a little worried about the accommodation. I know the ships are luxurious, but I've heard the cabins can be very small – you know, cramped and stuffy. I want a bit of space and fresh air.

TRAVEL AGENT Yes, it's true most cabins are not quite like hotel rooms, but most companies do offer deluxe cabins as well. Let me see, I've got a brochure here … This company says they have the largest cabins in the Caribbean – for example, a lot of them have got their own private verandah.

CUSTOMER What about toilets and bathroom? We don't have to share, do we?

TRAVEL AGENT No, all the cabins have en suite facilities. They also say there's a lot of space for clothes and things – plenty of wardrobe and drawer space.

CUSTOMER And there'll be three of us.

TRAVEL AGENT OK, some cabins can take three people – you'd have to get a stateroom, though, because they're designed for three or four people. I think you'll find that even if you don't have as much space as a hotel room they make up for it in other ways. You get a bathrobe, for example, and a chocolate on your pillow every night, and so on.

CUSTOMER Yes, I see what you mean. What about the facilities in the room?

TRAVEL AGENT Well, you can watch films and other programmes on the TV, listen to music on the multi-channel radio. There's a telephone if you want to speak to friends back home, a personal safe for money and valuables, and a fridge for drinks as well.

CUSTOMER OK, so what cabin would you recommend for us?

TRAVEL AGENT Well, you definitely want an outside cabin so that you can see daylight. So there are three possibilities. If there are three of you I think you'll have to have a suite, which means you'll also get a verandah.

CUSTOMER Mmm, that sounds nice, but it's probably going to be a bit expensive, isn't it?

TRAVEL AGENT Well, it's not cheap, but if you go for the smaller one without the separate shower and dressing room you'll save a little bit.

CUSTOMER OK, and is that still available?

TRAVEL AGENT I'll just check for you ... .

Listening 1	Unit 7

A weekend break

TRAVEL AGENT Good morning. Can I help you?

MAN Yes, we're looking for information on a short holiday – you know, a weekend break or something like that.

TRAVEL AGENT Well, there are some good deals for long weekends – you go on a Friday and come back on the Monday. Obviously if you stay for a week you get longer, but then you do have to pay a lot more. You can do quite a lot on a three-night stay.

WOMAN OK, a long weekend it is.

TRAVEL AGENT Have you thought about where you'd like to go?

MAN We're not quite sure. We want to stay in this country, but I'd like to stay in the countryside, a nice quiet hotel where I can relax, whereas you'd prefer something else ... .

WOMAN Yes, I want something with a bit more to do. A small city where there's a bit of history, things to look at, and restaurants – that sort of thing.

TRAVEL AGENT Certainly the countryside is quieter and more relaxing than the city. However, there's a lot more to do in the city.

WOMAN That's the problem.

TRAVEL AGENT However, I think you can get the best of both worlds. Can I suggest something?

MAN Please do.

TRAVEL AGENT Why not go to Chester? It's a beautiful city. On the one hand, you've got some fascinating buildings, museums, ancient city walls, and old-fashioned shops. On the other hand, it's also very relaxing – and I can recommend a very peaceful hotel.

MAN That sounds good.

WOMAN Yes, it does.

TRAVEL AGENT OK. There are various packages. Here are the details ... As you can see, you've got some choice. You could go by train or you could go by coach. The train is quicker, but it's much more expensive.

MAN That's a point, maybe we should go by coach.

WOMAN On a Friday? We'd be on the road for ever!

MAN Yes, but think of the cost.

WOMAN Despite the cost, I think we should go by train. I don't want to be tired and uncomfortable from a long journey in a coach. You were the one who wanted a relaxing break!

MAN That's true. I do want to relax. Nevertheless, the idea was that this would be a cheap holiday.

TRAVEL AGENT There is another option. You could just book the accommodation package and then drive – you'd not only have more freedom, it would probably also be fairly cheap.

MAN Good point. What do you think, dear? We could share the driving.

WOMAN All right. Let's drive, although we'll probably end up arguing about the route!

TRAVEL AGENT Right, that's decided then. Now, can you give me some details ... .

Listening 2	Unit 7

Enquiring about a motorhome

REPRESENTATIVE Good morning, Motorhome Holidays, Cathy speaking. How may I help you?

CUSTOMER Yes, I was speaking to someone earlier about hiring a motorhome, and I've got a few more questions.

REPRESENTATIVE OK, what would you like to know?

CUSTOMER Well, firstly I was wondering if you had to be a certain age or if you needed a special licence.

REPRESENTATIVE A regular current driving licence is enough. You have to be

twenty-five years old if you're single, or twenty-three if you're married.

CUSTOMER OK, that's fine. Can we pick up the motorhome at the airport?

REPRESENTATIVE No, I'm afraid you can't. For safety reasons we have a policy that you pick up the motorhome the day after your flight. You will have just had a long tiring flight, and we need to make certain that we've trained you properly. There's a 45-minute training session when you'll be shown everything you need to know before you drive away.

CUSTOMER I see. So what do we do on the first night?

REPRESENTATIVE We recommend you book into the airport hotel. We can arrange this for you – there's a section on the booking form.

CUSTOMER Right. Now, I wanted to know exactly what's included in the price. I asked about insurance and all that before, but I forgot to ask about petrol and mileage. Could you give me a bit of information?

REPRESENTATIVE Certainly – of course all this will be in the brochure, but I'll just run through it anyway. Fuel is not included. As far as mileage goes, we include 100 kilometres a day in the price – any excess will be charged at twenty-two cents per kilometre.

CUSTOMER OK. There's just one more thing. Erm … the toilets – how do they work? We've never been in a motorhome before.

REPRESENTATIVE Oh, they're very modern – very similar to the bathroom in your own house. There are full instructions in the vehicle on how to maintain them – you won't have a problem.

CUSTOMER Good, and that's on all vehicles?

REPRESENTATIVE All motorhomes, yes. Do you know which model you would like?

CUSTOMER I'm not really sure. Perhaps you could advise me – sometimes brochures are a bit confusing. We didn't want anything too big, but there are going to be six of us including the children.

REPRESENTATIVE That's not a problem. Most models can take four adults and two children. The MHC31 is the largest, but that may be a little too big. Did you want a TV?

CUSTOMER It would be nice, but we came to look at the countryside, not the TV.

REPRESENTATIVE How about cooking? Do you plan to do much of your own cooking?

CUSTOMER Yes, but we don't want to spend all day cooking – we just need to pop a few things in the microwave, that sort of thing.

REPRESENTATIVE OK, then. I think you've got a choice of two models – both the same size, one's slightly more luxurious inside – bigger double bed and so on.

CUSTOMER That sounds good – you want a bit of comfort when you're on the road all day. Is it more expensive?

REPRESENTATIVE Just a little – five dollars a day.

CUSTOMER Oh, that's OK.

REPRESENTATIVE Right, what I'll do is put a note in with your brochure and indicate the model I think is best for you.

CUSTOMER Great, that would be very kind.

REPRESENTATIVE Can I just check I've got your name and address right?

CUSTOMER Certainly. It's … .

Listening 3 Unit 7

A disastrous tour

JUDE Hi, Lucy.

LUCY Hi, Jude. How was your holiday?

JUDE Don't ask – it was a complete and utter disaster.

LUCY Why? What happened? Was it the weather? It wasn't very nice here.

JUDE No, the weather was fine. The places we visited were fine – the cities, the scenery were all fine. The hotels were fine – more or less. Even the coach was fine, if you don't mind travelling on an out of date, broken down, rusty museum-piece!

LUCY Oh dear. But I thought you said it was going to be a luxury coach.

JUDE That was what the brochure said – spacious, modern, and reliable. In fact it was over ten years old. It did have air-conditioning, and that was fine at first – when we really didn't need it. But as soon as we got to the hotter places, just before Barcelona, it broke down.

LUCY Oh dear, that must have been awful.

JUDE And worse than that, the on-board toilets were filthy and disgusting – they didn't work properly and no one ever seemed to clean them out.

LUCY Oh no! That's the last thing you want. But the view was OK?

JUDE No, the windows all steamed up with condensation and you couldn't see a thing most of the time.

LUCY Oh Jude, it sounds terrible. Weren't there any good points?

JUDE Well, the escort was very nice. We all felt so sorry for her. She really did her best, but she was faced with such problems. The local guides were a different kettle of fish – they hardly spoke English and we couldn't understand a word. Jane, the escort, ended up interpreting a lot of the time.

LUCY It sounds like she had as bad a time as you.

JUDE She did. Oh, and the worst thing was the driver. He was just so unbelievably rude and ignorant. Every morning he was miserable and he swore at one of the passengers who was five minutes late one day. Then another day he left all the luggage at the hotel.

LUCY That's terrible. Did you get it back?

JUDE Yes, but only after there was nearly a riot. And there was one more thing. We lost two people, an American couple. We left them behind in Barcelona. We waited ages. Jane searched everywhere, phoned various places. You can imagine what mood the driver was in. After about three hours sitting on the hot sticky coach we left – it meant we had to miss out on one of the visits.

LUCY Do you know what happened to them?

JUDE No, they must have made their own way back. Actually, I prefer to think that they escaped!

LUCY Yes, probably glad to get away.

JUDE I tell you, it was the coach tour from hell! I need another holiday to get over that one.

LUCY Poor you! You'll have to complain.

JUDE Of course – I've already sent a long letter.

LUCY Come and have a coffee and we can talk about something else … .

Pronunciation focus 2 Unit 7

a Oh dear!
b Oh dear. That must have been awful!
c Oh no! That's the last thing you want.
d It sounds terrible!
e Poor you! You'll have to complain.

Pronunciation focus Unit 8

Did you say the single room supplement was £26.70?
No, it's £27.60.

Is the code for Eilat 9728?
No, it's 9727.

Listening 1 Unit 8

Stages in booking a holiday

There are a number of stages we go through when we're booking a holiday for someone. We like to be fully involved in every stage and have as much client contact as possible, right through from the initial enquiry to ticket issue and welcome home. The computer system is crucial to all this, but we also try to keep as much personal contact as possible.

So, after we've dealt with the initial enquiry, and the client has decided where they're going and what sort of holiday they want, we go into the computer system and create a file for the person – basic information like name, address, telephone number, number of people travelling. Or if they're an existing customer we add to what we call their 'client history'. Then we'll enter the details of this particular booking as a new transaction and this will produce a printed booking form, that's the booking authorization form.

Now, the initial payment or deposit is taken at the time of the booking – if it's less than eight weeks before departure then we have to ask for the full payment. We'll also offer insurance and other services at the same time. Once we've received the deposit we confirm the booking on our computer system, and this booking links directly into the tour operator's computer system. Ideally, all of that is done with the customer in the office on their first visit, and they walk out with a confirmation in their pocket. Of course, if the customer needs time to think or isn't quite sure, then we can put the whole thing on a 24-hour hold. That means the reservation is safe for another day, and then if we don't hear anything from the customer the next day we'll let it go.

The next stage will probably be weeks later when the tour operator sends out the tickets – to us. We check them against the computer booking to make sure the details are the same on the computer as on the tickets, and if everything's OK we'll let the client know, either by phone or by letter. We'll ask the client if they want to come and collect the tickets or if they want us to send them by post. That's it really. After the holiday we'll send them a 'welcome home' letter which invites them to give us any feedback they may have. Hopefully, it also reminds them that we're here in case they want to book their next holiday with us.

Listening 2 Unit 8

Selling an air ticket

TRAVEL AGENT Good morning, can I help you?

CUSTOMER Yes, I'm looking for a flight to San Francisco.

TRAVEL AGENT OK, when would you like to travel?

CUSTOMER I need to be there on the 3rd

of February. I want to leave as late as possible. What's the time difference – they're behind us, aren't they?

TRAVEL AGENT Yes, if you got a flight from Heathrow in the morning you'd be there by the afternoon or early evening local time.

CUSTOMER OK, fine. What have you got for the 3rd?

TRAVEL AGENT I'll just have a look … OK, there are five flights with availability on that day. All direct. Do you have a preference for a particular airline – there's a United Airlines, a Virgin, a Delta, a British Airways, and another United Airlines?

CUSTOMER No, it doesn't really matter. The main thing is to get there as early as possible.

TRAVEL AGENT Fine. Well, the United Airlines flight number 955 leaves Heathrow at 08.45 and arrives in San Francisco just after midday local time, at 12.05. At the moment there's availability in all classes – First, Club, and Economy.

CUSTOMER That sounds like the one. Just out of interest, what time does the British Airways flight get in?

TRAVEL AGENT That's not until 16.15.

CUSTOMER No, that's cutting it a bit fine. Is the United Airlines flight a Jumbo jet?

TRAVEL AGENT A 747? Let me see … No, it's a 763. Is that OK?

CUSTOMER Yes, that's fine. I just wondered.

TRAVEL AGENT What about the return flight? Do you have a date in mind?

CUSTOMER Yes, I need to get back on the 7th of February, because I've got to be back in the office on the 8th. So I guess I'll need a flight leaving San Francisco on the 6th.

TRAVEL AGENT OK, let's see what we've got … Any preference for time?

CUSTOMER Not really, but I don't want to get back too late.

TRAVEL AGENT There's one that gets you back to Heathrow just after 9 o'clock in the evening – flight number UA908.

CUSTOMER That's a bit late, actually. Anything earlier?

TRAVEL AGENT Flight UA954 gets in just after midday at 12.10, leaving San Francisco at 17.35. Is that too early?

CUSTOMER No, that's fine.

TRAVEL AGENT OK. Do you have a preference for seat type or price?

CUSTOMER The cheapest possible.

TRAVEL AGENT I'll see what we've got … . Right, the lowest basic fare we've got for those dates is £1,114, I'm afraid.

CUSTOMER Wow! Nothing cheaper?

TRAVEL AGENT I'm afraid not. It's because of those specific dates and the fact that you're staying less than seven days.

CUSTOMER Not to worry, the company's paying anyway! Are there any extras?

TRAVEL AGENT Yes, with tax and so on it comes to £1,132 and twenty pence.

CUSTOMER OK, go ahead and book it.

TRAVEL AGENT Can I just have your name and address … .

Listening 3   Unit 8
Holiday disasters

Dialogue 1 (Alberta)
ALBERTA Did I ever tell you about my disastrous holiday in Ireland?

FRIEND No, I don't think so. What happened?

ALBERTA Well, it was last time I was over in Europe with Tony.

FRIEND Who's Tony?

ALBERTA He was my boyfriend at the time. Anyway, we were having a great time in Ireland, but we were getting a bit bored with hitching or using buses. So we decided to hire a motorbike and just go where we wanted. I don't know if you know, but some of the roads out on the west coast are in pretty bad condition, and I suppose we were going a little bit fast. We'd just seen what looked like a gorgeous empty beach in the distance – you know, there are some great beaches out there – and we wanted to get there, and besides, there was no other traffic on the road. Anyway, we were heading for this deserted beach when suddenly we hit an enormous hole in the road and just flew off the bike!

FRIEND Oh no, that's terrible! So you were both on the same bike, were you?

ALBERTA Yes, that's right. Well, I got up fairly quickly, and I was a bit dazed but I could tell I wasn't badly hurt. But Tony was lying there yelling in agony, with the bike on his leg – and his leg was in this really odd position. So I panicked for a moment and then I remembered we'd just passed a little shop, so I ran as fast as I could and got the man from the shop to come and help Tony.

FRIEND Hang on. Are you saying you left poor Tony all on his own in that state?

ALBERTA Well, I had to. There was no one else around.

FRIEND I suppose so.

ALBERTA Anyway, his leg was broken. The shop owner was great – he called an ambulance from the town, which was miles away, and got Tony as comfortable as possible. So we ended up spending the rest of the holiday in a hospital!

FRIEND Gosh, how awful! It was a bit different to what you expected

ALBERTA Yes, and I saw a different side to Tony as well – he was so miserable the whole time. Never stopped whinging. I think that's where we started going off each other … .

Dialogue 2 (Brian)
REPORTER Mr Murray, you were at the scene of the explosion at the Plaza in San Francisco last night. It must have been something of a shock?

BRIAN I can tell you it was one of the most frightening moments of my life.

REPORTER Can you tell us exactly what happened?

BRIAN Well, we were staying there for a couple of nights. We'd been to the movies, and we'd just had a nightcap in the hotel bar and we were going back to our room. We got to our floor, and we were just coming out of the elevator when there was an explosion and the whole corridor seemed to burst into flames. Everyone in the elevator started panicking, but I managed to keep reasonably calm.

REPORTER Let me see if I've got this right – you were actually on the floor where the explosion took place?

BRIAN Yes, that's right. It was pretty scary, and I still can't believe I did what I did – I've never been particularly brave.

REPORTER And what did you do, Mr Murray?

BRIAN It was like this: one man tried to get the elevator to go back down, but I stopped him, because I know you're not supposed to use the elevators if there's a fire. I knew where the stairs were, but the corridor was in flames. Luckily I remembered where the fire extinguisher was and I rushed through the smoke and grabbed it. I sprayed it on the flames and managed to clear a path so that the guys from the elevator could get to the stairs. When we were all out we raced down those stairs like there was no tomorrow.

REPORTER So what you're saying is that you got the people out single-handed?

BRIAN Well, I suppose I did – the people in the elevator anyway. But it wasn't just me. The whole hotel had to be evacuated, and by a miracle no one was hurt.

REPORTER How did it feel afterwards?

BRIAN Later on people were saying I was a hero, but it's not something I want to repeat I can tell you!

Dialogue 3 (Colin)
TRAVEL AGENT Could you just go through the details again?

COLIN It was the third day of our holiday – it was our honeymoon, actually. We were on one of the islands, having a romantic meal in a little taverna by the harbourside – it was seafood. I was just popping a prawn in my mouth when I felt someone behind me. I looked round just in time to see this young kid – he couldn't have been more than ten or eleven – running away with my jacket.

TRAVEL AGENT Let me just go over this again – you were in the restaurant, and a young boy came up to you and snatched your jacket. Where was the jacket at the time?

COLIN It was on the back of my chair – it was a hot night and I'd taken it off. I suppose I should have been more careful – will that invalidate my claim?

TRAVEL AGENT I'm not sure. Go on – what happened next?

COLIN I chased him, but he was too fast. He dropped the jacket, but of course by then he'd already taken my wallet with my credit card and everything in it.

TRAVEL AGENT Did you report it to the police?

COLIN Yes, straight away, but there wasn't much they could do. But worse than that, later that night I was violently sick. It must have been the prawns or something. Anyway, I was ill with food poisoning for nearly a week.

TRAVEL AGENT Did you have to stay in your room?

COLIN For a few days, yes. It was a disaster!

TRAVEL AGENT Well, you may be able to claim something for that. You were confined to your room for two days, you said?

COLIN Three days.

TRAVEL AGENT Did you see a doctor?

COLIN Yes – and I told the resort rep, as well.

TRAVEL AGENT OK. I'll fill in this claim form for you, and then you can sign it.

Language focus 2   Unit 8

So you were both on the same bike, were you?

Are you saying you left poor Tony all on his own in that state?

Let me see if I've got this right – you were actually on the floor where the explosion took place?

So what you're saying is that you got the people out single-handed?

Let me just go over this again – you were in the restaurant, and a young boy came up to you and snatched your jacket?

You were confined to your room for two days, you said?

Listening 1   Unit 9

Enquiries at a tourist information centre

Part one

1 Where's the best place to get a panoramic view of the city? We want to take some photos.

2 I've heard there are some paintings by Andy Warhol somewhere in Sydney. Can you tell me where they are?

3 Is there anywhere in the harbour where you can see battleships or any other old historic ships?

4 We want to relax, hang out, just do a bit of swimming and sunbathing. Have you got any suggestions?

5 I'd like to take the kids somewhere educational but not too boring. Is there any museum with – I don't know – sea-life, sharks, crocodiles, that kind of thing? Someone told me there's a good display on the Great Barrier Reef as well.

6 I'm interested in seeing all the famous sights – the Bridge, the Opera House. Is there a boat trip or anything like that, that shows me all the sights?

7 What about the more ethnic side of Sydney? Is there anywhere we can go to get a different kind of food for example?

8 Where can we go for a bit of fun and excitement – rides, rollercoasters, that sort of thing?

9 Excuse me. Could you tell us the best place to get away from the noise and bustle of the city – a park or somewhere? You know, a bit of greenery and some fresh air.

10 Someone told us there's an old-fashioned indoor shopping mall with all the top designer shops and some nice bars and restaurants. Do you know the place?

Part two

1 There's one or two possibilities. The Tower is the obvious one – you get some outstanding 360 degree views of the city. But you can also get some good views from the Harbour Bridge – if you go up the Pylon Lookout – and the Opera House as well. I'd go for the Tower though, if you've got a good head for heights!

2 That's the MCA – it's got some wonderful modern and contemporary art.

3 You should go to the National Maritime Museum. You can visit twelve or so historic ships in the outdoor display and the indoor exhibitions are also well worth visiting.

4 You could go to Bondi Beach, or there's some great beaches to the north.

5 You could try the Powerhouse Museum – that's got a lot of hands-on stuff – but if they're interested in sea-life then it's got to be the Aquarium.

6 Yes, go down to Sydney Harbour – I'll show you where – and take any one of the cruises. There's a lot to choose from: I recommend one of the old square-riggers.

7 There's always Chinatown if you like Chinese food. Or alternatively, I could give you the names and addresses of some good Thai restaurants – they're my favourite.

8 The place to go is Luna Park. It was restored and modernized a few years back and it's great. You'll love it, I guarantee it!

9 If I were you I'd go to the Botanical Gardens – or the Chinese Garden.

10 I can recommend lots of places to go shopping, but I think the place you're talking about is the Queen Victoria Building.

Listening 2   Unit 9

Sydney Harbour Bridge

This is the Sydney Tourist Information Centre's recorded information line, giving information on all the major tourist attractions in Sydney. You will hear a menu of attractions. Please press the appropriate number when you hear the name of the attraction you are interested in.

1 National Maritime Museum
2 Aquarium
3 Chinese Garden and Chinatown
4 Sydney Observatory
5 Sydney Harbour Bridge … (*beep*)

Sydney Harbour Bridge, known to locals by the nickname of 'the coat-hanger' because of its shape, is one of the most famous sights in the world. It is many things – an essential link between the south and north sides of the harbour, the perfect postcard backdrop to the Opera House, and a great spot from which to take in the harbour panorama. It is the world's widest long-span bridge and it was completed in 1932. It took eight years to complete and a workforce of up to 1,400 men was employed. It is over 500 metres long and nearly 50 metres wide. Supported by massive double piers at each end, the bridge spans the north and south sides of the harbour in a single arch which has a height of 134 metres above the water at its highest point, with a clearance of 49 metres for shipping. It has two railway tracks and eight lanes for road traffic, the direction of which can be varied according to traffic requirements. There is also a cycleway and walkways for pedestrians. An average of 170,000 vehicles cross the bridge every day, although increasing traffic led to the building of a tunnel under the harbour which was opened in 1992. Keeping the bridge freshly-painted is a major job, and teams of painters are permanently employed. The actor Paul Hogan, star of the film *Crocodile Dundee*, was once a Harbour Bridge painter.

By far the best way to experience the bridge is to walk across it. From the city side, access to the walkway is via Argyle Street in The Rocks, while the northern entrance is near Milson's Point Station, where a ferry service also operates. In the south-east pier there is a museum illustrating the history of the bridge's construction. There is a 200-step climb to the look-out for magnificent views of the city and harbour. The museum is open daily from 10 a.m. to 5 p.m.

Pronunciation focus   Unit 9

wide   eight   thousand   road

a how	g house
b high	h nine
c south	i most
d height	j train
e five	k low
f lane	l rail

boy   near   hair   pure

Listening 1   Unit 10
Answerphone messages

Hello, this is Jenny Townsend. I'm afraid I'm not available to take your call at the moment, but if you'd like to leave a message I'll get back to you as soon as possible. Please speak after the tone. [*Beep*]

Message 1
Hello, Jenny, this is Alison from City Tours. I was wondering if you were able to do a half-day panoramic tour for us on Tuesday the 6th of August? It's in an open-top bus leaving from Baker Street at 9 o'clock. If you can, can you get back to me on 630 7144? Bye.

Message 2
Hi, Jenny. Remember me? It's John Bevan – you did a special guided walk for us last year – all about the London of Charles Dickens. Any chance of a repeat this year? Say Thursday the 15th in the afternoon? Can you call me anyway? I'm on 01532 289 164. Bye.

Message 3
Hello, this is the Capital Guide booking service. We're looking for a number of guides to work on a big incentive group we've got coming over on the week commencing Monday the 12th of August. It involves an early morning transfer from Heathrow on the 12th, followed by a London tour and evening theatre and dinner trip. Also an Oxford visit on the Tuesday, then a return transfer on Wednesday. Call us soon if you're interested. The number is 233 6060. Thank you.

Message 4
Hello, it's Alison again from City Tours. Do you think you could do another job for us? It's a half-day sightseeing and shopping trip, ending with tea at Harrods. Call me back, you've got the number. Oh, I almost forgot: it's Friday the 9th, 2 o'clock pick-up. Speak to you soon. Bye.

Message 5
Hello, this is CTS Tours. We're looking for a guide for our four-day Scotland tour leaving on Friday the 16th of August. It's the standard Edinburgh and Lowlands trip. Would you be interested? If you are, phone David here at CTS – I know you've got the number. Look forward to hearing from you.

Message 6
Paul Rogers here. I wanted to know if you could do a Hampstead Sunday tour for us. You know the sort of thing – a walk on the Heath followed by a pub lunch. Either the 11th or the 18th of August would be fine. It's for the American Friends of England group. Anyway, phone me back tonight if you can. The number's 737 8192. Bye.

Language focus 1   Unit 10

1 I was wondering if you were able to do a half-day panoramic tour for us?

2 Any chance of a repeat this year?

3 Call us soon if you're interested.

4 Do you think you could do another job for us?

5 Would you be interested?

6 I wanted to know whether you could do a Hampstead Sunday tour for us.

Listening 2   Unit 10
Guide instructions

JENNY Hello, Jenny Townsend speaking.

SUE Hi, Jenny. This is Sue, Sue Jameson.

JENNY Hello, how are you?

SUE Fine. I was just phoning about the Scotland tour. Did you get the instructions?

JENNY Yes, I did. Thanks a lot. It's all very clear.

SUE Ah, well, unfortunately there have been a few changes. Have you got the instructions in front of you?

JENNY Hang on … Yes, here they are.

SUE Right, well firstly, they've got the office number wrong. It's 6307, not 6370.

JENNY Oh, yes. I think I knew that.

SUE Now, with the actual tour, the number of passengers has changed – it's now forty-one. There have been a couple of cancellations. I'll get the office to fax over the revised passenger list later on.

JENNY OK.

SUE The client wants to leave a bit earlier, so the times have all shifted on day one. Departure's now going to be at 8.15 sharp – I've told the coach company so you don't need to worry about that. That means you should get to The George in Stamford at 10.45 – and could you keep the coffee stop down to thirty minutes?

JENNY OK, I'll try, but it's a bit tight. I've got to phone The George anyway.

SUE Right. I'll leave that to you. Can you also try to keep lunch fairly short? You should be able to stop somewhere around 1.30.

JENNY That should be fine – I know a few places where they get you through quite quickly. So this way we should get to Edinburgh much earlier?

SUE Yes, that's the idea, so that the group have time to have a rest and then enjoy the evening. Now, on day two there aren't any changes, but it's very important that the group get to the distillery by 1.45 at the latest, so please don't let them spend too long over lunch.

JENNY OK. Anything else?

SUE Yes, I'm afraid so. On the Sunday the time of the Loch Lomond cruise has been changed – apparently they're overbooked on the twelve o'clock so it's now at one.

JENNY They could have an early lunch or a drink in the hotel – it's quite nice there. The cruise is optional, isn't it?

SUE Yes, although we've told the company that there will probably be about thirty or forty people. You may want to phone them when you have more of an idea.

JENNY Yes, well, I was going to phone them anyway just to check a few things.

SUE Right. Now last but not least, the client wants to have more time in the Lake District on the way back. So they've asked for an eight o'clock departure, which means breakfast at seven, and bags need to be ready at 6.30.

JENNY Wow, that's an early one – especially after the Scottish evening! I expect there'll be a few sleepy heads!

SUE I know. Still, that's what they want. It means you'll get to Grasmere around one o'clock. Then they want to have a bit of a drive around the Lakes on the way back. I think you could probably keep the tea stop down to thirty minutes.

JENNY Right, I think I've got all that. Are you going to send me a revised programme?

SUE Yes, of course – with the passenger list. I just thought you'd want to know now.

JENNY Yes, thanks.

SUE Well, good luck. I'll speak to you if there are any more changes.

JENNY OK, bye.

SUE Bye.

Listening 3 — Unit 10
Guide commentaries

1

The elegant building you can see on your left with the lovely green lawns in front of it is, of course, one of the most famous buildings in America. It is also one of the most powerful. It was designed by James Hoban after the site had been chosen by George Washington. Building work began in 1792, and although it was burned early on by the British in the war of 1814, it was restored. John Adams was the first president to live here.

2

You are now standing in front of one of the most famous sights in the whole world. It is without doubt the finest example of Mughal architecture. The glorious white marble exterior stands as a symbol of purity and love. It was built by the emperor Shah Jahan as a mausoleum – a burial place – for his beloved wife Mumtaz, and it took nearly twenty years to build.

3

The magnificent structure we are now passing is 300 metres high and has stood on this site for over a century. It stands as a proud example of the technological and engineering achievements of 19th century France. It is said that the British planned to build a similar structure just a bit higher, but they only got as far as the first stage

when – so the story goes – the structure began to collapse.

4

Now, standing in the middle of this square we have a splendid view of the largest and most important church in the Christian world. The church was started in the early 16th century and took over a hundred years to complete. Bramante, Raffaello, and Michelangelo all worked on it. The centrepiece of the church is the magnificent dome standing over 120 metres high. We shall now go into the church and climb to the top for some wonderful views of the city – so I hope you are feeling fit!

5

The building in front of you is nearly two-and-a-half thousand years old. It is a masterpiece of architecture, reflecting the advanced development of the culture which produced it. It was built as a temple to the goddess Athena, but in its long history it has also been used as a Christian church and as a mosque. Over the years much of it has been destroyed, indeed a lot of the sculptures are held in the British Museum in London.

6

We're now approaching a very famous sight indeed. It has a main span of 1,280 metres, with a total length of 2,824 metres, making it one of the world's longest suspension bridges. As we cross, look to your left for some superb views of the city and the bay, and to your right you'll be able to gaze out to the blue horizon of the Pacific Ocean.

7

Soon we'll be entering one of the most famous ancient buildings in the world. Most of what you can see is original. Imagine the scene, if you can, over 1,500 years ago, as gladiators fought to the death seeking the favour of their emperor. Imagine the blood and the death, the cruelty, and the peculiar pleasures of the declining empire. It was here also the Christians are said to have been thrown to the wild beasts.

Listening 1 — Unit 11
Holiday advertisements

Conversation 1

REPRESENTATIVE Hello, can I help you?

CUSTOMER Yes, I saw your advertisement in the World Wildlife magazine and I'm interested in getting some more information.

REPRESENTATIVE Right, that was our safari holiday, wasn't it?

CUSTOMER Er, yes – the rhino one.

REPRESENTATIVE OK, what would you like to know? I'll send you a brochure of course, but I can give you some information now as well.

CUSTOMER Thanks. Where exactly does the tour go?

REPRESENTATIVE It's in the north-east of India, mainly in the eastern Himalayas – which as you can imagine provides some particularly spectacular scenery. But the tour also visits Delhi, Agra, and Calcutta.

CUSTOMER What about accommodation – the ad mentions first class hotels. Are the facilties really that good?

REPRESENTATIVE Well, you've got to remember that this region has only recently been open to tourism, so if you're looking for an endless succession of five-star hotels then you're going to be disappointed. But all the hotels we use are clean and comfortable, and you'll find that any small lack of amenities is more than made up for by the beauty of the surroundings.

CUSTOMER Oh, I'm sure. I'm not after luxury!

REPRESENTATIVE Well, in fact a lot of the places we stay at are quite luxurious – the Wild Grass Lodge in the middle of the Kaziranga National Park, for example, where we stay for three nights for the main rhino and elephant safari, is very charming.

CUSTOMER Sounds good. Now the advert said it's an eighteen-day tour. Is that the only tour you offer?

REPRESENTATIVE That's our only 'In search of rhino' tour but we do many other tours to different parts of India, and we can also arrange independent tours and help you with different itineraries which could include many of the places on the rhino tour. You'll see it all in the brochure – just get back to us if you want to arrange something a bit different.

CUSTOMER Great. Just a couple more questions if you don't mind.

REPRESENTATIVE Sure, that's what we're here for!

CUSTOMER I know we hope to see rhino and elephants. What other things will we see?

REPRESENTATIVE Well, with luck you'll see wild buffalo, deer, monkeys and gibbon, and possibly a tiger or two. There's also some beautiful exotic plants – orchids in particular. And, of course, there are man-made places – the Taj Mahal, temples, Buddhist monasteries, and so on. But I think the thing that impresses most of our clients is the amazing beauty of the

Himalayas – there's nothing like it.

CUSTOMER What happens about meals?

REPRESENTATIVE For most of the tour we include room and breakfast only, so that you get a chance to use local restaurants – they're very cheap in any case – but in some more remote places, such as the Kaziranga National Park we include full board. You'll see the details in the brochure and price list.

CUSTOMER Good. Well, thanks, you've been very helpful. Could you send me that brochure?

REPRESENTATIVE Certainly. What's your name?

CUSTOMER It's … .

Conversation 2

REPRESENTATIVE Hello, Peter speaking. Can I help you?

CUSTOMER Yes, I saw your ad in the paper and I wanted to find out a little bit more.

REPRESENTATIVE Certainly. I can send you a copy of our latest brochure.

CUSTOMER That would be great. Can I just ask a few things first, though?

REPRESENTATIVE Of course.

CUSTOMER On the Antarctica trip, whereabouts do we go? Presumably we don't actually get to the South Pole?

REPRESENTATIVE No, you don't. You start in Buenos Aires and then you fly south across Patagonia to Tierra del Fuego where you set sail for the Antarctic peninsula. You stay mainly on the coastal areas, where most of the interesting wildlife is.

CUSTOMER And accommodation is on the ship most of the time?

REPRESENTATIVE Yes. You're in hotels for the first two nights and then again for the last night, but the rest of the time you're on board the expedition ship.

CUSTOMER What are facilities like there?

REPRESENTATIVE Very good. Comfortable fully-furnished cabins, all with outside views. The ship has a dining room with waiter service – most meals are included, by the way. There's a library and laboratory, a heated plunge pool, and a sauna.

CUSTOMER I see. Sounds great. I wasn't quite sure how long the trip was?

REPRESENTATIVE We've got two different itineraries – 14 days or 16 days. The 16-day includes two extra days on the Antarctic peninsula.

CUSTOMER Right, so what can I expect to see on the trip? Apart from snow and ice that is!

REPRESENTATIVE You'll certainly see a lot of that – and it's beautiful, especially some of the glaciers. Mainly it'll be penguin and

seal colonies, but you'll also see whales, and of course you may even catch a glimpse of the rarest Antarctic species of all – the human being! We visit a research station and an abandoned whaling station.

CUSTOMER Well, thanks. Can I give you my name and address for the brochure?

Conversation 3

REPRESENTATIVE Hello, Maureen O'Connor speaking.

CUSTOMER Hello, my name's Linda Lloyd. I saw your advertisement in the local paper and I'm very interested to find out more, and maybe come along on the trip.

REPRESENTATIVE Good, well the first question is have you ever done any walking like this before? It's very arduous, you know.

CUSTOMER I'm a very keen walker, and I've been on similar extended trips before. I've never done anything this long, but I've always been fascinated by the Camino de Santiago.

REPRESENTATIVE Yes, it's a wonderful pilgrimage. I did one of the shorter routes two years ago and some of the scenery is breathtaking – I'll never forget the Pyrenees and the view from the Val Carlos pass. But of course, the most wonderful thing is when you arrive at Santiago and go to the cathedral.

CUSTOMER It must be a great feeling.

REPRESENTATIVE It is. Anyway, I'm holding a preliminary meeting next week. Would you like to come?

CUSTOMER Yes, I would.

REPRESENTATIVE Is there anything you'd like to know before then? I can give you some leaflets and books at the meeting.

CUSTOMER That would be great. There are just a couple of things. What happens about accommodation?

REPRESENTATIVE There are refugios along the way which are free for the pilgrims, but they're very basic and really just provide a bed and not much else. They tend to be in places like church halls. Often they don't have showers or anything. We'll stay in those a lot of the time, but we'll also stop at the occasional B&B or inn, and maybe even a hotel from time to time. It's a very long trip, after all.

CUSTOMER Yes, I was going to ask about that. The ad says April to late July – will it really take that long?

REPRESENTATIVE It depends. It'll probably take about three months in all, allowing for rest stops. The aim is to get to Santiago for the fiesta towards the end of July – it's a great sight.

CUSTOMER OK, I think that's all I need to

know now. I'd love to come to the meeting. Where is it?

REPRESENTATIVE I'll give you the address. Have you got a pen? …

The independent traveller

Well, thank you for asking me along tonight. I hope you'll enjoy looking at my slides of the Andes. I've also been asked to give you some advice about independent travel and how to be a 'good tourist', so that's what I'd like to do first.

I've been travelling now for about twenty years. When I was younger I used to regularly take off with my backpack and my camera and head for some remote place, maybe working, maybe just hanging out. I spent a whole year in India in my early twenties, I've backpacked all round Europe and the Middle East, spent some time in China, and I've also been trekking in Nepal and South America. So, I've picked up a bit of experience along the way.

In the early days I always used to take each day as it came and not really plan very much. Nowadays I plan a bit more, and I tend to go on more organized trips, using tour operators and travel agents, although I still like to be independent when I get to a place. Believe it or not, you can find responsible tour operators who care about the environment and the places they're taking you to – but you do have to look carefully and ask a lot of questions.

I learnt a lot in my early travels about how to take care and be responsible – to be what some people call a 'green tourist'. I still try to put it into practice. I think the most important thing is to ask yourself, 'Why am I going?' If you just need to relax or if you're only 'country-counting', then maybe that's not a good enough reason to visit a place – especially a developing country. If you're genuinely interested in a country then that's a different matter. Before you go, learn as much as you can about the place, go to the library, read up about it, learn a bit of the language – even if it's just 'please' and 'thank you'.

Also, before you go, think carefully about your packing and what you're going to take. Things like shampoo, lotions, sun cream, and so on should be kept to a minimum. Make sure you really need them and you're not taking too much – there's no point coming back with bottles that are still nearly full – and above all, make sure they're environmentally-friendly and made from natural substances. In the developing world in particular, they can easily find their way into the water supply and cause pollution. You've got to be especially careful if you're camping up river from a village.

Now, when I'm at my destination, or when I'm travelling generally, I do my best to minimize my impact. You can do this very simply – and it also makes your experience much more enjoyable. For a start, make sure you eat and drink in local restaurants and that you eat and drink local produce. Try not to go for the big international fast food chains. Most of that money doesn't stay in the country and you're not helping the local community by using them. Many rural areas in the Mediterranean, for example, are seeing their agriculture decline, and by eating locally-produced food you will help the local economy. I also try to stay with locals, preferably in bed and breakfast, and avoid the big foreign-owned hotel chains.

If you can, use public transport – it may not be as quick as hiring a car, but it's cheap and interesting, and it's certainly one way of meeting the local people. Also, you might find you get to see something more than the standard tourist sights – and of course, you're not adding to the pollution.

Choosing souvenirs and presents is another area where the tourist can be either a help or a hindrance. There's a lot of rubbish produced, nothing to do with the culture of the country, badly made, often made in a completely different country and imported. So, learn about the cultural heritage of the country first, then you'll know what the local arts and crafts should be. Ask local people to show you crafts being made – I've found they're often very happy to do so, and I've even picked up a few skills myself. Of course, it goes without saying that you should never buy anything that's made from an endangered species. Never pick any plants or flowers either. Take a picture instead – you'll find it lasts longer in any case!

As you know, I'm a keen photographer, so my camera is my most important piece of equipment. But be sensitive when you're taking photographs, particularly of people – the cultural rules are often quite different. In fact, if I can give you two final pieces of advice, they are firstly, be sensitive: think about what you're doing and the consequences for the people who live there – all the time. Secondly, don't be scared to complain if you see something wrong,

something that's damaging the environment, or whatever. Tell someone. If you come across a polluted beach tell your tour representative; if you see another tourist dropping litter ask them to pick it up. It's only by doing such things that we'll get people to change their ideas and their behaviour, and to get tourism to be a more caring and responsible industry.

Well, I think that's everything I've got to say at the moment … .

Listening 2   Unit 12
Sustainable tourism

INTERVIEWER All the experts agree that tourism is the fastest growing industry in the world. It is also the industry which is most difficult to control and regulate. Tourism has a tendency to destroy itself – this year's idyllic beach resort becomes next year's high-rise hell, as high-spending tourists are sought out and lured for the sake of a quick dollar. Can we do anything about it? In the studio today we have Professor Roger Spencer, author of *Greed or green? – the need for sustainable tourism*. Professor, what exactly is meant by 'sustainable tourism'?

PROF. SPENCER Sustainable tourism means, to quote from one of the early reports on the concept, 'development that meets the needs of the present without compromising the ability of future generations to meet their own needs'. In other words, it doesn't try to stop the growth of tourism – that would be foolish – but to make sure that tourism grows in a way that allows tourists to see what they want to see, experience what they want to experience, but does not destroy the very things they are seeing and experiencing. At the same time, the society and culture and environment of the people who live in the tourist destinations – indeed their whole way of life – is not damaged or destroyed either. The idyllic beach resort you mentioned in your introduction remains an idyllic beach resort.

INTERVIEWER That's all very well, but how does it work in practice? Are there any practical principles behind the theory of sustainable tourism?

PROF. SPENCER Indeed there are. We have defined ten such principles and perhaps I could talk about some of them.

INTERVIEWER Certainly.

PROF. SPENCER Well, the first principle is the importance of using resources – natural, social, and cultural – sustainably. There is definitely a growing awareness of

this problem. Places like Disneyland in Florida now adopt environmental policies towards waste disposal, recycling, and water conservation. But there are still too many examples of natural resources being destroyed. For example, in the Gulf of Thailand waste disposal from the hotels of Pattaya and Hua Hin has meant that the waters are so polluted that they are no longer able to support shellfish – ironically, one of the local dishes which these same tourists come to experience! With a little bit of education and investment the problem could be solved. All it needs is for tourists to take a little more care and to think about what they're doing, and for the hotels to invest in more effective water treatment and waste disposal systems.

INTERVIEWER What about cultural resources?

PROF. SPENCER Well, I think the most obvious example of this is the growth of the sex industry in places like the Philippines, at the expense of more traditional forms of entertainment. Again, it's a question of controlling and regulating new developments.

INTERVIEWER OK. What's the next important principle?

PROF. SPENCER Well, related to the first is the problem of reducing over-consumption and waste. To give western tourists the luxuries and comforts they are used to, forests are being destroyed, beaches are being eroded, and water is becoming scarce. In The Gambia, for example, swimming pools in the foreign-owned hotels are full, lawns are watered, showers always available, at the same time as the local inhabitants have to raise water from hand-dug holes. In Nepal, whole forests are cleared in order to make sure trekkers have enough fuel and accommodation with hot showers.

INTERVIEWER What do you recommend?

PROF. SPENCER I think it's a question of where there's a will there's a way. If you take the example of Western Samoa. Here, a hotel construction project uses traditional designs and techniques, it uses local materials, and most importantly the whole project is based on the ownership of the hotel sites by the local villagers. This means the employment of local people and the use of local agricultural produce for the tourists to eat and drink. In other words, the growth of tourism there doesn't rely on imports, but sustains the local economy and community. This leads on to another important principle of sustainable tourism, namely making sure that the tourism industry talks to local communities and organizations and involves them in development.

INTERVIEWER Have you got any examples where this has or hasn't happened?

PROF. SPENCER I think one example is Hawaii, where for many years huge ugly high-rise hotels have been built without any regard for the local people or the local culture. Often they've been built on sacred religious sites and the protests of local people just ignored. On the other side, in Costa Rica for example, there is the Eco Institute which brings together government officials, private developers, environmentalists, and the tourism industry to exchange ideas for constructive and sustainable tourism planning.

INTERVIEWER Is this the model you see working most effectively to achieve sustainable tourism?

PROF. SPENCER Yes, I think it is. We cannot exaggerate the importance of discussion and planning. If people would only think about what they're doing and the consequences of their actions we wouldn't have such problems. It is, after all, in everyone's interest to ensure that both tourism and the countries and cultures where tourists go are sustained for as long as possible.

INTERVIEWER Thank you Professor. We'll be hearing more from you later, but meanwhile … .

Acknowledgements

The publisher would like to thank the following for permission to reproduce photographs:
The Bridgeman Art Library p. 7 (Mona Lisa, Sunflowers)
British Airways p. 64
James Davis Travel Photography pp. 7 (Tsar's bell), 128, 133
The Walt Disney Company Limited pp. 131, 133
Eye Ubiquitous pp. 89, 129 (P Hutley/Humber Bridge)
Fundación César Manrique p. 14
Getty Images pp. 6 (P Correz/blonde female, female black/white jacket), 7 (J Cornish/Big Ben, S N Solins/Sagrada Familia, D Armand/Sphinx, J Horner/Machu Picchu, J Calder/Terracotta Warriors), 34 (D Bosler/flight, S Peters/hotel), 44 (H Sitton/Santorini), 123 (C Ehlers/Sydney), 124 (P Chesley/Spice Stall), 142 (D Paterson Rannock Moor)
The Image Bank pp. 6 (P Simcock/Teenage girl), 124 (P Hendrie/Grand Palace, S Dee/Yak Guard), 129 (Seto-Otashi Bridge), 142 (R Lockyer/Edinburgh)
Images Colour Library pp. 12, 80, 85
National Tourism Organization – Malta p. 15
Pictor International pp. 6 (male portrait), 7 (Michelangelo's David, Hollywood), 129 (Eiffel Tower), 135, 146, 171 (book cover)
Rex Features p. 14 (Freddie Laker)
Scope Features p. 41
Sunworld pp. 107, 109
Telegraph Colour Library p. 48
Thomas Cook pp. 14, 93, 94, 95

We would also like to thank the following for their help and co-operation:
American Embassy
Oxford Moat House

Cover illustration by
John H Hamilton

Illustrations by:
Gerry Ball, Eikon Ltd. pp. 78, 145
Karl Duke pp. 104, 149
Nicky Dupays pp. 29, 155
Stefan Chabluk pp. 64, 77, 79, 86, 133
Ian Kellas pp. 69, 76, 83, 108, 118, 168, 170
Claire Littlejohn pp. 80, 96, 98, 147
Technical Graphics Dept, OUP pp. 17, 18, 21, 27, 28, 84

Location photography by:
Rob Judges pp. 20, 25, 44, 169, 171
Bill Osment pp. 110

Studio photography by
Mark Mason pp. 105, 171

The author and publisher are grateful to those who have given permission to reproduce the following extracts from and adaptations of copyright material:
p.14 The Thomas Cook Group Ltd.; pp.14 and 127 © The Automobile Association, material reproduced by kind permission of The Automobile Association; pp. 21 and 23 adapted from *The Business of Tourism* by J Christopher Holloway, reprinted by permission of Addison Wesley Longman Ltd.; pp.21 and 57 Thomson Holidays; p.21–2 statistics reprinted by permission of the London Tourist Board; p.30 Earthwatch for extracts from 1997 Annual Expedition Guide; p.31 Eurobus for extracts from 1997 brochure; p.31 Travelbag for extracts from 1997–98 brochure; p.31 from Alastair Sawday's *Special Places to Stay in Spain* by Guy Hunter-Watts; p.31 Spanish National Tourist Board; p.32 Real Holidays Ltd.; p.35–6 Holiday Inn for extracts from leaflet (used in Europe, the Middle East, and Africa by Holiday Inn Worldwide since 1993); p.37 Vienna Hilton, Astron, and Radisson SAS hotels; p.41 from an article by Mark Hodson © Mark Hodson/*The Sunday Times*, 1996; pp.65 and 105 Monarch Airlines; p.73 HM Customs and Excise for extracts from leaflet; p.75 Costa Cruises for extracts from brochure; pp.80 and 177 Voyages Jules Verne for information taken from advertisement published 1992; p.85–6 Princess Cruises for extracts from Caribbean brochure 1995–96; p.91 Hoverspeed Ltd.; pp.91 and 150 Eurostar; pp.93 and 95 Thomas Cook Holidays, VIA Rail and Motorhomes from Thomas Cook Brochure 'Canada for the Independent Traveller 1995'; pp.96–7 and 178 British Airways Holidays and Alamo Rent-A-Car for extracts from Florida 1995 brochure – please note that for information purposes this is not up to date; p.99 Cosmos Coach Tours; p.105 Association of Train Operating Companies, Secretary of State for the Environment, Transport and Regions; p.105 York Viking Moat House, Brighton Thistle, British Airways; pp.106–7, 109, and 179 Sunworld Wintersun for extracts from brochure; pp.131–2 and 181 Disneyland® Paris for extracts from brochure; p.135 from an article by David Nicholson-Lord © *The Independent*; p.147 from *Collins Independent Traveller's Guide: Spain* by Harry Debelius with permission of HarperCollins Publishers Ltd.; p.150 United Airlines, Saga Holidays, The Iberia Group; p.156 Tyax Lodge Heliskiing, Ocean Adventures, Greaves Tours, Exodus Tours, Safari Desk; p.158–9 Tyax Lodge Heliskiing; p.161 The Georgia Department of Industry, Trade, and Tourism; p.165 from an article by Edward Welsh, *The Sunday Times* 25/5/97; p.168 Poem 'When The Tourists Flew In' by Cecil Rajendra; p.170 from an article by Katie Wood, © *The Observer* 31/3/91; p.170–1 Tourism Concern and the World Wildlife Fund; p.182 United Distillers; p.186 American Embassy London Consular Section.

Although every effort has been made to trace and contact copyright holders, this has not always been possible. If notified the publisher will be pleased to rectify any errors or omissions at the earliest opportunity.

The author would like to express his thanks to his family and friends, and to colleagues and students at St Giles College, Highgate. Too numerous to mention are the many teachers and students who gave us detailed and invaluable feedback during the research and piloting stages of this project. Special thanks, however, are due to Roger Andrews and his colleagues at the Escola d'Hoteleria i Turisme in Palma de Mallorca.

Oxford University Press
Great Clarendon Street, Oxford OX2 6DP

Oxford New York

Athens Auckland Bangkok Bogota
Buenos Aires Calcutta Cape Town
Chennai Dar es Salaam Delhi
Florence Hong Kong Istanbul Karachi
Kuala Lumpur Madrid Melbourne
Mexico City Mumbai Nairobi Paris
São Paulo Shanghai Singapore Taipei
Tokyo Toronto Warsaw

and associated companies in
Berlin Ibadan

OXFORD and OXFORD ENGLISH
are trade marks of Oxford University Press

ISBN 0 19 4574008

© Oxford University Press

First published 1998

Third impression 2001

Set in Adobe Minion and Myriad
Printed in Hong Kong